Georgine Kalil, Frances Kregler, Alan McElroy, Roisin Sweeny

Education For You

English for jobs in education

1. Auflage

D1666010

Bestellnummer 30327

Bildungsverlag EINS

Haben Sie Anregungen oder Kritikpunkte zu diesem Produkt?
Dann senden Sie eine E-Mail an 30327_001@bv-1.de
Autoren und Verlag freuen sich auf Ihre Rückmeldung.

www.bildungsverlag1.de

Bildungsverlag EINS GmbH
Hansestraße 115, 51149 Köln

ISBN 978-3-427-**30327**-5

Vorwort

Das Lehrwerk **Education For You** richtet sich an Lehrende, vor allem aber an junge Menschen, die sich in der Ausbildung zur Erzieherin und zum Erzieher befinden, sowie an Studierende der Sozialpädagogik beziehungsweise der Fachrichtung Erziehung und Bildung im Kindesalter. Es eignet sich für den fachsprachlichen Unterricht an Berufsschulen, Fachoberschulen sowie Hochschulen.

Das Buch ist für Lernende konzipiert, die über Vorkenntnisse auf der Mittelstufe verfügen, seine Inhalte entsprechen den curricularen Vorgaben für das B2-Niveau des gemeinsamen europäischen Referenzrahmens.

In 13 Units werden Themenschwerpunkte aus verschiedenen Bereichen der frühkindlichen Bildung, der Sozialpädagogik und der Heilerziehung behandelt. Jede Unit umfasst drei Module, die jeweils unterschiedliche Aspekte des Hauptthemas behandeln. Die Module sind in sich abgeschlossen und können einzeln durchgearbeitet werden.

Education for You bietet sprachliche Übungen an, die ein abwechslungsreiches und handlungsorientiertes Lernen ermöglichen. Die Aufgaben sind sowohl für eine individuelle als auch für eine kooperative Bearbeitung konzipiert. In praxisnahen Texten, Case Studies und Aufgaben, wie z. B. Activity-Tasks, wird der Lernende mit beruflichen Situationen des Alltags konfrontiert, welche die kommunikativen Fähigkeiten durch situationsgebundene Sprech- und Schreibanlässe fördern. Die Situationen haben die pädagogische Arbeit mit Krippenkindern, Jugendlichen und Menschen mit besonderen Bedürfnissen zum Gegenstand. Der allgemeinsprachliche Wortschatz wird durch die Arbeit mit dem Lehrbuch gefestigt und zu einem fachspezifischen Wortschatz ausgebaut.

Die Listening-Übungen sind zum Download zu finden unter www.bildungsverlag1.de/ audio-portal.

Das Autorenteam wünscht viel Freude beim Lernen und viel Erfolg im Beruf!
Frances Kregler, Roisin Sweeny, Georgine Kalil und Alan McElroy

Inhaltsverzeichnis

STARTER:

Getting to know each other

Who am I?

1 If you are planning to work with children and adolescents, now is a good time to reflect upon your childhood and on the things that made you the person you are today. Naturally, parents, siblings, friends and teachers have all left lasting impressions on you, but significant and small experiences have shaped your personality as well. Have you ever
5 thought about why you do things the way you do? Or, where your opinions and preferences come from?

You may already know the people in your class by name, but how well do you *really* know them? Before you get to know each other better, think about who you are first.

Activity

Task 1

Bring in a picture of yourself as a child and share it with a partner. Where and when was the picture taken? Is there anybody else in the picture? Do you remember the occasion? What were you doing? Ask each other questions to learn more about your childhood memories.

Task 2

Draw a picture of yourself. Don't worry – it doesn't have to be a work of art; it can be a simple figure. Write an interesting fact about yourself on each part of the body, for example: how old you are, what your name is, where you are from, something you love, your favourite food, a hobby, or something you're good at, your dream, etc.

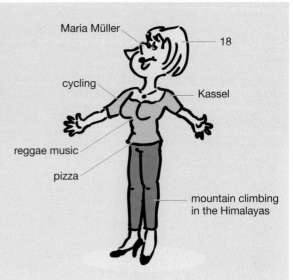

Maria Müller

18

cycling

Kassel

reggae music

pizza

mountain climbing in the Himalayas

Discussion

Task 3

Exchange drawings with a partner. Talk about the significance of the information in your picture. Ask questions to find out more about each other.

Activity

Task 4

Find out what you have in common with the other students in your class.

a. First, think of five interesting things about yourself, for example, "I was born in June", "My favourite colour is yellow" etc.
b. Then, think of how you would ask someone to get similar information about them e.g. "What month were you born in?", "What's your favourite colour?".
c. Next, circulate around the class and ask each other questions. If you find somebody you have something in common with, write it down.
d. When you've finished interviewing each other, tell the class who you have things in common with.

Writing

Task 5

Look at the pictures below and choose the door that looks the most inviting for you. It is the door to your future. Write a short piece about why you chose that door, and what or where you think it leads. Where do you think your future will take you? Write no more than 200 words. Exchange compositions with a partner and talk about your future plans.

Unit 1:

Working with children – working in institutions for childcare

Module 1: The childcare professional – practitioners and their work settings

1 Little did Friedrich Fröbel know when he founded the first play and activity institute in Bad Blankenburg in 1837, would become his concept of "kindergarten" so influential that the German word he coined would still be commonly used around the world today.

In fact, much more of Fröbel's work has become the foundation of early education in 5 English-speaking countries.

Although the term "kindergarten" is used in many countries, it isn't always used to mean the same thing. Because the development of the educational system is historically different in each country, the words for some concepts and professionals are often culturally unique and thus, difficult to translate into other languages.

10 The German word "Erzieher", for example, could be a *kindergarten* or *nursery school teacher*, an *educator*, a *childminder*, a *nanny*, or an *early childhood practitioner* largely depending on the setting the professional works in and the country.

The provision of childcare outside the home emerged contemporaneously with the Industrial Revolution when mothers of young children were increasingly drawn into the 15 labour market. *Infant schools*, as they were called in Great Britain, or *salles d'asile*, literally "rooms of the asylum" in France were merely daytime refuges for children who were still too young to attend school, or work themselves. The minding of the children was left to young women who generally had no training and earned meagre wages for their work.

20 It became apparent rather quickly that in the absence of their parents these young children required specialised care and upbringing. By the turn of the twentieth century the ideas of pedagogues such as Pestalozzi, McMillan and Montessori had helped shape the education and training of childcarers throughout Europe, greatly improving the quality of care they provided and giving the occupation a professional profile.

25 Today childcare professionals work in a number of different settings. In Germany, roughly two-thirds of all childcare professionals work in preschool settings, including nursery schools, crèches and kindergartens, and after-school care clubs. In most anglo-phone countries, "kindergarten" denotes the year of education in a primary or elementary school prior to the first grade. However, in England this year is commonly referred 30 to as "reception".

Childcare professionals are also employed in institutions of social welfare, such as approved or reform schools for delinquent juveniles, children's homes, youth centres, recreation programmes, welfare agencies for children and youth, and children's wards in hospitals. Additionally, childcare professionals may work in institutions for the care, 35 occupation and integration of people with mental and physical disabilities.

Comprehension

Task 1

The different names of childcare professionals and their work settings can be confusing. Try to match the term with its description. Use a dictionary to help you.

after-school care club – approved school – childminder – educator – kindergarten – nanny – nursery – reception

a. a general word for a teacher or an instructor, particularly in a school or university
b. the first year of compulsory schooling in England
c. a place school-aged children can go after school
d. a preschool setting for children 0–3 years
e. a person, usually a woman, who is privately employed to educate children in their homes
f. a non-compulsory year of education for children before they enter first grade in the United States
g. a registered professional day carer who works in her own home and provides care for up to three children under the age of five
h. an institution which educates and disciplines errant youths

Language

Task 2

Not everybody is suited to become a childcare professional. There are certain qualities a person should naturally have, or develop, to be able to work with children competently. Look at the words in the box and decide which of these personal attributes a childcare professional should have. Discuss your choices.

affectionate – alert – boring – calm – caring – cheerful – cold – conceited – considerate – cooperative – creative – dishonest – enthusiastic – friendly – honest – immature – impatient – inattentive – inconsiderate – indifferent – interested – interesting – intolerant – irresponsible – mature – observant – open-minded – organised – patient – polite – prejudiced – punctual – relaxed – respectful – responsible – sympathetic – tolerant – trusting – unimaginative – untrustworthy

Task 3

a. Using the adjectives from the box in Task 2, find as many antonym pairs as you can. Some words have more than one possible antonym. Use a dictionary to help you. The first pair has been done for you.

alert ≠ inattentive

b. Now, see how many noun forms correspond to the adjectives in the box and add them to the list. A first pair has been done for you.

honest	honesty

Task 4

What about you? Which of these attributes would you use to describe yourself? Now, choose a partner you know well and see how similar you are.

Grammar

Simple Present Tense

We usually use the Simple Present when we talk about:
- permanent conditions and states, including possession, relationships, illness and characteristics
- facts and opinions
- actions that happen all the time or on a regular basis
- habitual actions

Affirmative	Negative	Question / Negated Question
I work at a kindergarten.	I do not work at a kindergarten. I don't work at a kindergarten.	Do I work at a kindergarten? Don't I work at a kindergarten?
You work at a kindergarten.	You do not work a kindergarten. You don't work at a kindergarten.	Do you work at a kindergarten? Don't you work at a kindergarten?
Ann works at a kindergarten. She works at a kindergarten.	She does not work at a kindergarten. She doesn't work at a kindergarten.	Does Ann work at a kindergarten? Doesn't she work at a kindergarten?
We work at a kindergarten.	We do not work at a kindergarten. We don't work at a kindergarten.	Do we work at a kindergarten? Don't we work at a kindergarten?
They work at a kindergarten.	They do not work at a kindergarten. They don't work at a kindergarten.	Do they work at a kindergarten? Don't they work at a kindergarten?

Take a look at these examples:

• permanent conditions and states	*St. Mary's Nursery School accepts children under the age of three.*
• possession	*The mittens don't belong to Elena.*
• illness	*Jacob has a hearing impairment.*
• characteristics	*Cole doesn't like cabbage.*
• fact	*Grace is five years old.*
• opinion	*I think she is ill.*
• actions that happen on a regular basis, habitual actions	*The children brush their teeth after breakfast.*

Task 5

What do the children do all week? Look at the schedule and write down the group's weekly activities using appropriate verbs in the Simple Present Tense. A couple of examples have been done for you.

On Monday mornings the Busy Bees sing songs.
The Busy Bees sing songs on Monday mornings.

Busy Bees' weekly activities		
	Morning	Afternoon
Monday	singing	playground
Tuesday	art	yoga
Wednesday	storytime	science
Thursday	outing	music
Friday	free play	playground activities/ games

Task 6

You are a childcare practitioner in a kindergarten and you and your colleague are responsible for planning the group's daily activities for children aged four and five. What would your typical day look like? Use the simple present to prepare an activity schedule from 8 a.m. to 4 p.m.

Task 7

Early years teachers have a demanding job and a multitude of responsibilities. Use the following verbs in the left column with the activities from the right column to form meaningful sentences about their typical tasks. The first one has been done for you.

Early years teachers ... *assist the children for the development of basic skills.*

assist *helfen*	... a curriculum with a wide-range of activities that promote children's curiosity and knowledge.
devise *entwickeln*	... a positive and supportive working relationship with children, staff members and parents.
encourage	... care and support to children in a secure environment.
ensure	... children's creative development through stories, arts and imaginative play.
maintain	... each child on an individual basis and records their progress.
observe	... the children for the development of basic skills.
provide	... the children's learning abilities through access to new experiences.
stimulate *stimulieren*	... that the health and safety of children is maintained during activities, both inside and outside.

Handwritten annotations in left margin:
Ermutigen
Versichern
aufrecht~ erhalten
observieren
sorgen für

Writing

Task 8

What kind of day-to-day difficulties would you expect to have as a childcare practitioner? Write a short paragraph about what you see in the cartoon. Discuss your ideas as a group.

Module 2: A day in the life of a childcare professional

1 20-year-old Vivien Young works as an early years preschool assistant in Birmingham. She has a diploma in Health and Social Care, but is currently studying Child Care, Learning and Development at a local college.

Vivien's day begins at half past eight in the morning when she signs in. First she liaises 5 with the other staff members and starts to organise the morning's activities. Vivien greets the children and their parents when they start to arrive at quarter to nine. By quarter past nine, all of the children have arrived, and they can begin "Circle Time". Vivien takes the register and talks to the children about the weekly theme, the weather and the types of clothes that are appropriate for that day. She usually reads the children 10 a story that is relevant to the weekly theme.

They go outside until half past ten, and when they come back in, Vivien helps the children wash their hands, and prepares a fruit snack for them. At quarter to eleven the children get to choose which activity they'd like to do: crafts, manipulatives or dramatic play. While they're occupied with their activities, Vivien goes around playing with the 15 children, and noting any important observations.

Shortly before noon, she supervises the children with the tidying up. Once they have put everything away, Vivien helps the children take out their lunch boxes and makes sure that the children with food allergies do not eat foods they do not tolerate.

After lunch Vivien takes some of the children with developmental difficulties to the 20 local education authority building, where they will receive special attention. There she talks to the staff and reports any information.

She's back at the preschool by one o'clock to start setting up the afternoon activities using their planning sheets. While the children get dressed to go outside, Vivien checks the playground and makes sure the equipment is safe and in working order.

25 At around two o'clock they all have a snack and some juice. The children have time for free play until their parents come to collect them at three o'clock. Vivien signs the children out as they are picked up, passes on any important information to the parents and answers their questions. If a child has had an accident, Vivien asks the parents to sign the accident record book.

30 Before Vivien can go home, there are a few more things that need to be done. She clears the setting and checks to see if everything is safe and in order. She looks to see whether any belongings have been left behind and puts them in the lost property bin. Then she makes sure the heating is off and all the windows and doors have been secured. When her colleagues have completed their tasks, they exchange ideas about the next day and 35 close up. Vivien goes home at four o'clock after a long and exhausting day.

Comprehension

Task 1

What is Vivien Young's typical day like? Complete an activity schedule using the Simple Present Tense. Write the schedule on a separate piece of paper or in your notebook. An example has been done for you.

| 8.30 a.m. Vivien signs in at 8.30 in the morning. |
| At 9.15 a.m. Vivien… |

Task 2

Vivien Young's job is demanding and multifaceted. Not only is she responsible for the health and safety of the children, but also for their emotional and physical development and the acquisition of social skills. Together with a partner, find the tasks and activities in the text that correspond to these responsibilities and complete the table below. Can you think of any more?

Health	Safety	Physical Development	Emotional Development	Social Skills
			greets the children	

Grammar

Present Progressive Tense

We usually use the Present Progressive when we talk about:
- actions that are happening at the moment of speaking,
- actions that are temporary,
- repeated actions,
- developments and changes,
- things that are about to happen.

Affirmative	Negative	Question / Negated Question
I am taking a break. I'm taking a break.	I am not taking a break. I'm not taking a break.	Am I taking a break? Aren't I taking a break?
You are taking a break. You're taking a break.	You are not taking a break. Your're not / You aren't taking a break.	Are you taking a break? Aren't you taking a break?
Ann is taking a break. Ann's taking a break.	She is not taking a break. She's not / She isn't taking a break.	Is Ann taking a break? Isn't she taking a break?
We are taking a break. We're taking a break.	We are not taking a break. We're not / We aren't taking a break.	Are we taking a break? Aren't we taking a break?
They are taking a break. They're taking a break.	They are not taking a break. They're not / They aren't taking a break.	Are they taking a break? Aren't they taking a break?

Take a look at these examples:

• actions that are happening at the moment of speaking	*The children are listening to a story in the book corner.*
• actions that are temporary	*The light isn't working.*
• repeated actions	*Leah is having difficulty saying goodbye to her mum in the morning.*
• developments and changes	*Emil's language skills are improving every day.*
• things that are about to happen	*The children are going home in a few minutes.*

Task 3

Complete the sentences in the Present Progressive using the verbs and phrases in the box. Do the exercise on a separate piece of paper or in your notebook. The first one has been done for you.

a. Ssshh! The children *are having a nap*.
b. I'm afraid she cannot come to the phone at the moment. She ...
c. Quick! Matthew ...
d. It looks like we won't be going outside to play. It ...
e. What happened to Carla? Why ... she ...?
f. We have to go home now. It ...
g. I haven't seen the children for a long time. My goodness, they ...!

- to cry
- to change a baby's nappy
- to get big
- to get dark outside
- *to have a nap*
- to rain
- to run away

Task 4

Tense discrimination is the ability to recognise and use the two different aspects of a tense. Can you discriminate between the simple and progressive aspects of the Present Tense? Read the following text and complete the sentences with the verbs from the box in the appropriate form. Place the adverbs in brackets in the correct positions. Not all of the verbs will be used. Do the exercise on a separate piece of paper or in your notebook.

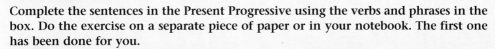

draw – prepare – try – seem – flush – come – put – hit – care – have – seem – get – cry – get – undress – take

Miss Madeleine's mischief-makers

Miss Madeleine's ...(1)... for five children; she is a live in nanny. She ...(2)... to keep her tots occupied, but it ...(3)... they ...(4)... (constantly) themselves into mischief. In the morning, while she is getting one child dressed, another one ...(5)... (already) himself again. And while she ...(6)... a meal for lunch in the kitchen, there's havoc in the nursery: James ...(7)... on the walls with markers. Sarah ...(8)... marbles in her mouth. Jude ...(9)... Asher and Asher ...(10)... Where's Peter? Oh no! He ...(11)... wax crayons down the toilet. Who ...(12)... to the rescue? Miss Madeleine, of course! She finally ...(13)... her break while the little darlings ...(14)... a nap.

Environment matters

1 The childcare environment can have a profound effect on the overall well-being of the children and the staff. Colour, lighting, sound and layout of an area all influence a
5 child's responsiveness as well as their ability to concentrate and learn.

Although nursery-aged children are particularly responsive to warm bright colours, too many primary colours can be over-
10 stimulating, or unsettling. Softer shades have a calming effect, and children are in fact less likely to show hyperactivity.

Likewise, sound levels in rooms have an impact on children's sensitivity. Carpeting, curtains and the height of a ceiling can help reduce excessive noise, producing an environment which is conducive to concentrated learning.

15 Both children and adults find a friendly and comfortable setting most inviting. Due to the lack of space, rooms are usually used for more than one purpose. Therefore, the layout of the room should be flexible and the equipment and materials well-organised.

Spaces for children are full of toys and learning materials to provide ample opportunity for different types of play and activities. Dividing the space into separate areas for dif-
20 ferent kinds of learning can help children orientate themselves in a special area, and also help the childcare provider monitor the children.

Comprehension

Task 5

a. Make a list of the words in the text that are unfamiliar to you. Try to understand their meanings from the context.
b. Now, find the words in the text which mean:

1. make smaller or less in amount
2. cause to feel anxious or uneasy
3. maintain regular surveillance over
4. the necessary items for a particular purpose
5. making a certain situation or outcome likely or possible

6. find one's position in certain surroundings
7. long window coverings
8. very great or intense
9. responding readily and with interest or enthusiasm
10. enough or more than enough of something

Grammar

Prepositions of place

Prepositions of place show someone's or something's position or location. Sometimes there's more than one possible choice. This can be confusing.

When do we use *at*?

- to talk about the position of something at a point, particularly in larger places, destinations, such as airports, and meeting points or social institutions
- before the names of places or buildings, especially when we are thinking of the activity inside the place
- in front of proper nouns, like the names of institutions and addresses containing a house number
- to talk about being at someone's house or at a firm

When do we use *in*?

- to talk about a dimensional position within a large area, like geographical location
- to talk about a position inside a three-dimensional space, including vehicles
- to talk about being within the surrounding environment
- to talk about being covered with or by a material

When do we use *on*?

- to talk about being on the surface of something
- to show that something is attached to something else
- to talk about a position by a lake or sea
- to talk about being inside some types of transport, e.g. on flight 587

We can use both *in* and *on* before nouns denoting enclosed open spaces, such as a field or a street. However, *on* is used when the space is considered a surface, and *in* when the space is considered an area.

When do we use *over* and *above*?

- to show that something is higher than a particular point, but not touching it

When do we use *under, underneath, beneath* and *below*?

- to show that something is lower than a particular point

When do we use *near, by, next to, between, among* and *opposite*?

- to show that something is close to a particular point

Task 6

Which prepositions are used with these places? Choose an appropriate preposition and write a sentence for each of the words in the box. Use a dictionary if you need help.

bus – cot – cubbyhole – door – first floor – fish tank – lavatory – library – playground – row – shade – swing – table – tree – tricycle

Activity

Task 7

Imagine you have to design a kindergarten room. What would it look like? Which age group would it serve? What would you put in it? Work with a partner and design your own preschool room. Use the area words in the box to help you. Share your designs with the other groups. There's an example below to help you.

arts and crafts – baby hygiene – construction – cookery – domestic play – dramatic play – growing and living things interest table – listening – make-believe play – making music – manipulatives – natural materials – naptime area – puzzles and games – quiet time – sand and water – technology – sensory development – small-world toys – workshop – writing and graphics

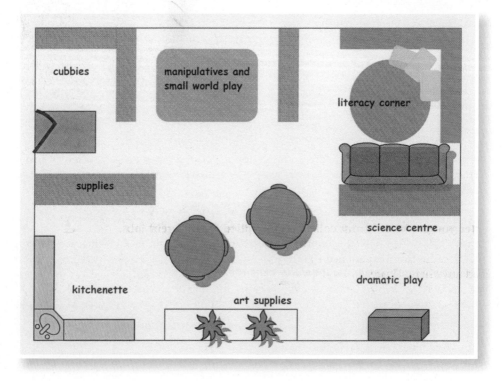

Conversation with René Dietrich, 29, preschool teacher in Berlin

1 **How did you become a preschool teacher?**
René: Well, after I finished my secondary education, I got my vocational training in business for wholesale and foreign trade. I worked at a car dealer. Afterwards I realised I wanted to go to college, but I didn't know what I wanted to study. But before I could 5 apply for college, I needed to obtain my diploma first. So, I went to a vocational school for economics and got my vocational diploma. Then I decided to study social pedagogy in Berlin. My focus was actually in education – primarily in early childhood education and social politics. And now I'm here with the Friedenau Rascals, where I've been working for about a year now.

10 **Did you have any practical experience?**
René: Yes, I did three month of practical training at a youth club. I organised a hip-hop project for kids. I also worked at another youth recreation facility for a while which provided programmes and rooms for music education. We helped organise lessons for youths who wanted to learn an instrument, or music rehearsals for teens who wanted 15 to play together in a band. We also helped the kids set up concerts and stages for their performances.

Why did you decide to study social pedagogy?
René: Well, after having worked in business 20 and trade so intensively, which was my personal area of expertise, I knew I wasn't going to learn much more that would truly interest me. I was more interested in working with people, the way people live together. 25 And so, I thought about social pedagogy because it leads to many different professions which all have to do with psychology, education and social politics.

Had you ever considered working in a preschool?
30 **René:** No, I had never really considered that. I was interested in early childhood education in my course of studies, but I didn't think that I would actually go into it professionally. In fact, I didn't even know during my studies that I would be able to work as a preschool teacher with my qualifications.

After you graduated from college you applied for different jobs.
35 **René:** Yeah, then I finally made the decision! By then I knew I was interested in education because from experience I knew that working in social work projects often didn't lead anywhere. However, I did have my problems with school. I thought about becoming a school social worker, but because I had had problems in school myself, I really didn't want to "go back to school". Since I really enjoyed working with young kids,

40 I thought I'd try applying to preschools. I did apply for other jobs, too, because my primary goal was to find employment. But then, I was glad that I got a job at a preschool after all.

So, after a year, you can probably judge whether this profession is one you'd like to stay in, or not.
45 **René:** I can't say yet whether it will be my profession for life, but I can say that I am quite satisfied with where I am at the moment and the fact that I am learning new things every day. As long as I can learn new things, I have fun with what I do. My interests may change as I get older; but at the moment I can have fun with what I am doing.

What kinds of things have you learned from your practical experience with
50 **children that you never learned in college? It's probably a very stressful job, isn't it?**
René: It can be quite stressful at times. That's something they don't write in textbooks. Someone once said bringing up children is like war, but it is also very rewarding. Of course you always have to deal with power struggles between some kids. And it can be
55 more difficult than anyone could imagine.

There are clearly fewer men in your profession than women. Do you think it's caused by blatant sexism, or prejudice?
René: Yes, I do. I think sexism definitely plays a role. I haven't been confronted with it myself, but I can also say that it didn't influence my career choice. It didn't matter to
60 me. I knew who I was, and I didn't think that I fitted the clichés, or expectations people had of men. I've never had a problem with that.

Can you understand why there's prejudice against men in early childhood education?
René: Sure. It has to do with paedophilia. I think that is the biggest misconception – that
65 male preschool teachers must be paedophiles. It's understandable when you take into consideration all of the scandals that have been in the press recently. I believe you have to judge each person as an individual, and give every individual a chance.

What are some of the positive things you experience in your preschool workaday life?
70 **René:** It's definitely being greeted in the morning. When I come to work in the morning there are always so many cheerful faces smiling at me. Kids come up and hug me. That's what I like about my job. I find it fascinating the way children can smile all the time. I'm also fascinated by the way they learn. They are constantly hyped up with feelings of happiness because they are learning. I have to admit that I'm often envious of them.
75 It's unfortunate that we gradually lose this ability. What I also like about my job is being a part of the whole, and being privileged to accompany these children during the first stage of their lives.

Comprehension

Task 8

Answer the following questions. Discuss your answers in a group.

a. What influenced René to become a preschool teacher?
b. Why does René believe only a minority of men work in his profession?
c. Why do you think sex discrimination is so apparent in this profession?

Writing

Task 9

What are some of the social benefits of having men as early childhood educators? How can children profit by this? Write a short response.

Module 3: Career opportunities – applying for a job

Listening

Finding a job

The transcript of the audio can be found on page 206.

Comprehension

Task 1

Listen to Sandra, Geoffrey, Julia and Claire talk about their qualifications. Use the table below to help you take notes. Copy the table onto a separate piece of paper.

Name	Sandra	Geoffrey	Julia	Claire
Age				
Education				
Experience				
Skills/Interests				

Task 2

Once you have listened to all four people, find the job advertisement on the following page that is best suited to each of them. Then explain your choices.

Job Advertisements

Title: Childminding Assistant
Terms of employment: permanent full-time
Working schedule: 22 hrs/week, Mon., Wed., Thurs. 8 am – 5 pm
Employer: Little Acorns Childminding Services
Salary: minimum wage
Experience: Previous experience would be an advantage but not essential as training will be provided.
Job description: Duties will involve assisting the childminder in the day to day care and supervision children aged 6 months up to 5 years providing a fun, playful and stimulating environment. Successful applicants are required to provide an enhanced disclosure.

Title: Early childhood educator
Terms of employment: temporary, part time, day
Employer: Developmental Disabilities Association
Work setting: Child care centre
Salary: £ 10.70 hourly for 27.5 hours per week
Anticipated starting date: As soon as possible
Education: Completion of college/CEGEP/vocational or technical training
Credentials: Early Childhood Education Diploma or Degree
Experience: 1-2 years; with children who have special needs, children with an intellectual disability
Responsibilities: plan and develop child care and nursery school programmes; provide supervision and guidance of daily activities; assess the developmental level of children; prepare progress reports and discuss with parents and other staff members; bathe, change nappies and feed infants and toddlers; prepare and serve snacks.

Title: Teacher's assistant
Working schedule: day shift, variable hours, up to 40 hours per week
Employer: Concord Hospital
Service Area: The Learning Centre
Minimum requirements: Must be at least 18 years of age and have a minimum of 9 credits in Early Childhood Education, or 3 ECE credits and 1500 documented hours in a licensed child care facility or alternatively have completed a 2-year vocational course in Early Childhood Education.
Certifications: Current certification in Infant and Child CPR, and Basic First Aid preferred, or must be achieved within 6 months of employment.
Responsibilities: Work in close cooperation with classroom team members to encourage the social/emotional, cognitive and physical development of the children. Assist in planning and offering individual and group activities, participate in the orientation process for each new family. In the position you will be working with a teaching team caring for infants from 8 weeks up to kindergarten aged children.

Title: Senior Youth Worker
Working pattern: full time, contract position
Employer: Islington Council
Service Area: Children's Services/Young People's Division
Salary: £33,110 – £35,738 / 35 hours per week
Job description: Toffee Park Youth Club is a dynamic and innovative youth project. We wish to recruit an energetic and committed individual to help us achieve our vision which is to create a caring and responsive service for young people. You will have had successful experience of working with culturally diverse groups and young people at risk, have a passion for developing young children's skills and talents. You will have designed projects to encourage participation and involvement and have a strong track record in engaging with and inspiring young people. Candidates should be qualified to a minimum of level 4 in youth work and understand the value of youth work in young children's development.

Grammar

Comparison of adjectives

			Comparative form		Superlative form
Rule 1: Adjectives with only one syllable	old shy cute	-er	older shyer cuter quieter feebler sallower angrier*	the + -est -st	oldest shyest cutest quietest feeblest sallowest angriest*
and adjectives with two syllables ending in -er, -et, -le, -ow and -y	tender quiet feeble sallow angry	-r			
Rule 2: Three letter adjectives (not ending on -y or -w) double the end consonant before adding the ending, e.g. fat → fatter → fattest, wet → wetter → wettest, fit → fitter → fittest					
*Rule 3: Adjectives with more than three letters which end in -y and are not preceded by a vowel: the -y is replaced by an -i before the comparative or superlative ending, e.g. dirty → dirtier → dirtiest					
Rule 4: Adjectives with two syllables that do not end in -er, -et, -le, -ow and -y, and adjectives with more than two syllables	helpful gifted nervous important adorable	more	more helpful more gifted more nervous more important more adorable	the most	the most helpful the most gifted the most nervous the most important the most adorable
Exceptions to the rules:	good / well → better → best bad → worse → worst far → farther / further → farthest/furthest little / small → less → least much / many → more → most				
There are some adjectives that can use both comparative forms.					

Task 3

Using the table in task one, compare the applicants' qualities and qualifications. Use the adjectives in the box to help you. You may also use the adjectives found in Module 1, Task 2. An example has been done for you.

active – experienced – interesting – lively – mature – old recent – reliable – tolerant – well-suited – young

Sandra Hare is the oldest applicant.

Language

Writing a curriculum vitae

1 A typical CV (curriculum vitae) in the United Kingdom or resumé in the United States
  does provides information about one's skills, work experience, education and special
  interests, as well as one's contact information, but it does not usually include a photograph, family status, age, nationality or racial background, as this could lead to discrimi-
5 natory treatment in the application process. Above all, the CV and covering letter should
  be brief.

Claire Peters
5 Priory Road · Warwick
Warwickshire CV34 4 · United Kingdom
52 83 37 71 · Email: cpeters@googlemail.com

Skills:	Nineteen years of experience working with children, of all ages First Aid and CPR certification • Ability to communicate in British Sign Language • Knowledge of dietary needs of children with food intolerance • Computer literate • Basic knowledge of Spanish
Work Experience:	
1996–2002	Ingfield Manor School worked with young children with physical disabilities and learning difficulties
1994–1995	Warwick Children's Centre assistant teacher, worked with children 2-4 yrs
1990–1992	Au pair in Sydney, Australia cared for infant and twin five-year olds
Education:	
1992–1996	North Warwickshire College BTEC Diploma in Children's Care, Learning and Development (equivalent to Level 3 Diploma Children and Young People's Workforce)
1987–1992	Warwick School, Surrey completion of Key Stage 4
Interests:	Cooking, travelling and spending time with the family

Writing a covering letter

The **return address (letter head)** with or without the sender's name, can either be placed on the left or right margin, or in the middle.

Claire Peters
5 Priory Road · Warwick
Warwickshire CV34 4 · United Kingdom
52 83 37 71 · Email: cpeters@googlemail.com

The **recipient's address** is always on the left margin.

20 January 2012

The **date** belongs either on the right margin or the left margin, but is usually placed between the return address and recipient's address.

Ms Andrea Randall
Developmental Disabilities Association
Clinic Drive
Coton Road
Nuneaton
CV11 5TY

The **regarding line** is not necessary, but it is a good idea in a covering letter to show which job advert you are responding to.

Dear Ms Randall

There is no punctuation in the British-style **salutation.**

Re: Your advertisement in the Warwick Courier, 14 January 2012

As you suggested in our recent telephone conversation, I am enclosing my resume for your consideration.

You should begin your introductory paragraph with the purpose of your letter.

You are looking for a temporary part-time child care professional with experience working with young children with special needs. I would like to draw your attention to my six-year working experience and the professional skills I have acquired over the years.

Why are you applying for the job? Why should the employer consider you?

As a mother of two school-aged children, I would describe myself as mature, experienced and responsible when it comes to working with children. I currently hold a level 3 Diploma in Childcare and Education qualification. I have six years of experience which include working in a worked day nursery with young children with physical disabilities and learning difficulties.

I particularly enjoyed building close bonds with the children and working closely with parents to ensure they were supported in leaving their child with someone other than a family member for the first time. I work on a 1:1 basis with children who have additional needs, and plan activities which can easily be adapted depending on a child's individual needs.

What kind of person are you? What credentials do you have?

You should also know that I regularly attend training courses including Makaton, how to overcome communication difficulties, and safeguarding.

In the final paragraph, you should welcome the potential employer to contact you. Show your eagerness.

You may call me anytime at 52 83 37 71 should you have questions. I look forward to hearing from you.

Yours sincerely

There is no punctuation in the British-style **closure.**

Claire Peters
Claire Peters

Enc.: CV, professional licence, letter of recommendation

Enclosures, also Encl.

Here are some guidelines to writing covering letters:

1 The date is written either:
20 January 2012 (UK-style)
January 20, 2012 (US-style)
It's best to write out the name of the month to avoid confusion.

5 The British-style salutation is written without punctuation marks. The American-style salutation takes (.) after the title *Mr., Mrs., Ms.,* and *Dr.* and commas, after the recipient's name.
Dear Mrs Smith / Dear Mrs. Smith,

If you don't know name of the person you are addressing, use:
10 *Dear Sir or Madam*

The subject matter is introduced in the *Re:* (regarding) line with a few key phrases. This is placed immediately following the salutation.

Unlike German letters, the body of the letter begins with the first word of the first paragraph after the salutation, and this is capitalised. The closure of the letter may use

15 *Yours truly*
Yours very truly
Sincerely yours

If you do not know who the recipient of the letter is and your salutation is either, *Dear Sir or Madam* or *Dear Sirs* then you must end your letter with *Yours faithfully*

20 At the very end of your covering letter, you should remember to point out that you are enclosing documentation of your qualifications. Below the closure and signature, you should include the abbreviation for "enclosed": *enc. or Encl.*

Here are some useful suggestions for your letter:

Introductory paragraph	*I am replying to your advertisement in the ....* *I read your advertisement in The Daily Paper and would like to apply for the position as ....*
Middle paragraph	*At present I am employed at ....* *I recently completed my three-year training course in ....*
Closing paragraph	*I would be very happy to discuss further questions in a personal interview.* *I look forward to hearing from you soon.*

Activity

Task 4

Use a newspaper or an employment database on the Internet to find a job that interests you. Then prepare your application as if you were applying for the job: write a CV and a covering letter. Trade job applications with a partner and compare.

Grammar

Asking Questions

There are two types of questions: yes-no questions and specific questions. Yes-no questions seek a confirmation of information, whereas specific questions seek detailed information.

Almost all questions require an auxiliary verb (e.g. *be, have, do*). Which auxiliary verb is needed depends on the type of main verb and its tense and aspect.

If the main verb is the stative verb *be* preceding a quality or attribute, another auxiliary verb is not needed. If the sentence already contains an auxiliary verb or a modal verb (e.g. *can, will*), the subject and auxiliary verb are simply inverted. Look at these examples:

She is disabled.	*Is she disabled?*

They are at home.	*Are they at home?*
I will help you.	*Will you help me?*
She will be home at six o'clock.	*When will she be home?*
She can speak three languages.	*How many languages can she speak?*

Sentences in the Simple Present and simple past tenses:
If the main verb is an action verb, the auxiliary verb *do* (*does, did*) is needed.

*They **live** in Cologne.*	*Do they **live** in Cologne?*
*She **works** in Bonn.*	*Does she **work** in Bonn?*
We don't live in England.	*Where do you live?*
*I **worked** in a kindergarten.*	*Where **did** you **work**?*

Sentences in the Present and Past Progressive and Present Perfect:
The auxiliary verb is inverted with the subject.

*I **am getting** ready to go home.*	*Are you **getting** ready to go home?*

*He's **going** home at five o'clock.*	*When **is** he **going** home?*
*They **were playing** on the playground.*	*What **were** they **doing**?*
*I **have worked** at a nursery for two years.*	*How long **have** you **worked** at a nursery?*

Task 5

At a job interview you are asked many questions. Complete the questions below with an appropriate question word or auxiliary verb. Do the exercise on a separate piece of paper or in your notebook.

a. *When* did you finish your teacher training?
b. ...(1)... do you want to be a teacher?
c. ...(2)... are your strengths and weaknesses?
d. ...(3)... did you previously work?
e. ...(4)... did you quit your previous job?
f. ...(6)... would you define a good teacher?
g. ...(8)... would you define an ideal classroom?
h. ...(9)... you know CPR?
i. ...(10)... you qualified in sign language?

Activity

 Task 6

In task 4, you prepared your job application. Congratulations! You have been invited to a job interview. This can be a daunting task, so you ought to be prepared. Make a list of questions you could expect to be asked at a job interview. How would you answer them? Conduct a mock job interview with a partner.

Unit 2:
Protecting children

Module 1: What is child safeguarding?

What is the difference between child protection and child safeguarding?

1 Alison Watts works as a child safeguarding officer for schools and learning in the north of England. She explains what it means:

Until a few years ago, we talked about child protection, and what it means to protect children from abuse and neglect. Now we talk about child safeguarding. The two words
5 have very similar meanings but the concept behind child safeguarding is broader. It includes the idea that as well as being protected from abuse, children also need to grow up healthily and be well cared for, with nothing to impair their health or development.

Any organisation which offers services or activities to children has a duty – both legally and morally – to safeguard the children it works with. Safeguarding means "to keep safe
10 from harm." In the workplace it means that you need to do everything possible to protect children physically and emotionally while they are there. So you need to do everything that you can to keep children safe while they are with you, but you also have a responsibility to think about children's safety when they're not with you. In particular, you need to know what to do if you have reason to think a child might be being abused.

15 When we want to show that we're thinking about protection from abuse, rather than general well-being, we use the phrase "at risk of significant harm". In these cases, it's very important that everybody who works with a child at risk (doctors, other health workers, care workers, social workers, educators and teachers) all communicate with each other and share important information. A lack of communication has led to prob-
20 lems in the past, although of course it is also important to remember confidentiality.

Even if children attend your workplace with one or both of their parents, you still have a responsibility to make sure that the children are safe. Accidents can happen even with parents there. That is why you should always carry out an assessment of all possible risks, and put a plan in place to reduce any risks to a minimum.

Comprehension

Task 1

Find five key words or phrases from the text which match the definitions below.

a. physical, sexual or emotional mistreatment
b. to fail to care for or pay attention to
c. in danger
d. to hinder
e. keeping personal information private

Task 2

Are the following statements true or false?

a. The verb to safeguard has a meaning that is almost the same as the verb to protect.
b. The term *child protection* includes more than *child safeguarding*.
c. To come to harm means to have something happen that hurts you in some way.
d. When you work with children, you only need to think about any harm which might come to them at your workplace.

Language / Discussion

Task 3

Work in pairs, each choose two of the words in italics in the text below and explain them to your partner. Use a dictionary to help you if necessary.

Here is an extract from a risk assessment. It shows the type of questions which professionals (social workers, teachers, early learning workers, health visitors) might have to answer about a child they are working with.

a. Are there any *concerns*?
b. Is there any known history of abuse?
c. Does the child have a lot of *injuries*?
d. Has the child been in hospital for any of these injuries?
e. Does the child appear *well-fed* and clean?
f. Are there any other signs of neglect?
g. Does the child have any problems with his or her *behaviour*?
h. If yes, what kind of problems e.g. aggression, *inappropriate* sexual behaviour?
i. Do you believe the child to be at risk?

Task 4

Have you ever heard about a case where child safeguarding went wrong? For example, a case in Germany when people were working with a child at risk, but the child was still hurt? Discuss this with your neighbour, see if you have heard about the same cases.

Listening

On the telephone

Part A

- Hello, Children and Families, can I help you?
- Hello, could I speak to Aneesha please?
- Speaking.
- Oh hi, Aneesha. This is Sarah Redmond, I'm calling from Lorimer Children's Centre, I run the Family Learning Sessions there. I got a message to call you.
- Hi Sarah, thanks very much for getting back to me. Yes, I wanted to speak to you about a child who I believe attends your sessions. His name is Jaydon Blake. Do you know this little boy?

- Yes I do. He comes in with his mum, they probably attend around half the time.
- That's great. Do you think I could ask you some questions? His mother has given her consent for me to talk to you. The reason is that there are some concerns about Jaydon's well-being, and I'd really welcome your input. I've just started working with the family, so you've spent much more time with him and his mum.
- Yes that's fine, do you want to ask me now?
- I'm a bit busy right now, but perhaps we could chat later this afternoon, or tomorrow?
- Later today would be great, shall I give you a call around 4 pm?
- Yes, that's fine.
- OK, speak to you then, bye.
- Bye!

Part B

- Well, thanks very much for your input Sarah.
- Is there anything that I should do?
- Just keep an eye on Jaydon, and see how he is in the sessions. If you see anything which gives you concerns, you should contact me as soon as possible. I have to write up a report, then we'll have to have a *Team around the child meeting*. Have you been to one before?
- Yes, once, about a year ago.
- Good, so you'll know what to expect. Everyone who works with the family must keep in touch with each other, although we should avoid giving any confidential details unless it's absolutely necessary. It's purely on a need to know basis, if we believe there is a risk of harm to Jaydon.
- Should I tell the other staff in the children's centre?
- No, you don't have to tell people who have no contact with the family. The only person you should tell is your line manager, who ought to be aware of what's happening. What we mustn't do is alarm or frighten Jaydon. We are here to give help and support when it's needed, we mustn't be seen as punishing either Jaydon or his mother.

Comprehension

Task 5

Listen to the first part of the conversation and answer these questions.

a. Where does Sarah work and where does Aneesha work?
b. Who made the first contact, Aneesha or Sarah?
c. Which of the two professionals has the most contact with the little boy?

Task 6

Listen to the first part of the conversation again and complete the following phrases, which are useful for making telephone calls.

a. How does Aneesha identify herself on the phone? ...(1)...
b. How does Sarah identify herself on the phone? ...(2)...
c. How does Sarah say where she works? "...(3)... Lorimer Children's Centre."
d. How does Aneesha thank Sarah for calling?
   "Thanks very much ...(4)..."
e. How does Aneesha say that she doesn't have time to talk? ...(5)...

Task 7

Listen to the second part, an excerpt from their later conversation. Decide if the following statements are true or false.

a. Sarah has to write a report about Jaydon.
b. Those who work with the family shouldn't give each other any information at all, because of confidentiality
c. Sarah ought to tell everyone else at the children's centre where she works about her conversation with Aneesha.
d. Sarah's line manager should know about the conversation.

Task 8

Listen again. What do you think the following phrases mean? Discuss them with a partner.

to keep an eye on – to keep in touch – a need to know basis

Discussion

Task 9

Role-play the following telephone conversation with a partner.

Student A: You are a social worker who wants to ask Student B to a meeting about a three-year-old girl named Alice Jacobs.

Student B: You are a kindergarten worker, and there is a three-year-old girl named Alice Jacobs who attends your nursery every week.

Task 10

In pairs, decide on what is the difference in meaning between the modal verbs *should, ought to* and *must*.

Grammar

Modal Auxiliary Verbs

Some Modal Auxiliary Verbs are used to talk about things which are advisable (a good idea), or which are necessary / obligatory. These Modal Verbs are *should, ought to* and *must*. We also use *have to*, although it is not a true Modal Auxiliary.

Task 11

Find the Modal Verbs in Task 7 and decide which has which meaning.

a. it's necessary / obligatory
b. it's not necessary / not obligatory
c. it's necessary not to do it
d. it's advisable / a good idea
e. it's not advisable / not a good idea

Things to remember about Modal Verbs:
- Modal Verbs are used with the infinitive of the main verb (e.g. we should *be* careful).
- Modal Verbs have no -s on the he / she / it part of the verb (e.g. he *must* listen).
- Negatives are made by adding *not* or in contracted form -*n't* (e.g. you should*n't* ask too many questions).
- Questions are made by inverting the verb and subject (e.g. *must I* really write the report now?).
- There is no past tense of *must, should* and *ought to*.
- If you want to express obligation in the past, use the past of *have to* (e.g. I knew I *had to* meet him quickly).
- *Mustn't* and *don't have to* have different meanings (see Task 11 and Task 12).

Have to – because *have to* is not a true Modal Verb, it:
- changes in the he / she / it part (e.g. he *has to* do it).
- forms negatives with *don't / doesn't* (e.g. she *doesn't have to* worry).
- forms questions with *do / does* (e.g. *do* we really *have to*?).
- has a past tense (e.g. I *had to* meet my manager yesterday).

Task 12

Complete the sentences with either *mustn't* or *don't / doesn't have to.*

a. The details of the case are confidential, so you ...(1)... tell anyone who is not directly involved.
b. As a preschool worker, she ...(2)... wear a suit to work.
c. There's a play group at the children's centre, so local parents ...(3)...travel far.
d. We ...(4)... overreact to this, there may be nothing to it.
e. Whatever you do, you ...(5)... lose the file.
f. It's a holiday tomorrow, so he ...(6).... go to work.

Activity

Case study

Imagine you are working with a child at risk. He is a six-month old baby boy, whose mother is only 15 years old. His father is also young, and doesn't want to be involved with his son. The baby and his mother live with her parents – his grandparents, and his two uncles who are 12 and ten. The family has a three-bedroom flat, but the rooms are small and it feels very overcrowded.

Task 13

Work in groups of three or four. Think of five or six risks that this baby and this family might face. Design a risk assessment form in your notebook based on the format below.

Risks identified		High / Medium / Low
1.	Write the first risk you think of here.	Decide using the risk matrix below.
2.	Write the second risk you think of here.	Decide using the risk matrix below.

RISK MATRIX					
	If something happens, how severe could it be?				
How likely is it that something will happen?	Very slightly	marginal	moderate	severe	very severe
very unlikely	low	low	low	low	low
unlikely	low	low	low	medium	medium
possible	low	low	medium	high	high
probable	low	medium	high	high	high
very likely	low	medium	high	high	high

Module 2: Making plans together

Working in a Sure Start children's centre

1 Natalie Bremner is 29 and works as an Early Years Educator at a children's centre in Birmingham. She has worked here for four years.

What is a Sure Start children's centre?

5 These centres were introduced by the government in 1998. The core aim is to give the best help to children right from the beginning of their lives, and to improve outcomes for children from birth to five or six years old, with a target of particularly helping 10 those who are most disadvantaged. Most centres offer childcare and early learning, but they do much more than this. They bring together children's and parents' health services, such as health visitors or help with breastfeeding. Most centres give advice 15 on parenting, or run parenting courses. The centres also signpost families to other childcare options, and help to find specialist services such as speech therapy. Some centres run sessions to help children with behaviour issues. Many also offer direct support to parents, helping them to find jobs or training courses, or give advice on money problems. Some run classes for parents such as English for Speakers of Other Languages (ESOL).

20 Why do you think children's centres are important?

Evidence shows that children's early years are really important, and that a good foundation in the first few years sets kids up for how they'll progress later in their lives. There are so many things children need at this age. Good childcare is important, but so are good parenting and a healthy home environment.

25 What other services does your children's centre offer?

Our centre is one of the bigger ones, so you can see a dentist here, or a social worker, and we have physiotherapists too. We run a "stop smoking" clinic. We also offer short-term breaks for parents of disabled children.

What qualifications do you have?

30 I have an NVQ Level 3 (National Vocational Qualifications = englisches nationales Berufsbildungssystem) in Early Years Care and Education.

Who else works at the children's centre?

We have family support workers, nursery assistants, nursery nurses and room leaders, a nursery manager, a children's centre coordinator and a children's centre manager.

35 How old are the children that you work with?

Between three and five.

Tell us about your typical day.
I work with the children as part of a team of six. In the mornings we put out various
playthings or craft activities which the children can choose from when they feel like it.
40 When they arrive we get them settled, and it's free play. We sometimes do focus activities, when one of us leads the activity and the children can come and take part if they
want, for example, reading a story. We also sometimes walk around looking for chances
to sit down and play with one or more children in ways which will help with their
development.

45 **Do you enjoy your work?**
Oh yes, I love it!

Comprehension

 Task 1

Replace the words in italics with words from the text that have the same meaning.

a. This first qualification will give him a good *basis* for working in childcare.
b. She hopes that her work will produce positive *results*.
c. In our work we *direct* families towards the services they need.
d. So far, there has not been much *movement* towards achieving our aims.
e. You need to show that you have *proof* of your claims.

Discussion

 Task 2

In groups of three to four, discuss the following questions.

a. Would you like to work in a children's centre?
b. Do you think it would be a good idea to introduce children's centres in your city or
   town? If yes, why?

Language

 Task 3

Look at the text of this email, and decide which word on this list would fit into
each numbered gap.

grateful – attend – co-operation – sessions – concerns

???	Felicia Okimbola, Social Services Children and Families
???	Yasmina Rahab, Pembury Children's Centre
???	12 October 2011
???	Child at risk

Dear Yasmina

I'm writing to you concerning David Prentice, date of birth 03/06/2010. I'm aware that he comes to your play group ...(1)... on Wednesdays at 9 a.m.

I can disclose that some ...(2)... have been raised about David's well-being. Would it be possible for you to ...(3)... a Team Around the Child meeting at 10.30 on 15 October 2011? The meeting will be held at Pembury Children's Centre.

I would be very ...(4)... for your ...(5)... in this matter.

Best regards,

Felicia Okimbola

Task 4

What else is missing from the email? Can you think what words should be written in the top left-hand column?

Task 5

Is the tone of this email formal or informal? How can you tell?

Activity

Task 6

Write a reply to the email, saying that you will be happy to attend.

Task 7

Imagine that Felicia and Yasmina know each other very well and have worked together many times before. Rewrite the email so that it is in a much more informal tone.

Hint: Informal emails are usually much shorter than formal ones.

Confidentiality vs. sharing information

1 When working with young children, there is sometimes a difficult balance to be found between the need to keep personal information confidential, and the need to share infor-
5 mation in order to make sure children are safe from abuse.

In Britain over the last few years there have been some serious case reviews which have

found that a failure to record information and to share it with other professionals has
10 had serious consequences. In particular, there has been a lot of publicity around the
2007 case of two-year-old Peter Connelly, who was seen 60 times by doctors, social workers and other childcare professionals in the eight months leading to his death. Despite
all of these visits and the injuries he had, nobody prevented him from dying at the
hands of his mother, her boyfriend and his brother. People who work with young chil-
15 dren need to be aware of which types of information need to be passed on to others,
and to know the correct way to do this. If you believe that a child is at risk of abuse it
is very important to speak to your manager about it.

Comprehension

 Task 8

Answer the following questions using the text.

a. What do you think a serious case review might be?
b. What do you think was the problem relating to information in the case of Peter Connelly?

Discussion

 Task 9

Discuss these questions in groups of three or four.

a. Do social workers and children's workers get unfair blame in cases when child safe-guarding goes wrong?
b. Is the way that the media reports such cases helpful or unhelpful?
c. Refer to specific cases which you discussed in Module 1, Task 4.

 Task 10

Here is an excerpt from the minutes of the Team Around the Child Meeting held about the little boy David Prentice. Find all the verb forms which express the future.

1 **Felicia Okimbola (Social Worker)** stated that David's mother Shaneka has already decided that she's going to attend a parenting course for teenage parents.
Jo Mink (Family Support Worker) agreed that she'll make sure that Shaneka gets appropriate budgeting and debt advice to help her to manage her money.
5 **Jane Sillitoe (Children's Centre Coordinator)** asked who will accompany David's mother to the housing office to apply for her own housing.
Jo Mink said that she'll do it.
Paul Giles (General Practitioner = family doctor) reported that he is going to refer David for an assessment on his hearing, in response to Shaneka's previous statement
10 that she thinks he can't hear her when she talks to him.

Jacinta Shah (Health Visitor) said that she'll visit David and his mother once a week for the next month, to give advice and help on issues relating to healthcare.

Yasmina Rahab (Room Leader) agreed that she'll monitor David at the Wednesday play group.

Grammar

Future forms – going to and will

	Going to	Will
Form – positive Form – negative	be (am / is / are) + going to + infinitive am not ('m not) are not (aren't) + going to + infinitive is not (isn't)	will ('ll) + infinitive will not (won't) + infinitive
Use 1	• Planned intentions. • Decisions already made.	• Spontaneous intentions • Decisions made at the time of speaking • Offering, deciding, promising, requesting
Use 2	Predictions based on visible evidence	All other predictions

Task 11

Put the verbs in brackets into the will ('ll) or the going to future.

A: I don't know how to input data into this system.
B: Oh it's quite easy, I (show) you.
A: Has Paul decided what to do when he finishes the NVQ?
B: Yes, he (work) in a nursery school.
A: Why are they looking at those catalogues?
B: They (order) some new books.
A: Should I bring a coat, do you think it (be) dry later?
B: No, I'm sure it (rain), there are lots of dark clouds.

Module 3: Solving problems

Two case studies, two problems

1 Tanya lives in a foster home. She's four years old, and has been in foster care for three months. She is in care because her mother has a problem with drugs and alcohol misuse and is now on a rehabilitation programme. Tanya attends a nursery school three times a week, she comes with her foster mother but stays on her own. The nursery worker has a
5 problem, because Tanya's behaviour can be challenging. As well as a social worker, there is also a psychologist working with Tanya. She has reported that Tanya may have some form of Post Traumatic Stress Disorder as a result of the neglect she has suffered. The nursery

worker needs to make sure that Tanya's specific needs are met, while at the same time considering the other children in the nursery school.

10 Sharmila is in hospital. She's four years old, and has been in and out of hospital since she was two because she suffers from a congenital heart defect. She doesn't always go to the same hospital, sometimes she's in her local children's hospital in Leicester and sometimes 15 she's in a specialist hospital in London. Her parents are concerned that she's falling behind in her early development because of all this disruption. This is especially true now that she's due to start at her local primary school. She has a preschool keyworker at Leicester Chil-20 dren's Hospital School, who is working with her and her parents to address this problem.

Comprehension

Task 1

Answer the following questions, working in pairs.

a. Which of the two children is a legally looked-after child?
b. Which of the two children is disruptive?
c. Which of the two children would be termed to be a vulnerable child at risk? Or would they both be?

Task 2

Find words in this list which match the definitions below.

challenging – disorder – disruption – to suffer – especially – in care – to address

a. in particular
b. undergo or feel pain or distress, illness or injury
c. when a child can't stay with his / her family so goes to a foster family or a children's home
d. try to solve
e. interruption in the progress of something
f. difficult
g. an illness or disability

Discussion

Task 3

In groups of three, think of possible actions that a) the nursery worker and b) the keyworker could take to improve the situation for these two children.

Language – Suggestions

Asking for suggestions:
– What shall I / we ...?
  e.g. What shall we do tonight?
– Do you have any ideas about ...?
– What do you think we should ...?

Making suggestions:
– How about + -ing / noun
  e.g. How about going out?
– What about + -ing / noun
  e.g. What about the cinema?
– We could ...?
  e.g. We could go out for dinner?
– Why don't we ...?
  e.g. Why don't we go dancing?

Let's (let us) ...!
e.g. Let's have a party!

Accepting suggestions:
Yes, I agree.
Yes, great / fine / ok / that's a good idea.

Rejecting suggestions:
I think I would prefer to ...
I don't think that's a good idea.

Task 4

Complete the gaps with the words above from the boxes. They are excerpts from conversations that take place when the nursery worker and the keyworker meet their line managers.

First excerpt

we should – any ideas – how about – would be – could we – could try

Anne: Do you have ...(1)... as to how we can improve this situation?
Silvia: I think ...(2)... put an IEP (individual education plan) in place for this little girl.
Anne: Yes, I agree. ...(3)... if we also get a specialist education support worker to work with her on a one on one basis?
Silvia: Yes, I think that ...(4)... a really good idea, some extra personal attention and input could really help her.
Anne: What else ...(5)... try to manage this situation?
Silvia: Well, I could put some strategies in place during my daily work with her.
Anne: Yes, that would be great. What sort of thing do you mean?
Silvia: I ...(6)... using positive modelling to encourage positive behaviour?
Anne: Yes, that's a very good idea.

Second excerpt

> you could – would be – shall we do – don't you – else should

Pritpal: What …(1)… about this little girl?

Jeannette: How about if we put an IEP in place?

Pritpal: I'm not sure we need to take that step just yet. She hasn't reached school age yet, and I think it would be better to do an IEP when she turns five.

Jeannette: What …(2)… we do then, to make sure that she doesn't fall behind before she starts school?

Pritpal: Why …(3)… makes a smaller plan, not a full IEP? You could set some social targets, because she's missed out on some key social development by not attending nursery school consistently.

Jeannette: Yes, that …(4)… a good idea. Also, I can continue to spend time with her every morning.

Pritpal: Yes, and while you're doing that, …(5)… make sure you read her plenty of stories, and play early learning games.

Jeannette: Yes, ok.

Discussion

Task 5

Which conversation is between the nursery worker and his / her manager, and which is between the keyworker and his / her manager? Discuss and decide with a partner. How were you able to tell?

Language

Task 6

Correct the mistakes in this dialogue. Each sentence has one mistake.

A: What about read a story to the children now?

B: I don't think are they ready to sit quietly.

A: Then why don't you setting up the painting activity?

B: OK. What shall we ask them paint?

A: How about to ask them to paint their families?

B: Good idea, could you getting out the paints?

A: OK, but let's to try keep the room clean!

Activity

Task 7

Role-play

Student A: Imagine you work in a nursery. One of the children in your nursery lives in a children's home. He, or she, has some behaviour problems, and you don't know why.

Student B: You are a care worker in a children's home. One of the children you work with has been upset due to recent contact with their family. Mum has mental health problems, which is why the child lives in the home.

What to do if a child discloses to you that he or she is a victim of abuse

1 Anne is a nursery manager. She wants her team to know what to do if, or when, a child discloses abuse. She gives them the following guidelines:

1. **Listen.** Give the child your full attention, nod understandingly or make supportive sounds as the story comes out. Let them tell the story in their own words, don't press
5   for details or 'interview' them. If you start questioning the child or asking for specific details, then this might cause problems with investigations later on.

2. **Take the child seriously, and say that you believe that the child is telling the truth.** The child is probably frightened about disclosing the abuse, because the abuser may have told them that if they tell this secret something bad will happen
10 to them. Even if the abuser doesn't say this, children will often feel that the abuse is their own fault.

3. **Remain calm.** Control your own feelings of anger, horror or sadness. You'll make the child feel worse and more afraid if you react in a way that shows you are shocked or upset. Don't make any judgemental statements about the alleged
15 perpetrator. The child may well love the person, and only want the abuse to stop.

4. **Reassure the child.** Tell them it is not their fault, and that they're doing the right thing in telling somebody. Let them know you will do something to help, and that they will be kept safe. However, only tell them things you are certain you can do. If you make promises that you can't keep, the child won't feel he, or she, can
20 trust you (or anybody) in the future.

5. **Explain what action you will take next.** Explain that you'll need to tell somebody else. If you promise that you'll keep the disclosure a secret, then you'll have to break that promise, because you do need to report this to someone else – you need to tell your line manager immediately.

Comprehension

Task 8

Answer the following questions.

Will the workers be helping the child if they:
a. look angry or become distressed?
b. criticize the alleged perpetrator?
c. listen openly to what the child freely wants to tell them?
d. conduct an investigation?
e. avoid asking too many direct questions?

Task 9

Copy this table into your notebooks. Decide which word matches which definition.

disclose	unhappy or distressed
supportive	give confidence to
upset	sympathetic and helpful
reassure	reveal

Grammar

Conditional I – What will happen if …?

We use Conditional I (If Clause Type 1) to talk about things which may happen in the future. The things are not certain but they are possible. We often use this to give advice.

Form	
If Clause	**Result Clause**
If + present tense e.g. If you eat healthily, you'll live longer.	will / won't + infinitive of main verb e.g. If you don't exercise, you won't get fit.

Task 10

Find six examples of Conditional I in the guidelines "What to do if a child discloses to you that he or she is a victim of abuse."

Task 11

Complete these sentences with your own ideas.

a. If I don't go out too often …
b. If I study hard …
c. If my best friend has time this week …
d. If I learn to speak English perfectly …
e. If I live to be 90 …

Activity

Task 12

Imagine that you have attended a Team Around the Child meeting about a child in the nursery school where you work The meeting took place because he has behaviour problems. You need to give feedback to your line manager at the nursery. Prepare this as a summary to give to the class. It should include the reason for the meeting, the desired outcomes and the action points which were agreed.

Unit 3:
Social background

Module 1: Child poverty

More than 600,000 young Londoners are living in poverty

1 Children living in families where no one works face the highest poverty risks, but children in lone parent families, or families where only one parent works also face significant risk. Almost half of London's children in poverty live in families where only one parent works.

5 The employment rate of parents in London is much lower than in the rest of the UK. In 2008 only 60 per cent of mothers in couples were in employment in London, compared to 73 per cent in the rest of the UK. There was a similar gap for lone parents: 42 per cent work in London, compared with 55 per cent in the rest of the UK. [...]

The costs of housing, transport and childcare are higher in London [than in the rest of 10 the country]. For example, families in temporary accommodation awaiting permanent social housing in London face very high rents, often over £300 a week. This is a deep poverty trap [from] which some families [find it] impossible to escape.

Only a quarter of jobs in London are part-time, compared to a third in rest of the UK, reducing the [employment] opportunities for parents of young children.

15 The high cost of living in London is not reflected in the wages of many low skilled workers. This means that wages are worth less to low income families.

Parents with English as a second language have low employment rate. 60 per cent of non-employed fathers and 40 per cent of non-employed mothers have English as a second language. Refugees, asylum seekers, gypsy and traveller families all face very high 20 levels of disadvantage.

Poverty has a negative effect on children's housing, health, risk of crime and accidents, education and in turn employment. Although the majority of poor children won't grow up to be poor, the issues associated with early poverty can increase the risk of poor outcomes, such as ill-health and unemployment, in later life. We need to eradicate child 25 poverty in London to make sure that Londoners fulfil their potential. [...]

The Mayor [of London] is campaigning to reduce low pay in London through the promotion of the London Living Wage. The plan will make sure that the low paid workers who contribute to London's economic success, workers from cleaners to care-workers, are provided with an acceptable standard of living. [...]

30 Since 2005, the London Development Agency has been supporting action to promote access to employment through the Childcare Affordability Programme. It aims to offer help to low income families, who want to access the childcare that will give them the time to go out and work, [and the support they need] to pay for childcare and find employment. [...]

Extract from: Child poverty, in: Greater London Authority (ed.), www.london.gov.uk/child-poverty, accessed January 23, 2012., Text modified by the author.

Comprehension

Task 1

Find words or expressions in the text which mean:

a. a single father or mother
b. substantial threat
c. the number of people who have jobs
d. accommodation provided by the state
e. being unable to improve one's standard of living or social situation due to low income levels
f. the level of expense involved in living in a certain area, e.g., paying for rent, food, services etc.
g. a term applied to people who have had to leave their country of origin for political or economic reasons, or to escape war
h. a term applied to people seeking the right to live in another country to escape economic hardship or political and religious persecution in their home countries
i. the greater number of people in a group
j. results / consequences
k. to eliminate
l. to be able to pay for, and make use of, services, e.g. childcare

Task 2

Are the following statements true or false? Correct the false statements and indicate in the text the passages supporting the true statements.

a. In London 60 per cent of mothers in a partnership are working.
b. In the rest of the UK 73 per cent of mothers in a partnership are employed.
c. In London 55 per cent of lone parents are in employment.
d. In London 25 per cent of jobs are full time.
e. In the rest of the UK about 33 per cent of jobs are part-time.

Task 3

Answer the following questions.

a. Why is the incidence of child poverty higher in London than in the rest of the country?
b. Why are the employment opportunities for parents of young children fewer in London?
c. What factor reduces the real value of wages in London?
d. What are some of the negative effects of poverty on children living in London?

Grammar

When comparing things that are different *than* is used.

Examples:
*The standard of living in the outlying areas of London **is higher than** in the inner-city areas.*
*Peter's report on child poverty **is more cautious** in its findings **than** Robert's.*

We can also make comparisons using *as ... as*, or negative comparisons using *not as ... as*.

*Example: The population of Munich is **as great as** that of Manchester, but **not as great as** that of London.*

Task 4

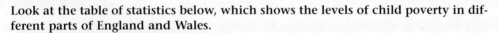

Look at the table of statistics below, which shows the levels of child poverty in different parts of England and Wales.

Children living in poverty 2008/09			
Region	**Local Authority**	**Children in poverty**	**Per cent of children, 0–18**
North West	Manchester	25,000	27
London	Tower Hamlets	12,000	27
London	Newham	14,000	25
London	Westminster	9,000	24
East Midlands	Leicester	16,000	24
East Midlands	Nottingham	12,000	23
[...]			
Scotland	East Dunbartonshire	1,000	6
Scotland	Highlands	2,000	6
[...]			
Scotland	Shetland Islands	0	3

Extract from: The child poverty map of Britain, in: The Guardian, February 23, 2011, www.guardian.co.uk/ news/datablog/2011/feb/23/child-poverty-britain-map#zoomed-picture, accessed January 20, 2012.
Source: Save the Children.

Now, using some of the comparative phrases below, write sentences to compare the level of child poverty in one area with that of another area.

Example: *The level of child poverty in Manchester is as high as that in Tower Hamlets.*

as low as – the same as – lower than – the lowest – not as high as – not as low as – the highest – higher than – as high as

Task 5

Transform the adjectives in brackets in the text below into the comparative or superlative where appropriate.

Example:

In Britain many families from immigrant backgrounds are (poor) than those who have lived in Britain for generations. The (poor) people of all are often those who are (educated).

In Britain many families from immigrant backgrounds *are poorer than* those who have lived in Britain for generations. The *poorest* people of all are often those who are *least educated*.

(Low) levels of education are often cited as one of the chief causes of poverty. People who lack skills and qualifications find it (hard) to find work than those who have received a good education or training. Poverty is also (prevalent) in urban than in rural areas. This is partly due to the fact that rents are (high) in towns and cities and the cost of living in general is (expensive) than in the countryside. Cities also have (big) immigrant populations than rural regions and immigrants are often amongst the (educated) social groups. It is not as difficult for native-speaking citizens to avail themselves educational and job opportunities. Immigrants who speak English as a second language experience (many) problems finding work than their native-speaking counterparts. When they do find work it is often of the low paid variety. The Mayor of London has initiated the Childcare Availability Programme to help (poor) families achieve a (good) standard of living. He feels that this programme may offer the (good) solution to the problems experienced by the socially disadvantaged in the city.

Task 6

Compare the city, town or area in which you live with London. Does your area suffer the same problems as London? Draw up a list of comparisons between your area and London and say whether you think children have a higher, or lower, standard of living / quality of life in your part of the world than in London. Share your conclusions with the rest of the class.

Module 2: Trends, causes and effects of poverty

Child poverty in Germany and across the world

1 The number of children living in poverty in Germany has been rising more rapidly than in other advanced industrialized countries. The children of single parents and immigrants are amongst those most at risk. The significance of claims made by Ursula von der Leyen, Minister for Family Affairs, that child poverty levels fell in Germany between 5 2006 and 2011 have been disputed by social commentators.

In three quarters of the world's most affluent countries child poverty levels have increased, sometimes considerably, over the last 10 to 15 years. One cause of this rise is that governments' attempts to protect families and children from the circumstances that lead to poverty have declined since the end of the Cold War and the advent of globaliza-10 tion. It may surprise many people that an increase in wealth has been accompanied by a rise in poverty. This development points to the fact that there has been a failure to distribute wealth evenly and fairly in society.

Western governments seem to have gradually abandoned the ideals they once held of wishing to create an egalitarian society where people are paid a fair wage for an honest 15 day's work. Nowadays, the social and familial circumstances into which children are born often have a decisive influence on their future educational opportunities, employment prospects and earning power.

The lack of commitment at state level to creating opportunities for people from disadvantaged backgrounds has meant that many children are condemned to live in circum-20 stances of persistent poverty throughout the period of their childhood. Experts in this field have urged governments to make a greater commitment to combating child poverty.

In Germany, where one in six children under the age of fifteen is dependent on Harz IV, welfare payments have seen a 1.5 per cent fall in the figures in the period from 2006 to 25 2011. This however still means that 15.1 per cent of children (or 1.64 million) are growing up in families with income levels below the poverty line. One of the reasons for this modest decrease may simply be that there are fewer children in Germany today than there were in 2006. Furthermore, these children will be virtually excluded from taking up job opportunities later on, as they will lack the education and skills to do so. The 30 problem of child poverty is particularly prevalent amongst single mothers and immigrant families, especially those from the former Soviet Union.

Experts believe that the government must first take action quickly to provide women with more opportunities to join or return to the workforce. Secondly, the education system has to be reconsidered and improved at the lower levels and greater efforts made 35 to integrate non-native speaking children into their school and social environments. If state financial support is provided to address the needs of poor children, poverty levels can be reduced.

Based on statistics from: Spiegel Online, Kinderschutzbund warnt vor trügerischer Statistik, January 26, 2012, www.spiegel.de/wirtschaft/soziales/weniger-hartz-iv-kinder-kinderschutzbund-warnt-vor-truegerischer-statistik-a-811697.html, accessed July 10, 2012.

Comprehension

Task 1

Answer the following questions.

a. According to the text, why have levels of poverty increased even though the world has become wealthier over the last decade and a half?
b. Why have some commentators argued that the slight fall represented in the latest figures for child poverty give a misleading picture of the true situation?
c. What do you think the German government should do to better address the problem of unacceptably high levels of child poverty

Task 2

Find words or expressions in the text which mean:

a. to be going up
b. fast / quickly
c. rich / wealthy
d. substantially / significantly
e. to have gone down / fallen
f. the start / beginning of something
g. a social system in which values such as fairness and equality are respected and nurtured
h. the chances of finding suitable work
i. the ability to make sufficient amounts of money
j. ongoing / continuing / uninterrupted / constant
k. fighting against the effects of a problem
l. the level of income below which a person or family are officially considered to be living in poverty

Listening

Listen to the following interview between a reporter and Sue Lynn, spokeswoman for a UK children's charity.

Have child poverty levels increased over the past few years?

1 **Lynn:** Yes, they certainly have. Since the effects of the latest economic crisis have begun to be felt, poverty rates have risen steadily. In 2008, just before the crisis struck, poverty levels stood at
5 around seven per cent. Since then they have gone up dramatically by a further eight per cent to the current figure of 15 per cent.

What factors, more specifically, have caused this rise?

Lynn: Well, the government has instituted a series of cutbacks that have hit the financial
10 provisions for education, training and childcare facilities very hard. Reductions in educational and training subsidies have led to fewer people being able to take up places in
universities and on training programmes. This has resulted in a more unskilled workforce
who can't find jobs. The freeze in government funding combined with a fall in levels of
income has given rise to a situation where parents either cannot afford, or cannot find,
15 preschool places for their children.

How does the future look?

Lynn: With the crisis appearing to worsen and unemployment on the increase, it looks
as if the continuing crisis will lead to rising rates of poverty.

Comprehension

Task 3

Answer the following questions.

a. By how much have poverty levels risen since 2008? What is the current percentage
   of the population living below the poverty line?
b. Explain the connection between government cutbacks, inadequate education, unemployment and poverty.

Grammar

Adjectives describe nouns and adverbs describe verbs.

Adjective: *There was a **dramatic increase** in poverty in London last year.*
Adverb: *Poverty **increased dramatically** in London last year.*

Formation of adverbs
Most adverbs can be formed by adding **-ly, -y, -ally,** or **-ily** depending on the spelling of the
adjective or noun on which they are based:

Examples: *high / high**ly**   full / ful**ly**   dramatic / dramatic**ally**   happy / happ**ily***

Some adverbs and adjectives have the same form.

Examples: *daily   fast   monthly   quarterly   weekly   hard   late*

*This publication on paediatrics is a **monthly** journal. (adjective)*
*This paediatrics journal is published **monthly**. (adverb)*
*He had an **early** night. (adjective)*
*He went to bed **early**. (adverb)*

Adverbs can also be used to describe adjectives, Past Participles and other adverbs.

Adverb + adjective: *She is **really** careful when handling babies.*
Adverb + Past Participle: *That child has been **well** raised by its parents.*
Adverb + adverb: *She works **extremely** well with young children.*

Verbs and adjectives

Some verbs are modified by adjectives rather than adverbs. These are often stative verbs rather than action verbs and typically relate to appearance or the senses.

Examples: *appear*   *be*   *look*   *feel*   *smell*   *sound*   *seem*

*I'm glad John is no longer sick. He **looks healthy** once again.* (i.e. not: *healthily*)
*Jane sounded **happy** when I rang her today.* (i.e. not: *happily*)

Good and *well*

Well is the adverbial form of **good**. *Well* is an irregular adverb.
Adjective: *John is a **good** worker.*
Adverb: *John works **well**.*

Mary is a good teacher.

Mary teaches well.

Task 4

Complete the following sentences by transforming the adjective in brackets into an adverb where appropriate. Not every adjective needs to be changed into an adverb.

Example:
Childcare services are (heavy) dependant on government funding.
*Childcare services are **heavily** dependant on government funding.*

a. He's really done his job very (good).
b. Poverty levels in some countries have declined (significant).
c. The post is delivered to our kindergarten twice (day).
d. I (full) agree with you that something must be done urgently to improve the quality of basic education in this country.
e. Many parents must work very (hard) to afford childcare.
f. She is (extraordinary) well paid for the work that she does.
g. When dealing with very young children she works (incredible) carefully.
h. Her job is (extreme) demanding as she has to put in long hours without a break.
i. We couldn't offer James a place at our kindergarten. His father looked very (disappointed) when we told him the bad news.
j. These parents always arrive (punctual) with their children at the kindergarten.

Describing trends and developments

1 Sue Lynn talks in the interview about poverty rates increasing and the number of job vacancies decreasing. We often use graphs to describe changes that have taken place in lev-
5 els of income, living standards, employment rates etc. over a period of time. The graph depicts rises and falls, increases and decreases, and rates of growth and decline. To describe these upward and downward movements we
10 use verbs and nouns to express the direction of the movement, and adverbs and adjectives to indicate the degree of change (e.g. great or small) represented by the movement:

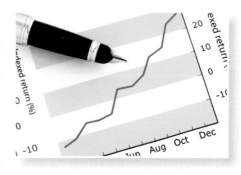

- Child poverty levels have increased (verb) drastically (adverb) over the past few years.
- There has been a drastic (adjective) increase (noun) in child poverty levels over the past few years.
- Government support for families has slightly decreased since 2005.
- There has been a slight decrease in government support for families since 2005.

Language

Verbs indicating upward movement: increase, rise, go up, grow, reach a peak, boom, soar, climb
Nouns: an increase, a rise, a growth, a boom

Verbs indicating downward movement: decrease, decline, fall, shrink, drop
Nouns: a decrease, a decline, a fall, a drop

Adjectives indicating a big change: great, enormous, dramatic, substantial, considerable, significant
Adverbs: hugely, enormously, dramatically, substantially, considerably, significantly

Adjectives indicating a small change: moderate, modest, slight
Adverbs: moderately, modestly, slightly

Adjectives indicating a gradual / slow change: gradual, steady, constant, consistent
Adverbs: gradually, steadily, constantly, consistently

Adjectives indicating sudden / fast changes: sharp, sudden, quick, rapid
Adverbs: sharply, suddenly, quickly, rapidly

Prepositions used in graphs: from, to, by, at

Number of preschool places	
2010	2011
500,000	600,000

Examples:

1 The number of preschool places available increased **from** 500,000 in 2010 **to** 600,000 in 2011.

The number of preschool places increased **by** 100,000 between 2010 and 2011. (i.e. the difference between both figures)

5 In 2010 the number of preschool places stood **at** 500,000 and in 2011 **at** 600,000. (i.e. the number at a particular point in time)

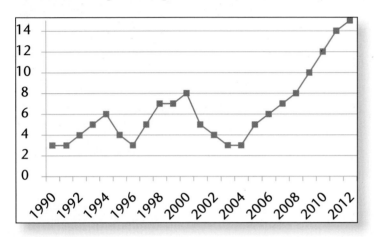

Task 5

Look at the graph above and write six sentences describing its movements using the verbs, nouns, adjectives and adverbs from the previous page.

Examples:
There was a **steady increase** in child poverty rates from 1992 to 1995.
The level of child poverty **dropped sharply** from eight per cent to five per cent between 2000 and 2001.

Task 6

Sue Lynn uses causative verbs in her interview to indicate the connection between causes and their effects.

1 "Reductions in educational and training subsidies *have led to* fewer people ..."
"This in turn *has resulted* a more unskilled workforce ..."
"The freeze in government funding combined with a fall in levels of income *has given rise to* a situation ..."

Causative verbs	
to lead to	to result in
to give rise to	to bring something about

What do you know of the prevalence of child poverty in Germany? Are some parts or regions of Germany more badly affected than others? With a partner discuss what you think might be the cause and effect of poverty on families and children in Germany. Then, using the verbs and phrases in the box above, write a text of approximately 80 words clearly illustrating the connections between the causes and effects of poverty (see example below). Finally share your thoughts, ideas and opinions with the rest of the class.

Example:

1 Low levels of education and training *lead to* vulnerable members of society being unable to find employment. This *results in* higher levels of poverty in these groups which in turn means that their children suffer the effects of social disadvantage. Ultimately these developments *bring about a* self-perpetuating cycle of poverty across the generations
5 which many find difficult, or impossible, to escape.

Module 3: The provision of day care places

Parents scramble for day care places in Germany

1 Veit is eleven months old and he isn't in the least bit shy of strangers. [...] His parents, Mario and Irina Gaul are looking for a kindergarten place for him. Irina, 37, is a sociologist at Caritas, the largest Catholic social welfare association in Germany. She first began looking for a day care place for her son when he was just five weeks old. [...]

5 Germany has proportionally fewer children than any other European country, with just 16.5 per cent of the population under 18. Ten years ago, the figure was 18.8 [per cent]. And according to a report by the Federal Bureau of Statistics published on Wednesday, that trend is expected to continue. One reason for the shortage is the difficulty families have of combining work and parenthood. [...]

10 Marlies Mertens runs a Catholic daycare centre in the Rhineland city of Bonn. She says she is regularly forced to turn away parents who want to register their children for a place in her nursery. Mertens is less worried about families in which both parents go out to work. But she is concerned about poorer families with several children to care for, or families who don't speak much German, or where the parents are poorly educated. Mertens says she
15 always fights for such children to be given a place in her nursery. [...]

Irina Gaul learnt at the beginning of February that there would be no space for Veit in a daycare centre. Almost all of the places were given to younger siblings of children already attending the centres, which meant new families didn't stand a chance. From the autumn, therefore, Veit will be looked after by a child minder. More and more people are recognising
20 the gap in the care system and training as nannies. It is estimated that there are around 35,000 child minders in Germany, most of them in the western states. Veit's new male

nanny has received all the training and looks after five children in his home. Irina says this isn't a bad solution, but it is less flexible than a kindergarten. And twice as expensive. [...]

Extract from: Daphne Grathwohl: Parents scramble for day care places in Germany, in: Deutsche Welle, August 3, 2011, www.dwworld.de/dw/article/0,,15293678,00.html, accessed January 23, 2012.

Comprehension

Task 1

Answer the following questions on the above text.

a. How would you describe the social and professional background of Irina?
b. How has the percentage of people under the age of 18 in Germany changed over the past 10 years?
c. What possible reason is given in the text for this change? Can you think of any other reasons that might account for this trend?
d. To what kinds of applicants does Marlies Mertens give preference in the kindergarten she runs? Why do you think she does this?
e. Why was Veit not offered a place in the kindergarten to which his parents applied? What might be the justification for this policy, and do you think this is fair?

Parents speak out

1 [...] Three-year-olds are supposed to be offered a year of preparation before going into primary school. But finding a suitable place in some areas has become very difficult. [...]

[Mary:] "I have tried to get my 5th child into a nursery school nearby, but [she] did not gain entry as she did not meet the criteria. The system is unfair. The unemployed seemed
5 to get [preference] over everyone else." [...]

[Jennifer:] "I would like to know the reason why families who work only get part-time places in nursery, whereas families who don't work get full time [places]. Surely families who don't work have more time to look after their children than families who work."

[John:] "I can't get my child into our local school. Our family has been involved with
10 the school for 40 years. Children who can't speak English seem to get in. Classroom assistants have to learn Polish over the summer. Parents who speak out are called racists."

[Brenda:] "I am absolutely disgusted that my daughter has been turned down by our local nursery school which my entire family have attended. I feel I am being discriminated against because both my husband and myself work, not like others who claim
15 [unemployment] benefits while [also working]." [...]

Extract from: Maggie Taggart: Lack of pre-school places in Northern Ireland leaving children unprepared, in: BBC, May 6, 2010, http://news.bbc.co.uk/2/hi/uk_news/northern_ireland/8665777.stm, accessed January 18, 2012. Text modified by the author.

Comprehension

Task 2

Answer the following questions.

a. Why do Mary, John and Brenda feel unfairly treated by the admissions policies of the preschool system in Northern Ireland? Do you agree with their point of view? Why or why not?

b. Do you think his John's attitude to the issue of language is racist? Explain.

Task 3

Complete the following text using the terms below.

siblings – gain entry – criteria – part-time – classroom assistants – preference – discriminated – unemployment benefits – turned down

1 Many parents are finding it very difficult to secure kindergarten places for their young children. This is not only a problem in Germany, but in many European countries such as Britain. In order to ...(1)... to a kindergarten, families have to meet certain ...(2)... such as having a low income level and being socially disadvantaged. These families can get ...(3)...
5 for scarce places over their wealthier rivals. Many children from better off families are only offered ...(4)... places, meaning that they have to be picked up from the kindergarten by their parents in the middle of the day. Alternatively, they are offered nothing at all and are simply ...(5).... Some children are rejected because they have no ...(6)... (brothers and sisters) in the kindergarten. Many working parents feel ...(7)... against and are angry that
10 the children of jobless parents claiming ...(8)... are favoured over their own offspring. Some parents complain that ...(9)... have to learn a foreign language in order to communicate with their young charges.

Grammar

Present Perfect

The Present Perfect is formed using the present tense of the verb *to have* plus the Past Participle of the main verb.

I / you / we / they **have taken** *the job.*
He / she **has taken** *the job.*
It **has happened** *twice this week.*

When we refer to events that have taken place in the past and have no connection to the present, we use the past tense. When, however, we refer to events that have taken place in the past but which have a direct influence on or connection to the present, we use the Present Perfect.

Examples:
John **worked** *at this preschool for many years.*
Mary **has worked** *at this preschool for many years.*

In the first sentence John is no longer working at the preschool. The sentence uses the Past Simple Tense and therefore must refer to a situation which has finished.

Mary, however, is still working at the preschool, although she started working there many years ago. The sentence uses the Present Perfect and therefore refers to a situation which started in the past but is still ongoing.

since / for

Since is used together with the Present Perfect to indicate a point in time when an event or situation began.

*Example: Mary has worked here **since** 2002.*

For is used with the Present Perfect to indicate the period of time up to the present over which an event or situation has taken place.

*Example: It is now 2012. Mary started working here in 2002. That means she has worked here **for** the past ten years.*

Task 4

Complete the following sentences using *since* or *for*.

*Example: She has worked with these children **since** they started here two years ago.*

a. Robert has been the director of this facility ...(1)... the last three years.
b. Franziska has worked in the field of early learning ...(2)... over ten years.
c. ...(3)... our voluntary worker, Chris, left last week the children have really missed him.
d. We have been able to completely reequip and refurbish our kindergarten ...(4)... receiving extra state funding last year.
e. I don't know where Chris is working now. I haven't seen him ...(5)... ages.

Task 5

Rewrite the sentences using the negative form of the Present Perfect, with *for* or *since*.

Example:
The last time I saw Chris was two months ago.
*I haven't seen Chris **for** two months*

a. The last time we received a new intake of pupils was six months ago.
b. The last time we received a government subsidy was January 2009.
c. The last time we bought new equipment was a year ago.
d. The last time we raised our teachers' salaries was in 2010.

Activity

Mr Mertens in the article above pursues an admissions policy of giving first preference to applicants from socially disadvantaged backgrounds.

Imagine that you, like Ms Mertens, run a kindergarten in a German city with a substantial immigrant population. You have just one place remaining in your kindergarten for the coming year. The following families present themselves to you, each wishing to have their three-year-old child accepted for admission to your kindergarten:

Family A: A working German couple. Both parents work during the day and need a place for their child. Between them the parents earn an average income and cannot easily afford to pay for private day care, although could manage to meet this expense if they save money in other areas of their lives. They need a full-time place for their three-year-old son. They have no other children.

Family B: An English-speaking couple. The father is well-educated, earns a good income, works for a German firm and is on a three-year contract. The mother hopes to take up full-time work next year, but she has a two-year-old child to take care of at home and wishes to attend private German language classes this year to improve her proficiency in the language. They want their son to be immersed in a German-speaking school environment so that he can make friends and develop socially amongst other children during their time in Germany.

Family C: An immigrant family that arrived in Germany five years ago. Both parents are moderately well-educated and speak reasonably good English but only rudimentary German. Their child, a girl, speaks the parents' language and only a few words of German. The father works long hours on low pay in a local factory. The mother is unemployed but is taking German lessons at the local vocational college and hopes to find full-time work in a low-skilled job in the near future. The parents are anxious for their child to attend your kindergarten, both to give them the time to work and, equally importantly, to provide their child with the opportunity to become socially integrated in a German-speaking social environment. The parents see the admission of their child to your school as essential to her future in the country. They have no other children.

Task 6

In pairs draw up a set of admissions criteria which will help you to decide between these three families. There are a number of factors you should consider when setting out your criteria e.g.:

a. How well will each of these children fit into your existing group of children (mainly German children from middle to high income families in the local area)?
b. What is the level of need of each of the three families?

c. How easily can these families avail themselves of alternative forms of care and schooling?

d. Which child will receive the greatest benefit in educational and developmental terms by being placed in your kindergarten?

Task 7

Now, with another pair playing the role of one of the families, conduct an interview to determine how well or how poorly the child in question fulfils the admissions criteria you have set out in the previous exercise. Be sure to phrase your questions tactfully. After you have considered the case, make a decision either to accept the child for admission or turn him down. Explain to the parents the reasons behind your decision. Then switch roles with the other pair and, choosing a different family to role-play, repeat the exercise.

Discussion

Task 8

Consider the following questions on your own, then discuss them with a partner and share your ideas and opinions with the group.

a. What do you think the real function and value of a preschool is?

b. Is a preschool really a day care facility whose main purpose is to provide a safe, controlled and supervised environment where children can play with each other while their parents are away working?

c. Are preschools essentially educational establishments whose chief purpose is to provide children with a crucial grounding in the social, cognitive and academic skills that will later be further developed at primary and secondary school level?

d. Do preschools really provide pupils with a significant head start in school-life over children who have not had the opportunity to attend one?

e. Would most children be better off remaining at home with a parent or grandparent up to school-going age, or do they benefit emotionally and socially from being away at home in the company of other children and adults?

Unit 4:

Living in a family

Module 1: What does a family mean to you?

1 Families are a basic component of societies across the globe. What we think of as family
(especially in Western societies) has changed significantly over the last 50–60 years. We
no longer think of a family as only being made up of mother, father and children. The
definition and scope of this institution and word has broadened and developed enor-
5 mously with the changing times. Or is it just the appearance of the family that has
changed? In this unit, we will explore living in a family in the twenty-first century.

Discussion / Language

Task 1

**Reflect and write a short comment on the following questions. Discuss your answers
with a partner or in a small group.**

a. What does a family mean to you?
b. Who do you include in your family?
c. What do you think your future family will be like?
d. Who is the most important person in your family? Who was the most important
person in your family during your childhood?

Giving opinions

**The following expressions are commonly used to give opinions. Try to use them in
your discussion.**

I think that a family is ...   I consider a family to be ...   I believe that ...
My point of view is ...   In my opinion ...

Grammar

Non-continuous verbs

There are some verbs that can be used to present your opinions or beliefs that are never used in the continuous form. For example, *I believe, I think* (not pondering but expressing general opinion), *to believe, to consider, to find*, and so on. They are not action verbs but are static verbs and are used for mental or emotional states.

I *believe* … (correct)	I am *believing* … (incorrect)
I *like* … (correct)	I am *liking* … (incorrect)
They *think* … (correct)	They are *thinking* … (incorrect)

What is a family?

María E. Huerta [from Mexico] feels the most important element of a family is love

1 From my standpoint, I think a family is a group of persons whose members love and try to help each other. One of the characteristics of this group is the motivation to help by thinking about the benefits for family
5 members.

I think a traditional family is formed by a father who is the wage earner, a mother who is the housewife, and brothers and sisters. The role of each member is very important because it influence the development and
10 behaviour of the children who live inside the family. The main factor for maintaining a family is love, but it's also important to be conscious that this feeling is pure.

Other factors that help to keep families together are respect and trust. Each member of the family in the fam-
15 ily must show respect to the other members because nobody is more important than the others. Some people think that only the parents deserve respect, but I consider that this is not true. […] In brief, I think that a family is a group of people united not only by blood, but also by love.

Antoinette Ferté [from France] feels the
20 **family is very important to the French people**

The word family is very important for me, because when you are young, the people around you are very precious. I love my fam-
25 ily, and I can't stand it when someone criticises them. When someone says "family", I think about a lot of people because my family is very big, and it is not always a biological family.

30 In France, I think that the notion of family is very important. The function of the family is very important in the lives of the French people. But we have – like in the other countries – a lot of kinds of families. We have the traditional family where you have the mother and the father and the biological children. After that, it is more complicated. You have some extended families, often in the country and especially those who living
35 on land which is used for farming. Childless families where the two parents work and haven't the time or the money to have children. We have a lot of single-parent families and more and more blended families. I think that in France the number of single-parent families has tripled. The way of life has changed in France, and today we have lots of different kinds of families. I hope that my family will remain a traditional family.

40 **Caroline Behne [from Germany] writes about how important her family is to her**
In a family you can talk about anything. You can tell them everything because they are like your best friends. You have fun with your family no matter what you do. Even if there is a fight or a misunderstanding, you have to tolerate each person because when you fight with someone, you notice how much you miss that person and how much
45 you love that person. You just can't live without that person. [...]

I think it is very important that you have a family because you learn so many things. You learn to live with other people, you learn to share things, and you learn to show consideration for someone. I just can't live without my family because I would miss them so much. I would even miss the mistakes they make.

Extract from: What is a family? in: Topics Online Magazine, Issue 8(3), 1997–2008, www.topics-mag.com/ edition8/family.htm, accessed March 21, 2012.

Comprehension

Task 2

Answer the following questions about the above text.

a. What does Maria consider the most important element of a family?
b. According to Antoinette, why has the number of single-parent families increased?
c. Why does Caroline think families are important?
d. Which one do you agree with? Which one do you disagree with? Why?

Task 3

Match the following definitions to phrases that were used in the texts above.

a. the person who works and financially supports the family
b. opinion, view or perspective
c. a theory or belief held by a person or group
d. to put up with something
e. of great value, cherished

Activity

Task 4

Do one or both of the following activities with a partner.

a. Create your own family tree.
b. Write questions to ask somebody else in the class about their family and do an interview. Write a short presentation about your classmate's family to present to the rest of the group.

Listening

A woman talks about her family

1 I am American and have been living in Germany since 1999. My *immediate family* stayed in the USA. They are spread out over the entire country. My parents still live in the area where I grew up in Upstate New York. My father's parents came from Lebanon and my mother's from Italy. At the turn of the twentieth century they emigrated to America.
5 Unfortunately, they have all *passed away*. Both of my parents were born and raised in Utica, New York. They even went to the same high school, but did not meet until afterwards. To avoid a big wedding in a church, they ended up *eloping*. For their *honeymoon* they went to Niagara Falls. My mother worked as a nurse until she started having children. My father is still working as an accountant.

10 I am the sixth child out of seven. I have five sisters and one brother, who is the oldest. Since I have been an adult, I can say it was quite nice growing up in a big family. Of course, I did not always think that way. At home I never had space for myself and had to share everything all the time. However, I always had somebody there for me, my sisters. They are still there for me even though I live so far away.

15 My brother and three of my sisters are married and have children. My brother has one child of his own and two *stepchildren*. He is also a grandfather of three grandchildren. Three of my sisters have two children each, ranging in age from seven to 13. I am an aunt to four nieces, three nephews, one step-niece and one step-nephew. Despite the distance, they know who I am, and I have been speaking to them on the telephone a
20 lot more lately. They are my family and I love them.

I have a partner, but live alone and have no children of my own. Besides my *biological family* in the States, I have a family made up of my friends here in Berlin. To me, family includes the most important people in my life, not only *biologically related* ones. I consider myself very lucky to have a family which spans the whole world.

Comprehension

Task 5

Answer the following questions on the text.

a. Where did her grandparents come from?
b. How many nieces does she have?
c. How many siblings does she have?
d. What does family mean to her?

Language

There are italicised words in the text. Translate them into German and write a definition of these terms in English.

Family types

1 Families in the Western world nowadays come in different shapes and forms. No longer do families only descend from biological or marriage ties. What we used to call non-traditional or dysfunctional are now common and prosperous groups of people who live and develop together. In the box are some of the main types of families.

Nuclear families	Extended families
This family consists of a mother and a father with one or more children. This form used to be the one of the most common in Western societies. This is no longer the case. The average number of children in European households is 1.6 (as of 2008) and that of North American households is about 2.1.	Extended families have changed a lot over the years. In the past, an extended family consisted usually of parents, children and grandparents and/or aunts and uncles and their children all living under one roof. Nowadays extended families do not usually live in one house but may live many miles away from each other. Because of the economic downturn, extended families under one roof are on the rise again.
Single-parent families Over the past 20 years, the number of single parent families has increased. Mainly headed by mothers, the number of single-parent families headed by the father has also been increasing. The reasons for single-parent families have changed. In the middle of the twentieth century, death was the cause of most single-parent families. In the 1970s and 1980s, divorce was the main reason. The twenty-first century has parents who do not get `married and/or who want to raise their children alone.	
Blended families Blended families consist of two previously married parents and their children from their former marriages. Two families blend to form a new step or blended family. In a blended family you have a stepmother / father and a biological mother / father as well as stepchildren and biological children.	**Patchwork families** In a patchwork family, each person is an individual patch in a patchwork quilt. Each person can stand alone, and stands for each person's unique self. When someone becomes part of the family – by birth, adoption, due to divorce and remarriage – the individual person is not changed, but can enrich the family (quilt). In this kind of a family, the interaction between the individuals shapes and forms the family unit.

Comprehension

Task 7

Are the following statements true or false? Correct the false statements.

a. A blended family always has biological and step-parents.
b. In a patchwork family, the family group is the most important unit.
c. Extended families do not exist anymore.
d. Single-parent families are an important part of many societies today.
e. Nuclear families are the main form of families in European countries today.

Task 8

Answer the following questions based on the text describing the different types of families.

a. Why do you think that extended families were important in the past? Why do you think the popularity of extended families declined for a while, but is gaining currency again today?
b. Why do you think the reasons for single-parent families have changed several times? Why do you think this type of family is becoming more common?
c. What is the difference between a patchwork family and a blended family?
d. In what way is the experience of being a mother today different than it was in the past (i.e. 60 years ago)?
e. Lone mothers are a quite new concept. Who do you think lone mothers are?

Task 9

Answer the following questions based on the knowledge that you already have.

a. Do you know any other types of families?
b. Can you think of another way to describe the other family members?

Modern British families

1 Father leaves for work in the morning after breakfast. The two children take the bus to school, and mother stays at home cooking and cleaning until father and the
5 kids return home in the evening. This is the traditional picture of a happy family living in Britain. But is it true today? The answer is – no! The past 20 years have seen enormous changes in the lives and
10 structures of families in Britain, and the traditional model is no longer true in many cases.

The biggest change has been caused by divorce. As many as 2 out of 3 marriages now end in divorce, leading to a situation where many children live with one parent and
15 only see the other at weekends or holidays.

There has also been a huge rise in the number of mothers who work. The large rise in divorce has meant many women need to work to support themselves and their children. Even when there is no divorce, many families need both parents to work in order to survive. This has caused an increase in childcare facilities, though they are very expen-
20 sive and can be difficult to find in many areas. In addition, women are no longer happy to stay at home raising children, and many have careers earning as much as, or even more than men, the traditional breadwinners.

There has also been a sharp increase in the number of single mothers, particularly among teenagers. Many of their children grow up never knowing their fathers, and some
25 people feel the lack of a male role model has a damaging effect on their lives.

However, these changes have not had a totally negative effect. For women, it is now much easier to have a career and a good salary. Although it is difficult to be a working mother, it has become normal and it's no longer seen as a bad thing for the children. As for children themselves, some argue that modern children grow up to be more independent and
30 mature than in the past. From an early age they have to go to childminders or nurseries, and so they are used to dealing with strangers and mixing with other children.

So while the traditional model of a family may no longer be true in modern Britain, the modern family continues to raise happy, successful children.

Modern British Families, in: BBC World Service, June, 2007, www.bbc.co.uk/worldservice/learningenglish/ newsenglish/britain/070601_family.shtml, accessed February 23, 2012.

Comprehension

Task 10

Are the following sentences true or false?

a. Divorce is common in Britain.
b. In Britain childcare is inexpensive.
c. Women earn more than men in Great Britain.
d. Many mothers nowadays get married very young.

Task 11

Answer the following questions based on the text above.

a. What has had the greatest impact on the modern family? What has also been effecting the family structure?
b. What positive outcomes have resulted from this change in families?
c. How does this compare to families in other countries? In Germany? Do research with a partner.

Language

Task 12

Read through the list of adjectives. Which ones do you know? Do you know their opposites?

a. close
c. dysfunctional
e. harmonious
g. estranged

b. traditional
d. active
f. close
i. broken

Task 13

Answer the following questions and exchange ideas with a partner.

a. Which adjectives would you use to describe a perfect family?
b. Which adjectives are missing? How would you describe your family?

Module 2: Does a child need both biological parents?

Being a child of same-sex parents

1 Studies have shown that children living with same-sex parents develop just as well as children with their biological parents and / or a mother and a father. They seem to be also just as happy and healthy as those children raised by heterosexual parents.

In 2009 and 2010 the Centre for Family Research at the University of Cambridge inter-
5 viewed 82 children and young people of lesbian, gay and bisexual parents between the ages of four and 27 throughout England, Wales and Scotland.. Some of the key findings are the following:

[...]

How I feel about my family

10 • Many children of gay parents see their families as special and different because all families are special and different though some feel that their families are a lot closer than other people's families.
 • Some children feel that their family is a bit different if they have lesbian or gay parents but this is something to celebrate, not worry about.
15 • Other children [...] realise that children with gay parents are less common than other sorts of families, but don't feel this means that their families are any different to other people's families because of it.
 • Very young children don't think their families are different from other people's families at all.

20 **How other people feel about my family**

- Most people, including friends at school, are fine about children having gay parents. They think it is a good thing, or don't really care.
- When children are younger they can be a bit confused and many don't understand that someone can have two mums or two dads because their family isn't like that. 25 This means they sometimes have lots of questions for children who have gay parents.
- Sometimes other children can be mean about gay people because they have never met any gay people and don't know much about them.
- Some people make judgements about what it's like to have gay parents. They think 30 children will have a certain type of life and not as good an upbringing. Children with gay parents can find these judgements upsetting.
- Children with gay parents like having gay parents and wouldn't want things to change but wish other people were more accepting.
  [...]

Extract from: April Guasp: Different families, in: Centre for Family Research, 2011, www.cfr.cam.ac.uk/news/ documents/StonewallReport.pdf, p. 3, accessed March 21, 2012.

Comprehension

Task 1

Answer the following questions about the above text.

a. Why do children of gay parents find their families special?
b. Why do they feel that their family is a bit different?
c. What do other people think about children having gay parents?
d. What do you think about these results? Are they different than what you would have expected?

Two case studies

Here are examples of two different families that were interviewed in the study that was mentioned at the beginning of this module.

Maheen (13), Faariha (9) and Megan's (23) family

1 Maheen and Faariha live in a large northern city with their two mums, Barbara and Andrea, as well as with their two grandmothers and grandfather. Maheen, who 5 has a hearing impairment, and Faariha were adopted along with their older sister, Megan, who is [...] away at university. Both mums work part-time, one as an artist and one as a writer, and share childcare. Their mums ensure that the girls' Asian herit-10 age is incorporated into their daily life [...].[...] [p.5]

Maheen [...] and Faariha [...] see their family as different from other families, but once again not because they have gay parents. Maheen explains "well, one of my best friends and her dad argue all the time, and for me it's really shocking what she does. Yeah, we don't really do that sort of thing. It was kind of a shock." Faariha adds "like some shout
15 a lot, some let you do anything you want and mine don't, they just ... well, care. Their mums and dads don't really look out for them as much." Faariha says what she really likes about her family is that "they're caring and they look after you". Maheen and Faariha agree the most important thing about their family is that "we all love each other". [...] [p.8]

20 **Alfie (4) and Briony's (6) family**
Four-year-old, Alfie and his sister Briony, six, live with their Mum and Mummy in their home in London. Each mother is the biological parent of one of their two children. Alfie and Briony have the same daddy, a friend of the family who was the sperm donor and who is also gay. Mum works as a lawyer and Mummy is currently a full-time parent.
25 [...] [p.7]

When Briony, six, is asked if her family is like other families or if she thinks her family is different, she says "I think it might be a bit different, but I don't think very different". Briony explains that this is because "most peoples' families you don't have to explain to everybody about your whole family, but I do in the playground. People will
30 be like oh, how come you've got two mummies, you can only have one, and then I have to explain it all, but other people don't really have to do that". [...] Alfie says he sees his family as different to his friends' families "because it's more nicer and more ... better". [...] [p.8]

Extract from: April Guasp: Different families, in: Centre for Family Research, 2011, www.cfr.cam.ac.uk/news/ documents/StonewallReport.pdf, pp. 5, 7–8, accessed March 21, 2012.

Task 2

Answer the following questions based on the text above.

a. How do the children and teens feel about their families? Why?
b. How can these families be supported by schools and preschools? Do they, in fact, need to be supported?
c. How do you think role models could affect their situations?

Not without any bullying

1 Children with gay and lesbian parents are still being bullied and teased in school. Often it is not dealt with by the teachers or authorities.

[...] Recent research shows that 98 per cent of young gay
5 people hear 'that's so gay' in school and we know from polling evidence that teachers don't necessarily respond to it when they hear it. Children with gay parents told us that it affects them too. While some young people with gay parents say they don't find this language personally
10 upsetting, more often children are bothered by it."
Maheen, 13, explains [...]

"this guy I know, Sam, he said 'oh, your pumpkin's turning gay, Maheen' ... I'm like what's that supposed to mean? And everyone thought that he wasn't being mean, but I knew that he was saying something about gay people." [...]

Extract from: April Guasp: Different families, in: Centre for Family Research, 2011, www.cfr.cam.ac.uk/news/ documents/StonewallReport.pdf, p. 17, accessed March 21, 2012.

Activity

Task 3

Answer the following questions with a partner. Prepare your answers to present to the rest of the group.

a. What can schools and preschools do when they are witness to these kinds of seemingly innocent incidents?
b. How can teachers respond to homophobic language?

Grammar

Noun and verb agreement

Collective nouns, like *family, team, crowd* and *staff* may be either plural or singular, depending on how they are being used in the sentence.

Examples:
*My **family is** great.* (the unit)
*My **family get** along very well.* (the individuals)

*The **staff** of the preschool **is** in a meeting.* (staff as a unit)
*The **staff are** in disagreement about how to deal with the bullying of a specific child.* (the staff as individuals)

Task 4

Choose the right form of the verb.

a. The staff (work / works) together well.
b. The whole staff (is / are) not available today.
c. The family (live / lives) in Berlin.
d. The family (talk / talks) to each other at dinner every evening.
e. The club (is / are) meeting tonight.
f. The couple (is / are) coming tonight.
g. The couple (is / are) breaking up.

Activity

Task 5

Do one of the following activities.

a. Write a dialogue between the pupils Briony, Maheen and the preschool teacher (or other member of staff). The teacher reacts to the homophobic language in an appropriate way. Perform this dialogue in front of the rest of the group.
b. Participants debate on the same-sex marriage. One group develops arguments in favour of gay marriage and another group presents arguments against it.

Module 3: Divorce

1 Divorce can be tragic, but is a part of many cultures. Only two countries do not have a civil procedure for divorce, the Philippines and the Vatican. In many countries, divorce rates increased significantly during the last
5 century. In the United States, the United Kingdom, Canada, Germany, Australia and Scandinavia, divorce is a normal part of everyday life.

Discussion

Task 1

Discuss with a partner or small group one of the following questions. Prepare your results to present to the rest of the group.

a. What do you think of when you hear the word divorce?
b. Do people get divorced too easily and quickly?
c. Would you still be friends with somebody after you divorced them?
d. How does divorce affect the children involved?
e. Is getting, or being, divorced socially disapproved of in your country?
f. Some people stay married for over 50 years. What do you think the secret of their success is?

Activity

Task 2

Read through the list of reasons or grounds for divorce. Rank them with your partner or group from the most understandable to the least understandable. Can you add any other reasons?

adultery – boredom – greed – lack of physical attraction – physical / verbal abuse – freedom – one does all of the housework – no similar interests – growing apart

Experiences of divorce

Mum moved out – it was terrible

1 My parents got divorced in the 70s. My dad kept us and my mum moved out. It was terrible and traumatic; tragic to grow up without a mum. I felt ashamed and lonely. I got married at 38 and have been married for 12 years. For the sake of my child, I cannot even think about divorce as I don't want him to go through what I did.

5 I wish my parents had divorced

I wish my mother had divorced my father when I was seven years old – when he downed a bottle of whisky and 80 sleeping tablets and was in a coma for two weeks. He continued to emotionally blackmail his wife and leave his three kids bewildered throughout their childhood, leaving us on welfare for 30 years with zero future. [...]

10 Dad was abusive and angry

My parents divorced when I was around three years old, so I have few memories of them being married. During my childhood and teens my mother rarely, if ever, spoke 15 badly of my father. She definitely had cause to though; he was pretty abusive on occasion and didn't contribute much towards my, or my brother's, upbringing.

My dad would visit fairly regularly. He 20 would (and still does) get wound up by my mum [...]. The anger from him, especially when directed towards my mother, definitely affected how our relationship developed with him. [...] As for how it might affect me and my own relationships, I take comfort in the advice a teacher gave me at school – 25 according to her, children of divorcees were likely to be more discerning in their relationships and not make assumptions that they just happen magically. [...] I admit I've been prone to having too many expectations of those I am in a relationship with.

Extract from: Where did it all go wrong?, in: The Guardian, February 9, 2011, p. 9, http://www.guardian. co.uk/lifeandstyle/2011/feb/09/where-did-it-go-wrong, accessed February 26, 2012.

Comprehension

Task 3

Answer the following questions with a partner and write down the answers.

a. What do you think about the advice the teacher gave the third person?
b. In your opinion, why can the person in the first example not even think about divorce?
c. Why did the second person wish that the parents had got divorced? Can you understand this?

Writing

Task 4

The above examples of divorce involving children are not happy ones. Can you think of an example (either from your life or from the media) which was happier? Describe this situation on paper.

Language

Prepositions of time: *while, during* and *for*

During is used with a noun to express when something happened:
During my childhood and teens my mother rarely, if ever, spoke badly of my father.

While is used to express the same thing but with a verb:
While I was growing up, my mother never spoke badly of my father.

For is used to talk about the duration of periods of time over which an event has taken place:
My mother never spoke badly of my father *for* 15 years.

Task 5

Complete the sentences using *during, while* or *for.* Do the exercise on a separate piece of paper or in your notebook.

a. My parents have been married ...(1)... 50 years.
b. ...(2)... my childhood, my parents got divorced.
c. ...(3)... their marriage, they never fought.
d. ...(4)... they were living together, they travelled a lot.
e. I fell asleep ...(5)... the film.
f. We were on welfare ...(7)... 30 years.

Unit 5:
Stages of development

Module 1: Concepts of development in early childhood

Theories of development and learning

1 In order to develop good pedagogical practice at a preschool, it is first necessary to acquire an understanding of the stages through which young children grow and develop. Child psychologists and educational specialists have develop theories concerning the physical, cognitive, emotional and social development of children at the preschool age.
5 Many of them have identified specific stages that all children go through as they grow and mature, developing new skills and a deeper understanding of the world they live in. The development of these skills and understanding enables children to increasingly control and interact with their immediate environment, and to assert and express themselves as individuals within it.

10 Amongst the best known developmental and educational psychologists are John Dewey (1859–1952), Maria Montessori (1870–1952), Jean Piaget (1896–1980), and Erik Erikson (1902–1994).

In his works, John Dewey emphasised the importance of basing learning programmes on the immediate experience of the children, as well as on the teacher's observations of
15 what interests the children. He believed that the learning experience should be closely related to the life experience of the children. He was also a strong advocate of the guiding role of the teacher and was opposed to the tendency he saw in progressive teaching methods of allowing children too much freedom to have fun and do as they please. He felt it was important that teachers had the confidence to use their own understanding
20 of their pupils, as well as their own experience of the world to provide a meaningful context for learning. He felt that without clear guidance, direction and structure, learning programmes could have little real educational value.

Maria Montessori's ideas have become so widespread in the field of early childhood education that they are now often perceived as self-evident. When she first published her ideas at the turn
25 of the twentieth century, her pedagogical concepts were revolutionary and controversial.

Montessori believed that children had a natural desire and impulse to learn and would do so independently if the conditions were created for them by their teachers.

30 Jean Piaget is well known for his work on explaining the cognitive development of children. He believed that children passed through certain clearly defined stages of intellectual development. The development phase that children go through
35 between the ages of three and seven, he termed the "preoperational stage". This stage of development is characterised by the child's egocentric perspective on the world and his place in it. Piaget conducted a number of experiments in which he
40 demonstrated that children in this age were incapable of seeing something from another person's perspective. He also showed that children in the preoperational stage can only focus on one aspect of a thing at a time. For example, a child in the preoperational stage finds it difficult to understand that his own mother
45 also has a mother, i.e. that his grandmother is also his mother's mother.

Erik Erikson concentrated on the psychological development of human beings and observed that children go through a process of establishing their independence between the ages of two and three.

The child may develop feelings of shame and doubt at this stage, if it is thwarted by
50 adults in its attempts to establish her autonomy. At the next stage of development, between the ages of four and five, children are at a stage of developmental maturity where they are ready to acquire a sense of purpose. At this stage the danger is that instead of developing a healthy sense of initiative, the child may be reprimanded by adults for mistakes it makes and, as a result, be burdened with a sense of guilt.

55 All of these developmental psychologists believed in the importance of providing children with concrete situations in which to test and develop their experience and understanding of the world.

Comprehension

Task 1

Match the words and expressions in italics in the following sentences with the appropriate word or expressions from the box below.

widespread – advocate – self-evident – reprimanded – autonomy –
guidance / direction – immediate – thwarted – a sense of initiative – enables

a. The ideas of pioneers, such as Maria Montessori, in the area of child psychology and development were considered revolutionary in their day, but are now so *common* that they are seen as very *obvious*.

b. John Dewey was a *supporter* of the idea that teachers had an important role to play in the development of children. He felt that teachers had a responsibility to use their own experience and knowledge of the world as a means of providing structure and *orientation* to their pupils' development.

c. Dewey also believed that pedagogical concepts and teaching practices should be based fundamentally on the children's *direct* experience of the world they live in.

d. The learning and application of new skills *facilitates* children in exercising more control over their environment, and interact more productively with it.

e. Children are often *frustrated* by adults in their efforts to achieve in interacting.

f. When children are *criticised* for making mistakes, it often discourages them from developing *the power to make and act on their own decisions*.

Discussion

Task 2

Some preschool teachers feel that the theories of child development they learn while studying aren't very relevant to the practical, everyday business of managing a class and dealing with the desires and demands of their young pupils.

With a partner discuss the question of whether or not the principles of theory can be usefully applied to the processes and procedures of classroom practice.

Report your ideas and opinions to the rest of the class.

Erik Erikson's eight ages of man

Erikson's stages of psychosocial development		
Age	Stage	Strength
0–1 year	Trust vs. Mistrust	Hope
2–3 years	Autonomy vs. Shame and Doubt	Willpower
4–5 years	Initiative vs. Guilt	Purpose
6–12 years	Industry vs. Inferiority	Competence
Adolescence 13–19	Identity vs. Role Confusion	Fidelity
Young adulthood 20–39 years	Intimacy vs. Isolation	Love
Middle age 40–64 years	Generativity vs. Isolation	Care
Old age 65+	Ego Integration vs. Despair	Wisdom

1 Erik Erikson divided human development into eight distinct but interconnected stages, from birth to old age. His work was based on that of Sigmund Freud, but also considered the vital role social and cultural influences play in developing our sense of self, and in determining how we interact with the people who make up our social environment.
5 Erikson believed that at each stage of life (listed in the table above), a person has to successfully resolve what he called an identity crisis in order to develop healthily and move on to the next stage of their psychosocial development. For example, in the first stage of life, babies need to develop a sense of trust in the people around them by feeling that they are being properly cared for and loved. Once this sense of trust has been
10 instilled, the infant is then ready to deal with the crisis awaiting it in the next phase of

its development. Thus Erikson saw human development as a cumulative process in which the successful resolution of one
15 stage provides the inner strength necessary to meet the challenge of the next.

In their first year of life children learn to develop a sense
20 of hope and optimism within themselves, if given the proper level of care and love by parents and other caregivers. According to Erikson it is par-
25 ticularly important for the child at this stage to enjoy a close relationship with its primary caregiver who should always be available and willing to comfort the child when it feels insecure and needs lots of loving attention. The presence and availability of the caregiver will reassure the child that it is safe and can always rely on the caregiver to protect it from danger or
30 harm. Children who are raised in an environment where their need for security is neglected, grow up with feelings of anxiety, fear and insecurity towards the world. They tend to distrust instead of trust, and develop a sense of doubt rather than hope in a world they fear will harm them or let them down.

Between the ages of one and three Erikson emphasized the need for parents and caregiv-
35 ers to allow the growing child the freedom to explore their environment and to do things on their own. Children at this age will feel a natural desire to develop a sense of independence, and they experience a great sense of pride and joy in any task they manage to accomplish by themselves. A sense of self-worth develops in children in this phase, if they are allowed the scope to develop their ability to do certain things by
40 themselves. Of course, it is also important for caregivers to get the balance right and not allow the child so much freedom that it places itself in danger. Erikson felt that the main risk to the child's development at this stage was presented by authoritarian or overprotective caregivers, who – out of a misplaced anxiety for the safety of the child – may criticise him for acting on his own impulses and for exercising his will. Such treatment
45 may lead the child to develop feelings of shame towards itself which will undermine its will to do and achieve things for itself.

Erikson believed that between the ages of three and six, children should be allowed to plan simple activities such as play dates with their friends and encouraged to contribute to the organisation of events like their birthday parties. This sort of freedom and scope
50 for action instils a sense of initiative in the child. The child will thus feel encouraged to make its own suggestions and know that they will be positively received and taken seriously by the people from whom the child seeks affirmation and approval. In this phase the child who is allowed to plan and make proposals about how events and activities should be organised will develop a sense of self-belief and purpose. "I did it all by
55 myself" is a proud claim made by children at this age. Problems at this stage arise when parents are critical or contemptuous of the child's ideas or lack confidence in its ability to achieve the goals it sets itself. This will result in the child thinking its ideas and opinions are valueless and not worth acting on. Thus failure to resolve the identity crisis

60 at this stage of psychosocial development can produce an adult who constantly apologizes for himself and is afraid to offer an opinion for fear of being ridiculed or criticised.

For further reading on Erik Erikson, see: *Childhood and Society,* Erik Erikson, various editions, first published in 1950; and *Erik Erikson: His Life, Work, and Significance,* Kit Welchman, Open University Press, 2000.

Comprehension

Task 3

Answer the following questions on the text.

a. Explain how Erikson's work was both similar to and different from Freud's.
b. In Erikson's first stage of development, explain how the effects of proper care and upbringing can instil feelings of trust in the child.
c. Why is the development of feelings of trust crucial to the establishment of personal autonomy in the next phase of development (from one to three years)?
d. How can the behaviour and actions of parents and caregivers produce feelings of shame and doubt in a child at this age?
e. What can parents and caregivers do to help to inculcate a sense of initiative and purpose in the developing child?

Task 4

Match the words below with words or expressions from the text.

a. very important / essential / indispensable / crucial
b. the developmental issue that needs be resolved at each stage of psychosocial growth
c. the belief or feeling that things will turn out well
d. the person in a child's life that is most responsible for its care
e. to have failed to do something that should have been done
f. to get to know an environment by moving around and examining it
g. an adjective that describes people, often parents, who believe in the importance of obeying rules
h. the impulse and willingness to realize an idea or wish
i. to be thought well of by someone
j. to be laughed at or mocked

Discussion

Task 5

First reflect on your own experience of childhood between the ages of three and six or on the experience of a child of that age that you know well or with whom you work closely. Think of common, everyday situations at home or activities at school where children have the opportunity to assert their initiative in making decisions to perform a task in their own way. This could be, for example, allowing the child to decide what she wants to eat for breakfast and permitting it to prepare the meal the way it wishes.

Note down your answers to the following questions, then discuss them with a partner and finally with the class.

a. In what ways can children at this age be supported and encouraged to develop a capacity for independent decision-making and action?
b. What concerns and anxieties of parents and caregivers might hinder this process and result in the generation of guilt feelings rather than a healthy sense of self-esteem?

Module 2: Applying theory to classroom practice

Applying Erik Erikson's theory in the preschool classroom

1 Two of the psychosocial developmental crises identified by Erik Erikson occur in early childhood, at the ages in which children attend preschool. The second of these crises involves the child developing a sense of initiative, which is itself essential to the generation of a feeling of purpose. Preschool caregivers should be aware of these crises and
5 know to manage them to help ensure that the child will develop in the right way. This is a crucial stage in the development of children. If handled badly the child may grow up with a feeling of guilt and a lack of self-belief. If dealt with correctly the child will develop a sense of competence and confidence in its own abilities to perform and complete tasks independently.

10 It's important at this stage to strike the right balance between allowing children the freedom to make their own decisions, while not presenting them with tasks and activities that are excessively challenging. For this reason it is vital to provide children with structured, planned activities that are broken down into small, manageable steps.
15 Each step involves the child making a small decision when carrying out of a concrete, practical activity.

In order to support children's development at this stage, teachers should: encourage children to act
20 independently; focus on the progress the child makes and not on its mistakes; set expectations that are commensurate with each child's abilities; focus on setting activities that involve the performance of real tasks.

25 Classrooms should be set up to allow the children to act with as much independence as possible. Children should be able to fetch and reach drawing materials and tools themselves. This allows them the power to decide for themselves, for
30 example, what pencils and crayons to choose for an art activity.

According to Erikson it is important to send a signal to children that their efforts are taken seriously and valued. For example, in a writing activity, where the children were encouraged to draw a sequence of pictures to tell a story, the children were told
35 that their first efforts were merely a draft. They were told by the teacher that in drafts you can experiment with ideas, especially crazy ones, and it didn't matter if you made mistakes and had to cross out a picture and begin again. This approach encouraged the children to focus on the progress they were making with the activity and to understand that making mistakes and changing your ideas were all part of
40 the creative process.

Erikson also emphasised the importance of designing activities that cater to the individual capacities of each child, as well as being sensitive to the needs of the individual at any given time. For instance if Heike has a new brother and has to share her parents with this newcomer, it might be unreasonable to expect her to share a toy or book with
45 another child. If Heike is forced to share this may give rise to guilt feelings concerning her unwillingness to share Mum and Dad with her little sibling.

Erikson, together with Montessori, emphasised the importance of providing children with real activities to perform. This could be preparing a meal in the kitchen. By performing tasks such as these the children feel a sense of pride and achievement in doing
50 something "grown-up", and therefore real and useful. Learning to use real utensils properly, such as sharp knives, gives the children a feeling that they are trusted and boosts their sense of competence and responsibility. Learning a real skill helps them to feel that they are moving forward in their development towards adulthood. A real skill can also be practised at home and elsewhere, increasing their feeling of control
55 and competence.

Comprehension

Task 1

Answer the following questions

a. According to Erikson what kind of process influences and shapes the development of human identity at each psychosocial stage?
b. Why is it so important that teachers focus on the child's conflict with itself at each stage of its development?
c. What kind of conflict characterises the third psychosocial stage?
d. Explain how inadequate, insensitive or inappropriate upbringing can lead to the production of guilt feelings in the child.
e. Why is it important at this stage in their development that young children are presented with activities that are broken down into small steps?
f. Explain the logic behind giving children real tasks to do and concrete goals to achieve.

Language

When breaking a process down into its component steps, we often use signal words such as *first . . ., secondly . . ., then . . ., next . . ., after that . . .* and *finally,* to clearly distinguish each step of the process from the next and indicate what point of the process has been reached.

Example: Planning a painting activity

- First, ask the children to select an object to paint. This could be a ball, a simple toy, a colourful box, a kitchen utensil or a flower.
- Secondly, clearly inform the children about the activity and what you would like them to do.
- Then, ask the children to put on their aprons.
- Next, ask the children if they know where the painting materials are stored and get them to fetch them themselves.
- After that, ensure that each child has provided him/herself with a paintbrush and has access to the full range of paints laid out on the activity table.
- Then, ask each child to look closely at the object in front of them and to note its shape size and colour.
- Next, ask them to try and reproduce the object on the sheet of paper in front of them using their brushes and paints. Tell them they are free to use their imagination in their representation of the object. They can change or add details to the object in their painting as their imagination dictates.
- Then, ask the children to remove and clean their aprons, and to hang them up.
- Finally, gather the children together in a circle and ask them to talk to the group about their experience of creating their painting. The children should be listened to attentively and praised for their efforts, in order to promote their sense of self-confidence.

In the example above, the process is presented as a sequence of instructions. To give instructions the imperative is often used. There is only one imperative form for both singular and plural cases, and this is simply the infinitive form of the verb.

Examples:

Take the first left, go straight on and the kindergarten is on the left.
Children, *go* to the cupboard and *fetch* the paints and brushes.
Fill some beakers with water, Jenny, so we can clean the brushes.

Task 2

Complete the following sentences using the imperative form of an appropriate verb selected from the "painting activity" text above.

a. ... (1)... an object for the children to paint.
b. ...(2)... the children to put on their aprons.
c. ...(3)... each child has a paintbrush of his/her own.
d. ...(4)... the children they are free to use their own imagination.
e. ...(5)... the children together in a circle.

Task 3

Erikson, like Dewey and Maria Montessori, emphasised the importance of creating environments where children can play and learn using real objects and achieve concrete results by performing meaningful tasks.

With a partner, think of an activity requiring peer interaction and teamwork, carrying out the activity, such as the making of papier-mâché Halloween masks.

a. Think the activity through carefully and list all the steps involved in the performance the activity.
b. Work together on writing out the process, as in the example given above, using verbs in the imperative and signal words to help indicate the beginning of a new step in the process. The activity should be organised in such a way that the individual tasks are manageable for the children, while allowing them the freedom to complete the tasks independently.
c. Read out your activity plan and discuss the logic of how you chose to structure and organize it.

Grammar

Ability, possibility and permission – the verb *can*
Can is used to talk about ability, possibility and permission. The negative form is **cannot.** It refers to both the present and the future and is followed by the infinitive form (active or passive).

Examples*:*
I *can plan* (active infinitive form) a classroom curriculum (i.e. I have the ability to perform this task).
The classroom *can be converted* (passive infinitive form) into a play area by moving the furniture aside (i.e. it is possible to change the function of the room).
You *can* use this knife to cut the cake, if you wish (permission).
This room *cannot* be used as a play area because it is too small (impossibility).
Can has no infinitive or Present Perfect form. Instead the expression *be able to* is used.

Examples:
I'd like to *be able to* plan a classroom curriculum properly, but haven't yet received the training to allow me to do so.
The children *haven't been able to* go outside and play for the past week because the weather has been so bad.

Task 4

Complete the following sentences using *can*, *cannot* (or *can't*), *be able to* or *been able to*, and say whether the sentence refers to the ability to do something or the possibility/impossibility of doing something.

a. We ...(1)... send the children out to play today as the weather is fine.
b. I have ...(2)... plan my classroom activities far better since I attended a weekend seminar on this subject.
c. She ...(3)... work with us, I'm afraid, because she doesn't have sufficient training.
d. The children ...(4)... be trusted to use the sharp cutting tools responsibly, because we've already taught them how to do so.
e. The children would like to ...(5)... go to the technical museum today, but ...(6)... because it's closed.

Activity

Task 5

Think of a concrete learning activity, such as learning how to prepare a simple breakfast. You have a group of 4 six-year-olds. Explain how you would organise the activity to enable the children to act on their own initiative without overchallenging them.

a. What individual steps would you break the activity into?
b. How would you take account of the children's individual abilities to get each child to do what he's interested in?
c. How would you correct mistakes without making them feel they've done something wrong?
d. Write out the activity as a series of steps. How you would deal with the issues listed above?

Module 3: The development of a pedagogical concept for preschool children

The ideas of Maria Montessori

1 The theories of Maria Montessori have probably had more influence on the methodology and practice of early childhood pedagogy than those of any other educationalist.

Trained in paediatrics Montessori's work brought her into contact with children who were regarded as uneducable, i.e. with children who did not seem willing or able to
5 respond positively to any teaching methods. Knowing that problems arising through poor education and upbringing in childhood led to the development of psychological and behavioural difficulties later in adulthood, she set about devising teaching methods that would prove to be very effective with children who did not respond to conventional teaching techniques.

10 Montessori laid great stress on the importance of observing how children behaved by
themselves and interacted with one another.
She believed that it was crucial to create an
environment that was conducive to learning.
15 The educationalist considered it as essential
to make the kindergarten a child-oriented
environment. This means setting up the
rooms in the kindergarten in a way which
appeals to children and allows them the free-
20 dom to function independently, without the
assistance or interference of adults. This can
be done by using child-sized furniture, equipment and tools, and ensuring that shelves in
the rooms are set low enough so that their contents are accessible to every child.

The human aspect of the learning environment, however, is as important as the physi-
25 cal. This means that the kindergarten teachers need to be properly trained, sympathetic
to the children's needs and committed to meeting those needs through using the right
kind of approach. Montessori emphasised these environmental factors because of her
conviction that children learn naturally from their own experience of their immediate
surroundings, if left to their own devices.

30 Montessori thought that the experiences and activities made available in the learning
environment should be as real as possible if they were to have any true developmental
value. Performing real tasks with real tools was much preferable, in her opinion, to carrying out pretend tasks using toy tools, which couldn't be used outside the context of
imaginary play. This is why she insisted that the utensils and implements that the chil-
35 dren were given actually functioned as intended. Knives should be sharp to allow the
children to prepare their own snacks and meals. Hammers should be heavy enough to
drive real nails into blocks of wood. Montessori felt confident that children could be
trusted sufficiently to use such tools safely and responsibly. She also felt that children
should be allowed the space and time within the kindergarten curriculum to work and
40 play independently, in order to allow them the freedom to explore, experiment, learn
and develop on their own and through their interaction with each other.

For further reading, see: *The Montessori Method*, Maria Montessori, various editions, first
published in English in 1912; and *Montessori: The Science Behind the Genius*, Angeline
Lillard, Oxford University Press, 2005.

Comprehension

Task 1

Answer the following questions on the text, in your own words.

a. What early professional experiences led Maria Montessori to the area of child
education?
b. According to the ideas of Montessori, why is it so important to create the right kind
of environment for children to learn in?
c. Describe some of the ways in which such an environment can be created.
d. Why is it important to give the children real tasks to perform?

Task 2

Match the words and expressions in italics in the following sentences with the appropriate words or expressions from the box below.

methodology – laid emphasis on – is conducive to – conventional teaching techniques – immediate surroundings – uneducable – devised – curriculum – left to their own devices – carrying out – observing – conviction

a. Maria Montessori developed a *set of techniques* to help children who were thought to be *unteachable* to learn effectively.
b. She *developed / put together* a pedagogical system that was designed to replace *normal teaching methods*.
c. Carefully *watching* the behaviour and interactions of children *is helpful to* the creation of an appropriate *programme of educational tasks and activities*.
d. When *left alone* children can independently learn a great deal from their *direct environment*.
e. Montessori *emphasized* allowing children the freedom to explore, play and experiment on their own.
f. Most educationalists entertain a firm *belief* in the pedagogical value of independent learning.
g. By *performing* meaningful activities and enjoying the achievement of meaningful goals, children develop their ability to accomplish tasks and meet new challenges.

Language

In the comprehension text above, verbs such as *believe, feel, think* and *insist* convey the beliefs, opinions, ideas and convictions of a certain person:

Montessori *believed* that it was first of all crucial to create an environment that is conducive to learning.

Montessori *thought* that the experiences and activities made available in the learning environment should be as real as possible.

Montessori also *felt* that children should be allowed the space and time within the kindergarten curriculum to work and play independently.

She *insisted* that the utensils and implements that the children were given actually functioned as intended.

Task 3

Using the verbs above and some of the vocabulary in Task 2, write a short essay of approximately 250 words expressing your own ideas on the most important factors concerning the education of young children. In your essay consider the issues of peer interaction, independent play, the significance of the physical environment and, most importantly, the role of the teacher in the education of young children.

The Spreesprotten Kinderladen – a pedagogical concept

The concept of the kindergarten in Kreuzberg, Berlin, is based on many of the ideas and teachings of Maria Montessori.

1 Childhood is characterized by physical growth and change, the development of self, an increase in independence, the ability to form relationships with adults and other children, the experience of playing alone and with others, the ability to learn accommodate others and the experience of the world in general.

5 Each child is born with a multiplicity of needs and abilities: the need for contact and to explore, the will to survive and live, the ability to enjoy life, the capacity to understand and react, and the capacity to recognise the connections between things.

The expression "the child is an actor in his own development" means for us that the child has a need to develop and grow, and is provided with an environment that respects 10 this need and can be relied upon to meet the individual child's requirements. In this way, the child can play a part in its own development, but is also subject to outside influences and factors.

We accompany and support the developmental process of the child, offering a feeling of security and protectiveness. We have developed the environment of our kindergarten 15 in such a way that the child can learn holistically, become independent, develop a sense of self-confidence and acquire social skills. We respect the personality of the child, but also exercise an influence on its behaviour and development, in accordance with the tenets of our concept, as well as through active engagement with the child. We nurture the child's freedom of movement; its freedom to experiment; its freedom to express 20 feelings; its freedom to choose; and its freedom to be independent of adults.

eigene Übersetzung vom Autor, vgl. für weitere Informationen: www.spreesprotten.de/shared/pdf/ bildvomkind.pdf, Zugriff April 2012

Comprehension

Task 4

Answer the following questions in your own words.

a. Identify the elements of Montessori's teaching that the Spreesprotten Kinderladen have used to create their concept.
b. Using your own ideas, suggest ways in which you think the needs of the child as an individual can be reconciled with the necessity of developing and integrating the child as a social being within its peer group.
c. In what ways do you think this concept and its implementation can provide children with the support they need to positively resolve the identity crises that Erikson believed occurred at stages two and three in a child's psychosocial development? (see Module 1, Task 2)

Listening

Interview with Gabi, Antonia and Kathrin, caregivers at the Spreesprotten Kinderladen

Please tell me something about the pedagogical concept you have developed for your kindergarten.
Gabi: Well, we are basically "minimalists". We focus on developing relationships, individuality and independence. One of the best aspects of our philosophy is that the staff members are also keen to develop and find out more about who they are, so that each one of us, by understanding who we are, can relate to the children in an authentic way. It's more important for us, as caregivers, to develop meaningful relationships with the children than to follow a precisely formulated programme, point for point and goal for goal.

Kathrin: Yes, I think it's very important that the children learn how to get on with other children and to learn that others, apart from themselves, also have needs. This doesn't always work of course. Sometimes the children understand and accept others, and sometimes not.

Gabi: It's also important to emphasise that we don't take a "moral" approach to resolving disputes. There's no "you're bad" or "I'm bad", but rather we try to encourage the children to accept each other as they are.

Do you think the concept you've created is appropriate for the developmental needs of every child in your care?
Gabi: Yes, we do! It's appropriate for everybody, because if you treat the other person with respect, tolerance and openness, that person feels valued. This is the basis of a healthy relationship through which each person can help develop himself.

How do you see the role of the caregiver in the development of the children?
Gabi: We have to try out a lot of different things. It isn't the case that we can simply say right from the beginning that it works in such and such a way. Maria Montessori developed materials that are complete in themselves. There is no need for somebody to be standing by and providing correction. The child itself can use the materials in his/her own way and if it doesn't work, it can try it out again and again.

Maria Montessori wrote that teachers should "teach less and observe more". Do you sometimes find it difficult to stand aside and allow the children to do their own learning?
Antonia: It really depends very much on the specific situation. When the children are involved in a learning process and trying something out it's easy for me to sit on the margins and observe their play and interaction. But in conflict situations my instinct is to leap in and immediately

intervene. It can be difficult in these situations to stand aside, but this gives you an opportunity to reflect on where your limits lie and to ask yourself why you feel the need to intervene at a certain point.

Gabi: Yes, the concept has a great deal to do with us, the caregivers, and who we are as people. You have to ask yourself questions like "why is it difficult for me to be patient with a certain child", and so you have to examine what your own reaction is and see what it has to do with your own personality.

Do your pupils in the three-to-six age group learn a lot from each other?

Kathrin: Well, we recently had a situation where there was a conflict. One child was lying on the floor crying, while another sat on top of him and refused to move. The whole group were involved in dealing with this conflict. They all tried in different ways to resolve the conflict by saying things like "get off him please". One of them tried to push the offending child off the other, but was beaten away by him. Then one of the children came to us and said "we need help". We said that there were already more than enough people involved, and stood aside to observe the situation. In the end one of the boys came over and pulled the boy off the other from behind. The child who was crying was then comforted by three others and after two or three minutes they were all playing happily together again. Of course we could have quickly settled the conflict ourselves, but not in the way the children dealt with it. And we thought, yes, that's exactly how it should work, with the children being free to come to terms with each other without our interference.

Thank you so much for your time.

Task 5

Answer the following questions in your own words.

a. The interviewees lay great stress on the importance of the staff understanding themselves as individuals in order to establish productive and meaningful relationships with the children in their charge. Explain why you think this is.

b. How can the caregivers grow and develop as individuals through the relationships they establish with the children?

c. In the area of play, how do the Spreesprotten caregivers try to put the principles and teachings of Maria Montessori into practice?

d. What does Antonia say her impulse to intervene in conflict situations can tell her about herself?

e. Why does Kathrin feel the policy of non-intervention in conflict situations contributes to the development of the children?

Activity

Task 6

You and a partner wish to set up a kindergarten together. In order to do so, you first need to develop a clear concept on which to base your pedagogical practice. Using the Spreesprotten concept above as a model, think up and write out one of your own..

The concept should contain information such as:
- the principles your concept is based upon
- your understanding of the most important factors of a child's development
- how the teaching practices you employ, based on the theoretical principles you've outlined, can support and promote the emotional, cognitive and social development of the children in your care
- the overall developmental goal of your pedagogical practice, e.g. you are trying to help the children develop into happy, confident and motivated individuals

Task 7

Exchange your finished concept with that of another pair.

a. Note down the similarities and differences with your own concept. Are there any aspects of the other pair's concept with which you don't agree?
b. Draft a series of interview questions based on your reading of the other pair's concept.
c. Then conduct an interview with them which is designed to allow them to elucidate their concept and the thinking behind it. You can use the questions in the interview above to help you formulate your own.

Unit 6:
Working with children under three

Module 1:
Emotional relationships –
a matter of trust

Choosing the right childcare

1 Fewer families today can afford to live on one salary alone, and increasingly more mothers do not want to compromise their educations and careers for the sake of having children. 5 As a result, Germany's birth rate has been declining, falling in 2010 to its lowest level since 1946. Although this decline can be attributed to a number of factors, the unavailability of subsidised public day care and the unaffordability of private day care are among the strongest reasons why couples decide against having families.

10 In an effort to counteract the steady drop in the birth rate and to encourage women to return to the workforce quickly, the federal government has devised a scheme to provide access to day care for 35 per cent of all children under the age of three by the year 2013, while guaranteeing day care places to all one-year-olds. In 2011 only one in every four children under age three was cared for outside of the home, the greater percentage of 15 which was cared for by childminders in the old federal states, and in a nursery or kindergarten in the new federal states. In order to meet this ambitious goal by 2013, 30 per cent of these new places for the under three-year-olds are to be provided by childminders.

Due to the shortage of day care facilities in many areas of Germany, parents often do not have many options as to whom to entrust with the care of their children. Those who do 20 have the choice find it difficult to decide whether a nursery or a childminder would be best. The needs of children and their parents are different and the choice in day care is based on the suitability of the carer or facility to meet these individual needs. Regardless whether childminder or nursery, when parents look for an appropriate setting, the most important criteria include safety and cleanliness, the number of staff, the variety of equip- 25 ment and stimulating materials, but above all, the positive interaction of the carer with the child. A child's ability to develop a trusting and secure relationship with its carer is fundamental for its sound emotional and behavioural development. Also the parents' trust in the carer to validate and support their child's emotions is reflected in the stability of the child-carer relationship and is key to a positive working relationship.

Comprehension

Task 1

Which statements are not true? Correct the false statements with information from the text above.

a. Women are having more children than 20 years ago.
b. The lack of day care is one of the strongest reasons why couples do not have children.
c. Between 2011 and 2013 the number of day care places for children under three will have increase by 30 per cent.
d. More parents in the old federal states leave their children with childminders.
e. The relationship between carer and child plays a significant role the child's development.

Task 2

Discuss the following questions with a partner, then share your answers with the group.

a. Why are fewer women having children today?
b. Why do you think a greater percentage of children under the age of three is cared for by childminders in the old federal states, while in the new federal states, the greater percentage is cared for in a nursery or kindergarten?
c. Why is the positive interaction between carer and child so important?

Case study

Evelyn tells her story about finding day care for her one-year-old, Freddy.

1 We thought that Freddy would be better off at a nursery school, but at twelve months, it was very difficult to find a nursery school we felt comfortable with. Many of the nursery schools in our area
5 weren't accepting one-year-olds because of the shortage of staff members.

We finally happened to find a childminder in our area who, in her early sixties, was looking to take on two young toddlers. Although she
10 had no formal education as a child care professional, she was experienced, having raised two girls by herself as a single mom. She liked Freddy immediately, and Freddy warmed up to her quickly, too. She was willing to mind Freddy
15 from nine o'clock in the morning till three in the afternoon. This wasn't always that convenient for us, but between the two of us, we managed to pick him up punctually every day.

The childminder's apartment was clean, but small and on the third floor. She had a cat,
20 too, which was not very fond of children. Freddy was the first child in her care, so she
didn't have any problem carrying Freddy up and down three flights of stairs until
she took on a second toddler, Luisa, who couldn't walk yet. Though Freddy could walk,
he wasn't ready to climb up and down three flights of stairs by himself yet. The childminder had to rely on the help of a neighbour to mind one child while she fetched the
25 other. And when a neighbour wasn't available, Freddy was made to crawl up and down
the stairs by himself. We were concerned about Freddy's safety and didn't like the idea
of him being left alone in a crib while the childminder carried Luisa down the stairs,
but there wasn't much we could do about it.

As the year progressed, we noticed that the childminder was reluctant to answer all of
30 our questions and didn't seem to appreciate our concerns and suggestions. Although
Freddy seemed to be enjoying himself, we began to doubt her competency as a childminder. When the childminder announced that she would be taking a two-week summer holiday, we were faced with a problem. Neither of us could afford to take two weeks
off from work to stay at home with him. Furthermore, we didn't think that it would be
35 good for him to be in the care of someone with whom he wasn't familiar. After an emotionally difficult nine months, we made the decision to remove Freddy from the childminder's care. Freddy, now two, absolutely loves nursery school and we are very satisfied
with the nursery and its professional staff.

Task 3

Discuss the following questions with a partner, then with the group.

a. Evelyn was dissatisfied with her choice of day care for Freddy. Why was she unhappy
   with the situation? What could have been better?
b. The parents' choice in day care for their child is based on the suitability of the carer
   or facility to meet their individual needs. Make a list of the advantages and disadvantages of childminders and nurseries for children under the age of three.
c. If you had a young child, what kind of day care would you choose?

Language

Task 4

**Complete the sentences with a preposition. If you need help, look for clues in the
first two texts of this module.**

a. A majority of families cannot live …(1)… one income anymore.
b. Traditionally, mothers were expected to stay at home for the sake …(2)… their
   children.
c. Problems in a child's emotional development can sometimes be attributed …(3)… a
   disturbed relationship between carer and child.
d. Many nursery schools do not take …(4)… children under the age of two.
e. Ten per cent more children under the age of three will have access to day care …(5)…
   2013.

f. Many people believe young children are better ...(6)... at home with their mothers than in day care.

g. We are not fond ...(7)... the idea of leaving our child with a childminder.

h. Working parents have to rely ...(8)... competent professionals to care for their children.

i. Without day care for their children couples are often faced ...(9)... financial problems.

Grammar

Past Progressive

When we want to say that something (an action or situation) was in progress at a particular time in the past, we use the progressive aspect of the past tense – the Past Progressive form of a verb. It looks like this:

was / were + (verb)-ing

Only actions or events that are not instantaneous can be used in the Past Progressive Tense. For example, the verb *stop* expresses an action that occurs immediately; it does not require time to progress. The verb *stop* is therefore almost never used in the past progressive form.

The verb phrase *to have a snack,* on the other hand, does not occur instantaneously. It requires time to have a snack. We can say that at one particular moment of the day this action or event was in progress. Look at this example:

*What **were** the children **doing** at ten o'clock?*
*At 10 o'clock the children **were having** a snack.*

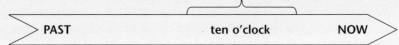

| PAST | ten o'clock | NOW |

Snack time might have begun at ten o'clock, but it continued beyond ten o'clock, perhaps until quarter past ten.

*At ten o'clock the children **were not napping**. (weren't napping)*

Task 5

Freddy has just turned three. He has learned a lot in the past three years. Look at the timeline and write sentences in the past progressive to describe the milestones in his development during his first 36 months. An example has been done for you.

birth	responds to voices	*After birth Freddy was responding to voices.*
	passes objects from hand to hand	
6	learns to crawl	
9	takes first steps	
12	says his first words	
15	learns to say his own name	
18	uses more than 200 words	
21	speaks in three-word sentences	
24	rides a tricycle	
27	counts to ten	
30	understands concepts of time	
33	gets dressed without help	
36		

The childcare dilemma

1 Academics, childcare experts, politicians and parents have been in disagreement for decades about the question of whether full-time day care for children under the age of two is harmful or beneficial. Over the years studies and news articles have presented contradicting conclusions about the linkage between day care and the emergence of 5 aggressive and risk-taking behaviour later in life. A study published in 1986 by Professor Jay Belsky sparked a heated debate about the long-term effects parental separation had on infants and young toddlers. Belsky found evidence that young children who spent many hours in day care facilities every day displayed higher levels of aggression, had poorer relations to teachers, and were more likely to use drugs and alcohol later 10 in life. Although Belsky admits that the negative effects are marginal on an individual basis, he warns that the multiplicity of aggressive behaviour in older children and teenagers can have a large-scale impact. Other research, however, has shown that nursery day care can have positive effects in cognitive and language skill development among the under two-year-olds.

15 Most parents grapple with the decision to return to work and are already laden with guilt for leaving their child with a childminder or in a nursery at an early age. This period of transition into day care is stressful for both child and parent. The results of a Dutch study in 2006 did not pacify parents' anxiety. The researchers (Vermeer and van IJzendoorn) found that cortisol levels in children younger than 36 months who 20 attended a day care facility were considerably higher than in those who were cared for at home. Cortisol is a hormone that is released in stressful situations. Although no longitudinal studies have been done to reveal the long-term effects of high cortisol levels, the researchers speculate that the interactions in a group setting is stressful for a young toddler. Some experts suggest that abnormal cortisol levels can not only cause 25 aggression and disobedience, but also emotional insecurity, fearfulness and hyperactivity.

British psychologist Dr Penelope Leach is concerned about the non-maternal childcare in the first year of life. She states that the advantages
30 of day care in nursery settings only become evident between the age of 18 and 30 months. Leach makes reference to psychoanalyst John Bowlby's attachment theory, which establishes that children between 8 and 36 months often
35 suffer from separation anxiety from their primary caregiver. Bowlby and Belsky's research has led to a greater emphasis in training childcare professionals on the importance of establishing continuity in the care-giving relationships
40 and the provision of attachment-friendly care. This involves assigning the child to a key person in the day care setting to whom it is able to develop a stable emotional relationship.

Comprehension

Task 6

Complete the table with the missing word forms. Write a sentence using one of the other word forms.

Noun	Verb	Adjective	Adverb
		beneficial	
aggression	–		
anxiety	–		
	suggest		
provision		–	–

Task 7

Answer the following questions in your own words. Then discuss your answers in a group.

a. Why is it believed that day care for the under two-year-olds can lead to more aggressive behaviour?
b. Why is a nursery setting stressful for toddlers?
c. How can day care in a nursery setting benefit toddlers?
d. What can practitioners do to make the nursery experience less stressful for a toddler?

Module 2: Language and motor skills development

Language development through movement

1 In the first three years of its life, a child is constantly multi-tasking as it grows and learns. It learns to use self-control and coordination over its own muscles, experimenting with physical movement, and discovering the meanings of words through interactions with others. Everything it experiences and does is connected to language. Each new move-
5 ment and each new sound or word is the assertion of the infant's own self. Without the use of its body as a medium, a child could not define itself through language as an autonomous person in a social environment.

First language acquisition is closely connected to the process of sensory perception. A child must use its sense of vision, hearing, touch, taste and smell to perceive its environ-
10 ment before it can learn to express its observations or feelings. The sensorimotor area of the brain requires exposure to feelings and movement to stimulate the environment of neural connections. The left and right hemispheres of the brain communicate across the corpus callosum when language is conveyed through movement, facilitating the development of all cognitive skills.

15 Although many childcare practitioners are aware of the importance of movement and play for language development, nursery and preschool teachers often feel pressurised to create structured curricula which are often inappropriate for young children. Today preschools are placing a stronger emphasis on traditional methods of early literacy and language arts rather than on physical education and free play in order to satisfy the
20 expectations that children achieve benchmarks.

Childcare practitioners can promote language development in toddlers by focusing on activities which combine language and movement. Children do this naturally without the guidance of adults when they play. When they invent games and rules for those games, they implicitly practise their negotiation skills while they expand their vocabu-
25 laries. By adding elements of rhythm and music, learning through movement becomes a kinaesthetic experience; children grasp and retain the concept of nouns, verbs, adjectives and prepositions more quickly and develop a keener sense of their meanings.

Comprehension

Task 1

Collocations are two words that are commonly used together as a fixed expression. Find the words in the right column that collocate with the words in the left column. Look for clues in the text to help you.

a. free	1. callosum
b. language	2. education
c. corpus	3. acquisition
d. cognitive	4. play
e. language	5. skills
f. physical	6. arts

Task 2

Which word makes sense? Choose the correct word in the brackets to complete the sentence. Look for clues in the text, or use your dictionary to help you.

a. Most experts agree that (exposure / disclosure) to television is harmful for the under two-year-olds.
b. The (exposure / disclosure) of confidential information without permission is unethical unless a person is in danger.
c. Babies are born with the innate ability to (grasp / understand) objects.
d. Very young children do not (grip / grasp) the difference between reality and fiction.
e. The email has replaced the letter as the most common (medium / facility) of correspondence.
f. Although it is quite unusual, some adults (retain / keep) their baby teeth their whole lives.
g. Many parents (retain / keep) their children's baby teeth as a keepsake.

Task 3

Answer the following questions in your own words. Then discuss your answers with a partner.

a. Why is physical movement advantageous for language learning?
b. Why are more nurseries and preschools designating more time to language arts than free play?
c. Why is free play important for the development of language skills?

Grammar

The Past Progressive vs. the Simple Past

We often use the Past Progressive in sentences which also use the Simple Past Tense for a different action. The verb in the Past Progressive form refers to a longer action, i.e. something that was *going on already* when the shorter action or event occurred. The shorter action or event uses the simple past. Look at this example:

*The children **were playing** on the playground **when it started to rain**.*

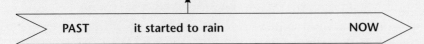

The children went out to play before it started to rain. Their playing was in progress when the rain started at once.

We can express the sentence differently. If we put the shorter action before the longer action in the sentence, we use the word *while* rather than *when* to connect the sentences.

*It **started to rain** while the children were **playing on the playground**.*

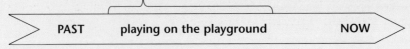

Task 4

Complete the sentences with the simple past or past progressive form of the verbs in the brackets.

a. Leonard (get) himself wet. He (drink) water from a cup and (spill) some on his jumper.
b. Victoria (hurt) herself. She (play) on the playground and (fall) from the swing.
c. Sarah (sleep) still when her mother (come) to pick her up.
d. Max (say) he (hit) Kyle because Kyle (tease) him.
e. We (plan) to take a walk to the park when it (start) to rain heavily.
f. The practitioner (not + see) the accident happen because she (not + pay) attention.

Hearing babies use sign language

1 A group of mothers have started their own sign language group for hearing babies to try to communicate with them before they learn to speak. Simple actions accompany
5 pictures at the Baby Boffins sessions in Hastings, East Sussex, using an idea originally pioneered in the US. It has been set up with the help of the government's Sure Start programme, which means it is free. Co-
10 founder Sarah Stone said signing relieved the frustration in babies. She said her children were signing sentences to her from the age of 13 months, and communicating their basic needs very clearly.

The method of signing with hearing babies by hearing parents was developed by Dr Joseph Garcia, an American child development expert. After working as an inter-
15 preter, he noticed how hearing babies of deaf parents could communicate their needs at a much earlier age than children of hearing parents who did not use signs. He also noticed how it reduced levels of frustration in a child and helped build up the bond between parent and infant.

Language experts have expressed concern that the use of signing could take priority over
20 the need for parents to talk to the children. But co-founder of Baby Boffins, Helen Cross, disagrees and says it actually enhanced their speech. "They grow in confidence, and a confident child will speak more, not less," she said.

Hearing babies use sign language, in: BBC, March 1, 2005,
http://news.bbc.co.uk/2/hi/uk_news/england/southern_counties/4307333.stm, accessed March 26, 2012.

Comprehension

Task 5

What are the arguments for and against teaching sign language to babies and young children? Discuss them with a partner and make a list.

Activity

Task 6

In a group of four or more people, discuss whether baby sign language can help improve language skills. Afterwards the class can divide into two teams. One team will support the motion that baby sign language can improve language skills, and the other team will oppose the motion. Refer to Unit 3, Module 3 about the rules of debates.

Grammar

The modal verb *should*

The modal verb *should* has several different uses:
We use *should* to make a recommendation, or to express an opinion. Here are some examples:
*You **shouldn't** go to work if you are ill.*
*You **should** stay home and rest.*

We also use *should* to talk about an obligation, or things that are good or important to do.
*We **should** call the child's parents.*

Should is also used to express something that is probable.
*We **should** be back by four o'clock.*

We use *should* to make a prediction, or to say what we expect will happen.
*The weather **should** be nice tomorrow.*

To talk about what a child, for example, is expected to do by a certain age, we use *should* followed by *be able to.*

should + be able to + infinitive verb

*At three months a baby **should be able to smile** when it sees its mother.*

Task 7

Look at the table of milestones in language development below and write a sentence using *should be able to* to express what a child can be expected to do at each phase of its development.

a. at 9 months	communicate with gestures, like waving its arms
b. at 12 months	use a few words like "dada" and "dog"
c. at 18 months	name some body parts
d. at 24 months	say two and three word phrases
e. at 30 months	ask questions with "what?", "where?"
f. at 36 months	speak in three- and four-word sentences

Module 3: Hygiene and toilet training

Good hygiene practice in childcare settings

1 Toddlers are more susceptible to illness than older children and adults because their immune systems are still too weak to ward off all bacteria and viruses. Therefore, child-care practitioners must follow public health guidelines and regulations, and maintain good hygiene practice in their settings at all times. Although day care staff may be aware
5 of the importance of proper hygiene, in reality, some may be too busy to practise it consistently. Here's what some of them say:

"I carry and comfort the little ones all day long. When they cry, I wipe away their tears and when they have a cold, I clean their runny noses. Of course small children don't cover their mouths and noses when they cough or sneeze, so I am in constant contact
10 with germs and body fluids. I have to remember to wash my hands frequently to try to prevent the spread of colds."
Cynthia, Leeds

"The children at our nursery not only have their own cubbyholes for their belongings, each of them also has a hook and a shelf space in the washroom which is
15 marked with a picture of the child, for their flannels, towels and toothbrush. That way there is no confusion about whose is whose. The flannels and towels are washed every other day."
Miles, Plymouth

"Because the babies are always putting the toys in their
20 mouths, we sterilise the toys regularly to reduce the risk of cross-contamination. Each child also has its own set of bed linens for its cot."
Judith, Cornwall

"Our nursery has a nappy changing policy. Nappies are
25 checked and changed if needed every two hours, or sooner if the child is soiled. All staff wear disposable gloves and aprons for each change. The changing areas are cleaned with disinfectant after each use. The soiled nappies are double wrapped in nappy sacks before they
30 are put in the covered waste disposal bin. The childcare practitioners are expected to wash their hands with warm water and liquid soap after they have finished."
Bret, Carlisle

Comprehension

Task 1

Find a word in the text to replace the word in italic print. Use the dictionary to help you.

a. The childcare practitioner must *comply with* state regulations.
b. The children's personal belongings are hung separately to try *to curb* the spread of germs.

c. Each child naps in its own *bed*.
d. The towels and linens are washed every day *to minimise* the chances of transmitting illness.
e. *Dirty* nappies must be wrapped in two plastic bags before they are disposed of.
f. The practitioners teach the children about the importance of *cleanliness*.

Grammar

Reflexive Pronouns

Reflexive Pronouns are pronouns following transitive verbs, or verbs that take objects, to show that the object and subject are the same person or thing.
*The girl looked at **herself** in the mirror.*

In this sentence the subject is the same person as the object.
It should be noted that English has far fewer verbs that take Reflexive Pronouns than other European languages. There are some verbs in German, for example, that are followed by reflexive pronouns, but not in English.

The boys washed themselves their hands. (incorrect)
The boys washed their hands. (correct)

I interest myself for music. (incorrect)
I am interested in music. (correct)

A reflexive pronoun is not used after prepositions of place or position.
*The girl took her teddy **with her** to bed.*

If the subject is plural and the verb is a reciprocating action, then a reciprocal pronoun *each other*, or *one another* is used.
*Lucy helps Louis, and Louis helps Lucy. Lucy and Louis **help each other**.*

Compare these sentences:
*The children **helped themselves** to fruit.* (reflexive pronoun)
*The children **helped each other** pick up the toys.* (Reciprocal Pronoun)

In the second sentence, the verb is a reciprocating action.

We also use reflexive pronouns to show that the action is done alone without help from someone else.
*A child should never be left **by itself**.*
*The boy was proud that he could climb the ladder **by himself**.*

Reflexive pronouns are also used to emphasise something, usually the subject.
*I'm caring for an ill child, though I feel ill **myself**.* (also)
*I was going to call the child's mother, but the mother called me **herself**.* (personally)

Task 2

Look at the sentences below and decide whether the reflexive pronoun or Reciprocal Pronoun is necessary. Rewrite the sentence correctly only if the sentence is incorrect.

a. After breakfast the children brushed themselves their teeth.
b. The baby recognised itself in the mirror and giggled.
c. Maggie isn't able to dress herself yet.
d. The children sat themselves down in a circle.
e. The children were playing hide and seek, and James hid himself behind the curtain.
f. Simon hurt himself in the playground.

Task 3

Translate the following sentences from German into English.

a. Die Kinder freuten sich über ihre Weihnachtsgeschenke.
b. Zoë musste sich selbst anziehen.
c. Er hat sich wahrscheinlich gestern im Regen erkältet.
d. Sie versteht sich gut mit den anderen Kindern.
e. Wir haben uns alle beim Zirkus amüsiert.
f. Leo hat sich mit der Schere geschnitten.

Writing

Task 4

Together with a partner, write a list of guidelines for maintaining good hygiene for the staff members at your preschool. Present the guidelines on a poster to the class.

Case study

1 Three-year-old Zoë Rosso, like many children her age, was having difficulty making it to the toilet in time. She had been potty training for a few months, and was dry by the time she started preschool. But when Zoë started preschool, the stress of the new situation caused her to have accidents from time to time. Zoë's mother saw no
5 reason for concern until the Montessori preschool Zoë was attending in Arlington, Virginia, suspended her for one month. The principal of the preschool claimed that Zoë was having too many accidents at her age; the county had a policy for the admission to preschool programmes requiring three-year-olds to be fully toilet-trained. If a child had more than eight accidents in a month, it would be suspended.
10 After the suspension Zoë returned to the preschool and shortly thereafter started having accidents again – too many. For fear that Zoë would be suspended again, her parents found a place at a new preschool that worked with children who were potty-training. Zoë's mother assured her that she would be going to a preschool where the teachers wouldn't be angry with her for having accidents. Zoë never had an accident
15 after that.

This text is based on the story "Three-year-old suspended from Arlington preschool for too many potty accidents" by Brigid Schulte that appeared in the Washington Post on January 30, 2011.

Comprehension

Task 5

Discuss the following questions with a partner.

a. Why do you think Zoë began having accidents?
b. Should being toilet trained be a criterion for admission to a nursery school? Why, or why not?
c. How should potty training be managed at a nursery school or creche?

Task 6

Discuss the following questions as a group.

a. How would you react if a child had an "accident" and didn't make it to the toilet in time?
b. How should the accident be dealt with?

Unit 7:
Growing up

Module 1: Growing pains

1 Growing up involves a lot of changes, the taking on of new responsibilities and learning on many different levels. These changes are usually accompanied by conflicts, discussions and debates. In this unit, some problems of growing up will be discussed.

Writing / Discussion

Task 1

Reflect and write a short comment on the following questions. After you have finished answering them, discuss your answers with a partner.

a. What did you enjoy about growing up? What did you dislike about growing up?
b. What is better now at your current age compared to when you were younger? What is not as good as when you were younger?
c. What would you change if you knew then, what you know now?
d. Did you have a happy childhood? Why or why not?

Quotes on growing up

"If you haven't grown up by age forty, you don't have to." – unattributed

"A grownup is a child with layers."
– Woody Harrelson, actor

"It is only because of problems that we grow up mentally and spiritually." – Morgan Scott Peck, psychiatrist

"We grow neither better nor worse as we get old, but more like ourselves." – May Lamberton Becker, journalist and literary critic

"All children are artists. The problem is how to remain artists once they grow up." – Pablo Picasso, artist

"To exist is to change, to change is to mature, to mature is to go on creating oneself endlessly." – Henri Bergson, philosopher and writer

"When I grow up I want to be a little boy." – Joseph Heller, writer

Discussion

Task 2

Discuss with a partner the meaning of the quotes. Which one can you relate to most? Share your ideas with the whole group. Can you come up with your own quote about childhood or growing up?

Caught between childhood and adulthood: the life of a teenager – it's all in the mind

1 Growing up isn't easy, and adolescents are stuck in the middle of it. They aren't quite adults yet, but they aren't children anymore either. Teens are in a period of metamorphosis called puberty that erupts in their brains when they are about ten, and not only causes rapid physical growth, but also erratic mood swings and unpredictable behaviour.
5 They go through a process of maturation that takes them through many ups and downs – conflicts with themselves and with others.

Teenagers often feel misunderstood by their parents and resent their parents' involvement in their lives. They seek their independence and demand the freedom to discover their identity and role in society. But the rules their parents lay down for them always
10 seem to prevent them from doing just this; conflict is inevitable. At the same time, teens secretly yearn for their parents' guidance and support at one of their most vulnerable stages in their lives. Although many parents feel their efforts are futile, their constant lecturing about responsible decision-making and proper social conduct is crucial for their offsprings' development and for their safety.

15 Scientists say that teenagers are not to blame for their less than desirable patterns of behaviour. Research on the development of the adolescent's brain has revealed that it undergoes a wave of overproduction of brain cells and synopses during puberty that is similar to that in infants in the first year of life. The executive centre of the brain, the pre-frontal cortex, does not fully mature until the mid-twenties. During adolescence, this part of the brain,
20 whose job it is to plan and think about consequences and to control impulses from other parts of the brain, is deluged by hormones, making it practically impossible for teens to think clearly, to understand the consequences of their behaviour, and to understand and follow rules of social conduct. Unlike an adult, an adolescent is unable to control impulses; instead, he seeks thrills and adventure and engages in activities that involve risk, without
25 being able to recognise the risk. These activities are usually prompted by group dynamics and a teen's eagerness to win the respect of his peers.

The miscommunication between adolescents and their parents also seems to be caused by a teenager's inability to interpret emotions through facial expression. While adults use the pre-frontal cortex – the rational part of the brain – to read emotion, adolescents
30 use the amygdala, the part of the brain that stores memories of emotional events and controls instinctive responses such as fear or the fight-flight response to threat. A teen has difficulty interpreting social cues, such as body language, facial expression and even the tone of voice. So, when a parent asks his/her child to clean up his/her room, this is probably not interpreted as a request, but rather as a threat or insult.

35 The tendency to overreact to harmless remarks makes teenagers particularly vulnerable to bullying and humiliation from their peers. They go to all lengths to "fit in" with their clique and to avoid negative attention. This usually expresses itself through their preoccupation with their appearances. Girls particularly become very self-conscious about their bodies and often have a distorted perception of themselves. Because they still lack
40 self-esteem, teens are easily embarrassed and hurt by their peers' criticism – even if it's a spiteful gaze.

Teenagers are fragile. Their brains take them on a roller-coaster of emotions that are more intense than at any other time of their lives. Although all people go through this stage of confusion and frustration, the adult, whose mature brain has made their behav-
45 iour more placid, often in later life they regret not being able to experience life with the same intensity as when they were teens.

Comprehension

Task 3

What are the meanings of the words in italics in the following sentences? Choose the correct synonym from the box.

calm – changeable – embarrassment – flooded – signals – unavoidable – useless – weak

a. During puberty, teenagers experience not only rapid physical growth, but also *erratic* mood swings and unpredictable behaviour.
b. The rules parents lay down for their children always seem to prevent them from venturing their independence; conflict is *inevitable*.
c. Teens need their parents' guidance and support at one of their most *vulnerable* stages of their lives.

d. Many parents feel their efforts in being a good parent have been *futile* when their children act irresponsibly.

e. During adolescence, a teenager's brain is *deluged* by hormones, making it practically impossible for them to think clearly and to understand the consequences of their behaviour.

f. A teen has difficulty interpreting social *cues*, such as body language, facial expression and even the tone of voice.

g. The tendency to overreact to harmless remarks makes teenagers particularly vulnerable to bullying and *humiliation* from their peers.

h. Once an adult's brain matures (by his mid-twenties), his behaviour becomes more *placid*.

Task 4

Answer the following questions based on your understanding of the text.

a. What happens to a teenager during puberty?

b. Why do conflicts often evolve between teenagers and their parents?

c. In what ways are teenager's brains different from an adult's brain?

d. Why do teenagers often overreact to their parents' comments and requests?

Growing up

What does it mean to grow up? Growing up can be divided into three major categories:

- **Growth** is associated with an increase in physical size, and can be measured by the height, weight and circumference of the head.
- **Physical development** refers to the increasing ability and function of the body, including motor skills, skills of coordination and balance.
- **Emotional and social development** relates to how children understand themselves as individuals and as part of a social group (i.e. friends, family). It also determines how they become more independent and self-confident and are able to express and control their emotions. This aspect of development affects relationships with others the most.

Comprehension

Task 5

Match the following skills or abilities to one of the three major categories of growing up. Can you name any other skills or competences?

a. hand-eye coordination

b. self-esteem

c. weight
d. body proportions
e. self-concept
f. autonomy
g. balance
h. motor skills
i. sensory development
j. friendship
k. relating to others

Grammar

Comment adverbs for viewpoint and opinion

Comment adverbs are words or phrases that express the speaker's, or writer's, opinion or attitude about the stated information.

Some comment adverbs evaluate the statement so as to reflect the speaker's, or writer's, preferences or viewpoints (i.e. *fortunately, honestly, importantly, luckily, personally, regrettably, surprisingly, thankfully, understandably, unfortunately*). These adverbs are placed at the beginning of the sentence and separated from the rest of the sentence by a comma to show they modify the whole sentence, rather than just the verb.

Some comment adverbs show how likely we think something is (i.e. *apparently, certainly, clearly, definitely, surely, probably*). If it is placed after the subject to add emphasis, commas are used to separate it from the rest of the sentence: *Our son, **clearly**, had no idea what he was doing.*

Other comment adverbs show our judgement of someone's actions (i.e. *carelessly, kindly, politely, stupidly, wisely*):

*He **stupidly** got himself in trouble with the law.*
*She **wisely** chose not to leave school.*

Comment adverbs should not be confused with **adverbs of manner**, which sometimes look the same, but are meant to modify the verb or verb phrase and are placed either before the verb or after the verb and its object.

Comment adverb: ***Happily,** she was able to find an apprenticeship that suits her.*
(I am happy that she found an apprenticeship.)

Adverb of manner: *She **happily** found an apprenticeship that suited her.*
(She is happy to have found an apprenticeship.)

Viewpoint adverbs are quite similar to comment adverbs, but are used to make it clear from what point of view we are speaking (i.e. *politically, financially, physically, biologically, from a medical point of view*):

From a scientific point of view, teenagers are not to blame for their rebellious behaviour – their brains are.

Task 6

Rewrite these sentences so that the word or phrase in italics is replaced with an appropriate comment or viewpoint adverb. Make any necessary changes to complete the sentence.

a. *It was understandable that* her parents were upset about her behaviour.
b. She *regretted* not having finished school.
c. I am not *biologically* related to my uncle.
d. You have few *legal* rights as a minor.
e. It's *probable* that she ran away from home.

Listening

Teenage confessions

The transcription of the audio can be found on page 207.

Comprehension

Task 7

Listen to Emma (17), Stephen (18) and Jane (16) talking about how they struggle with their problems. As you listen, take down notes on a separate piece of paper to answer the questions in the grid.

	Emma, 17	Stephen, 18	Jane, 16
What problem do they have?			
What are the causes of their problems?			
How are their problems similar?			
How do their problems affect them?			

Task 8

After you've listened to Emma, Stephen and Jane talking about their problems, compare your notes with a partner's. Discuss the answers to the questions.

Writing

Task 9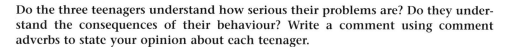

Do the three teenagers understand how serious their problems are? Do they understand the consequences of their behaviour? Write a comment using comment adverbs to state your opinion about each teenager.

Task 10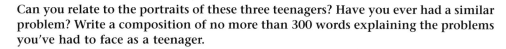

Can you relate to the portraits of these three teenagers? Have you ever had a similar problem? Write a composition of no more than 300 words explaining the problems you've had to face as a teenager.

Module 2: When parents can't let go

Until children reach adulthood, it's a parent's job to teach their children to be independent and self-reliant. As children grow up, parents become less and less involved in their children lives. However, some parents just can't let go. *Helicopter* and *velcro parents* are just two examples that put a name to a recent phenomenon in parenting.

Discussion

Task 1

Have you ever heard of these types of parents? What kind of parents do you think they describe? Discuss the questions with a partner.

When parents meddle

1 In recent years a new parenting phenomenon has cropped up. Parents are becoming much more involved in their children's lives than in previous generations. Helicopter parents constantly *hover* over their children and intervene in everything they do. They're always ready and waiting to *swerve* in and help their children out of *sticky* situations. A
5 *velcro* parent refers to an even more involved parent whose child has even less room to learn and develop *of its own accord*. They are so *devoted* to their children that they cannot let them go; they stick to them like Velcro. Instead of risking that their children could fail, they do things for them instead. This overly protective kind of parenting, experts say, is not only producing non-reliant, dependent children, it is also having a lasting
10 negative impact on the adolescents' personalities.

Although teens are hitting puberty ever earlier, they seem to be maturing to adulthood ever later; adolescence is being extended. Nowadays, it is not uncommon for young adults to marry in their thirties – living with mum and dad until they do – whereas forty years ago, men and women got married in their early twenties.

15 Though there isn't enough adequate research to explain why this phenomenon is happening, it is apparent that helicopter parenting results in children not being ready – or 20 capable of leaving the nest.

Some speculate it is because of the *ubiquitous* use of mobile phones and email communication that makes it easier for parents to check 25 in on their offspring at any time, anywhere. Others suggest that over-involved parents *meddle* in their children's lives because they want to relive their youth *vicariously* through the lives of their children.

30 When parents *mollycoddle* their children excessively and never give them the opportunity to manage their own affairs, they *deprive* their children of the space they need to learn how to make decisions for themselves; they will never be equipped with the skills they need to accomplish tasks and overcome problems. In fact, studies show that children of helicopter parents are more likely to be dependent, neurotic, more vulnerable and 35 self-conscious, and less open to new ideas.

Comprehension

Task 2

Match the following definitions to one of the words in italics in the text.

a. without outside intervention
b. a fastener that is usually sewn onto fabrics
c. something that can be found everywhere
d. change direction abruptly
e. involving problems that are difficult or awkward
f. to interfere unduly in someone else's affairs
g. to wait or linger close at hand; to remain in one place in the air
h. deny a person of something
i. experiencing something in the imagination or through the feelings or actions of another person
j. to dote on and pamper
k. dedicated and loving

Task 3

Answer the following questions based on the text above. Discuss your answers with a partner.

a. What is a helicopter parent?
b. What is a velcro parent? How is this different from a helicopter parent?
c. What are the possible reasons for this phenomenon in parenting?

Language

Linking words to express a contrast: *while, whereas* vs. *although, though*

While and *whereas* are used synonymously and show that two or more events or arguments are in direct opposition to each other.
*Helicopter parents hover over their children, **while** velcro parents stick to them wherever they go.*
*I let my children try to do things by themselves, **whereas** you do everything for them.*

Though and *although* are synonyms and are both conjunctions. They both contrast two different characteristics or events, but they do not have to happen at the same time.
*Katie does everything for her son, **although** he could do a lot for himself.*
*Children grow up, **even though** their parents sometimes do not want them to.*

Task 4

Complete the following sentences using *while, whereas, though* or *although*. There may be more than one possible answer.

a. Helicopter parents hover over their children, ...(1)... velcro parents stick to them.
b. ...(2)... Katie can cut her own meat, her mother insists upon doing it for her.
c. My mother gave me a cell phone so that I could call her from school, ...(3)... it was explicitly disallowed.
d. ...(4)... not enough research has been done to explain the cause of this phenomenon, it's clearly resulting in children not being ready to leave the nest.
e. ...(5)... 18-year-olds are allowed to vote and join the military in the U.S., they are not allowed to drink alcohol.
f. Daughters of teen mums are more likely to become teenage mothers themselves, ...(6)... sons of teenage mums are more likely to go to prison.

Writing

Task 5

Write down the negative and positive characteristics of helicopter and velcro parents.

The most spied upon people in Europe

France – Emma Jane Kirby

1 [...] Surveillance cameras are not just kept for the streets. Last year a company which manufactures GPS systems for cars launched Kiditel, a child-tracking device.

5 The games console-sized device slips into a child's pocket and allows parents to keep track of their child's movements via satellite images sent to their computers. Many parents welcomed a product they believed 10 would help their children keep safe, but psychologists like Jean Claude Guillemard were not so welcoming: "The children who

have this device will think of their parents as Big Brother," he said. "I think that scares me. I think it's dangerous for their mental health."

15 Similarly a French childminder caused a row last year when she became the first nanny to install an internet webcam in her crèche so that parents could still look in on their children – and see that she was taking good care of them – even though they were at work.

The parents loved it, but local authorities and the National Federation of Maternal
20 Assistants denounced the idea as undermining the relationship of trust between the parents and the childminder. [...]

Denmark – Julian Isherwood

[...] A Copenhagen kindergarten that recently suggested it would like to install CCTV monitoring around its premises gave up the idea following a public outcry.

25 Similarly, workplace monitoring is under strict control, preventing camera surveillance of employees, although the installation of CCTV in public areas and particularly in shops is permitted.

Extract from: The most spied upon people in Europe, in: BBC News, February 28, 2008, news.bbc.co.uk/2/ hi/7265212.stm, accessed May 1, 2012.

Discussion

 Task 6

Discuss the following questions in a group.

a. Why do you think the psychologist Guillemard warns that a tracking device for children can be harmful?
b. Would you agree that an Internet webcam in a day care facility undermines the relationship of trust between the parents and practitioner?
c. Do the advantages of this kind of surveillance technology outweigh the disadvantages? Explain why, or why not.

Module 3: When kids have kids – teenage mums

Children of teenage mothers need an early head start

1 Children born to adolescent mothers often face more obstacles in life compared to those born to older mothers. Teenage mums more often have premature births and their babies low birth weights. They are more likely to grow up in poverty, have behavioural problems and developmental delays, become the victims of neglect and abuse, and to
5 drop out of school. Daughters of teenage mums are more likely to become a teenaged mother themselves, while sons of teenage mums are more likely to go to prison. Studies have also shown that teenage mothers who live alone with their children are more likely to abuse or neglect their children than those living with another, related, adult. These children are also exhibit higher levels of anxiety and lower levels of self-esteem.

10 Having a child at such a young age is not only a burden to the mother herself and her family, but also to society as a whole. In an effort to offset and prevent this social encumbrance,
15 the Early Head Start (EHS) preschool programme was devised to reach out to children of teenage parents and other socially disadvantaged children under the age of three. It pro-
20 vides them with services and resources such as nutritious meals, regular medical check-ups and treatment as well as pre- and postnatal care for pregnant women. These
25 parenting services are especially geared towards adolescent mothers who are still developing cognitively, physically and emotionally.

Since the introduction of the pro-
30 gramme in the United States in 1995, surveys show that it has had positive impacts on the socio-emotional development of the children and on parent child interaction. Parents learn the importance of reading books to their children and of playing with them. Consequently, the children in the programme have better concentration, improved language development and exhibit less aggression. Parents under the age of 18 who partici-
35 pated in the programme were more likely to stay in school and were less likely to remain dependent on welfare.

Comprehension

Task 1

Are the statements true or false? Correct the false statements with the appropriate information from the text.

a. Children of teenage mothers are less likely to be born early.
b. Children of teenage mothers are more likely to be abused or neglected.
c. Children of teenage mothers tend to be more fearful and aggressive.
d. The partners of teenage mothers are more likely to go to prison.
e. Early Head Start (EHS) is a preschool programme for children from privileged families.
f. EHS offers food and health care.
g. Parents in the programme are less likely to receive government assistance over extended periods of time.

Discussion

Task 2

Why do you think children of teenage mothers are more likely to be socially disadvantaged? Discuss the probable causes in a group.

Case Study

Gemma Ray, 16: "Walking around town was the hardest thing I ever had to do when I was pregnant."

1 I gave birth to my son, Ellis, now 13 months, before my sixteenth birthday. When I found out I was pregnant, I was really scared and confused, didn't know who to talk to or
5 where to turn. My mum and dad were shocked. My mum quickly got over it and supported me, whereas my dad didn't talk to me for ages, which was really hard on me as I am a big daddy's girl. It really upset me, but
10 now he is really supportive and loves his grandson. When the people at school found out I was pregnant, one person smacked me in the stomach and said, "Bet you ain't pregnant now." I walked away, I didn't see the point in stooping to her level. I was transferred to a school for teenage mums. Walking around town was the hardest thing
15 I ever had to do when I was pregnant. Strangers on the bus looked down on me and called me a "Slag" or a "Whore", and I could feel people's eyes burning into me as they stared at what they thought was yet another single teenage mum. At secondary school, there wasn't much support available, but at the specialist school I had a lot of support, not just from the teachers, but also from the students as we were all in the same situa-
20 tion, so there was no one there to judge you. I felt really alone, but since coming to the YWCA I am very confident and don't care what people think. I know I'm a good mum and I'm proud of my son. I want to attend college in September to do my A-levels and then do a counselling course, and see where life takes me from there. My advice is: Don't be afraid to ask for help. Ignore petty people that think you can't do it. Believe in
25 yourself.

The experiences of two teenage mums, in: The Guardian, April 15, 2009, www.guardian.co.uk/society/ 2009/apr/15/teenage-mums, accessed May 1, 2012.

Comprehension

Task 3

Answer the following questions based on your understanding of the case study.

a. How did Gemma's parents react to her pregnancy?
b. How did the public react to her pregnancy?
c. In what ways was the special school able to help Gemma?
d. How, do you think, is Gemma's story different from the average teenage mother's?

Discussion

Task 4

Imagine you were in Gemma's shoes. What would you do in her situation? Would you carry the baby full term? Would you consider abortion? What do you think would the consequences of your decisions? Reflect upon these questions and discuss them with a partner.

Activity

Task 5

How can teenage pregnancy be better prevented? Develop a plan of action that can be put into practise in your town or community to help lower the teenage pregnancy rate. Present your ideas to the group.

Parents rebel over lessons on sex for pupils aged four and plans to teach homosexuality to six-year-olds

1 A primary school is facing a parents' revolt over the content of sex education classes for children as young as four. [...]

Under the plans, those aged six could be taught about same-sex relationships and the difference between 'good and bad touching'. Topics for ten-year-olds include orgasm
5 and masturbation. Grenoside Community Primary in Sheffield already offers sex education to pupils in the two oldest year groups, but is planning to extend it to the younger ones as well.

Some parents have been shocked by details of the lessons revealed in con-
10 sultation meetings. Headmaster Colin Fleetwood insists the material is not explicit and is in line with national curriculum guidelines. But parents including Louise Leahy –
15 who has four children aged five to ten at the 319-pupil school – are furious.

"There is a great deal of material in there which children don't need to know at such a young age," the 41-year-old said. "It's almost like the lessons and videos shown are saying, 'Put all your toys in the bin, now it's time to grow up'."

20 She said some of the vocabulary used for the first two year groups is inappropriate, and she objected to a DVD for older children showing a man lying on top of a woman.

Videos about people touching themselves encourage children "to think in a sexual way", she said, adding: "One governor told me her child needs to know this stuff because she watches Emmerdale and EastEnders, but mine don't and I don't want them to."

25 Katie Burrell, 26, whose six-year-old son Redd is at the school, agreed, saying:, "My boy still believes in Father Christmas, he doesn't need to be told these things."

"The lessons for six- and seven-year-olds are far too explicit. I think a lot of parents will take their children out of these classes."

"I am by no means a prude, but some of this is beyond stupidity."

30 Mr Fleetwood said governors will decide what can be taught following the consultation. He added:, "We want this to be a positive learning experience which will help our children make sensible and responsible decisions as they grow up."

His view was echoed by Dr Sonia Sharp, executive director for children, young people and families at Sheffield City Council, who said the lessons are widely taught at other 35 primary schools in the city.

More than a fifth of UK primaries offer sex education, the content of which is decided by governors. It is compulsory only at secondaries. Labour planned to make the subject compulsory from the age of five. Yesterday, the Department for Education said it is reviewing the subject.

Chris Brooke: Parents rebel over lessons on sex for pupils aged four and plans to teach homosexuality to six-year-olds, in: Daily Mail Online, November 17, 2011, www.dailymail.co.uk/news/article-2062249/ Parents-rebel-lessons-sex-pupils-aged-furious-plans-teach-homosexuality-year-olds.html#ixzz1tilLN8eO, accessed May 2, 2012.

Writing

Task 6

You and your partner are preschool teachers and you would like to implement a sexual education curriculum geared toward four- to six-year-olds. What do you feel is appropriate to tell children about sexuality and how? Plan a few activities in which you introduce young children to sexuality.

Activity

Task 7

Have a classroom debate on the appropriateness of sex education in preschool. Split into two teams. One team will support sex education, while the other team is opposed to it. Before you open the debate, each team should collect and prepare their arguments. Once both teams have presented their arguments, decide as a group which team was most persuasive.

Unit 8:
Food and health

Module 1: Healthy eating and obesity

Comprehension

Task 1

Match the pictures of the children with the quotes below.

Juan-Pablo, Mexico

Anish, India

Georgia, USA

Jasmine, Great Britain

Li-hua, China

a. "My favourite food is masala dosa, it's a savoury pancake filled with potatoes and vegetables and spices. I also love mangoes, and watermelons when it's hot."

b. "My two favourite things to eat are macaroni cheese, and spaghetti and meatballs. My favourite dessert is pancakes with maple syrup."

c. "My favourite things to eat are the enchiladas my mother makes, they're corn tortillas filled with chicken and then fried. I also love tacos filled with refried beans and cheese."

d. "I love rice with fish and vegetable stir fry, and my favourite soup is pork rib soup with water chestnuts. My favourite dessert is coconut ice cream."

e. "My favourite food is bangers and mash (sausages with mashed potato) but I also love pasta and pesto (with lots of parmesan cheese). And I really like chicken curry too."

Discussion

Task 2

In groups of three, decide which of the children's diets is the healthiest, and which is the least healthy. Give at least three reasons for each decision.

Language

Task 3

Look at the picture on the right. How many of the foods in the picture can you name in English?

Compare your list with that to the person next to you, and see if you can extend your food vocabulary.

Task 4

Now copy the food pyramid into your notebook and put the food words on your list into the main food groups in the pyramid.

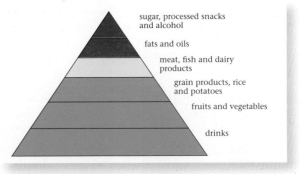

Discussion

1 Doctors and nutritionists agree that it is important for everyone to eat a diet which contains as much variety as possible, and 5 which is a balance of the food types from the main food groups. This is especially true for children, whose development depends upon their bodies receiving the right nutrients. Of course it's also important to limit how much unhealthy food (such as sugar) children eat, both for the sake of their bodies and their teeth.

Task 5

With a partner, discuss how you as a kindergarten worker could encourage children to limit the amount of sugar and unhealthy food they eat. What is a reasonable amount of sugar and fat?

Council "put child, five, into care for being obese"

1 A schoolchild aged five has become one of the youngest children in Britain to be taken into care for obesity reasons, it has emerged.

The child, who cannot be named for legal reasons, report-
5 edly had a body mass index of 22.6, which is considered clinically obese for such an age. [...] Social services from Tameside council, Greater Manchester, decided that the child's parents, who also cannot be identified, had failed to bring their weight under control.

10 He is the second young person the local authority has placed into care for being overweight. A teenager, who also cannot be named, was found to have had a BMI of 30.3, which is the equivalent of about 13 stone, which is five stone more than average.

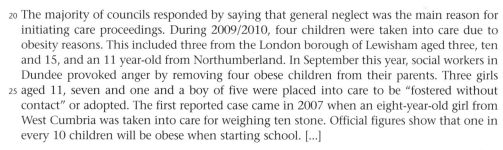

15 The disclosures came after requests, made under the Free-dom of Information Act, that were sent to all local author-ities in Britain. [...] The survey, by the Daily Mail, found another child was removed by Sunderland council, but officials refused to provide details of the age or weight, claiming it would breach data protection laws.

20 The majority of councils responded by saying that general neglect was the main reason for initiating care proceedings. During 2009/2010, four children were taken into care due to obesity reasons. This included three from the London borough of Lewisham aged three, ten and 15, and an 11 year-old from Northumberland. In September this year, social workers in Dundee provoked anger by removing four obese children from their parents. Three girls
25 aged 11, seven and one and a boy of five were placed into care to be "fostered without contact" or adopted. The first reported case came in 2007 when an eight-year-old girl from West Cumbria was taken into care for weighing ten stone. Official figures show that one in every 10 children will be obese when starting school. [...]

A spokesman for the National Obesity Forum said it supported placing obese children into
30 care but only as a last resort and only after all efforts had been made to reduce their weight. "We sincerely hope that such occasions will be rare ... but make the point that this will be the automatic response to a child at the other extreme – severe malnutrition," they said.

A spokesman for Tameside Council told the Daily Mail: "The point at which obesity turns into a child-protection issue is a complex and difficult area, and in these two cases
35 there were other determining factors that led to the children being placed in local authority care [...]."

Extract from: Council "put child, 5, into care for being obese", in: The Telegraph, December 5, 2011, www. telegraph.co.uk/health/healthnews/8934809/Council-put-child-5-into-care-for-being-obese.html, accessed February 15, 2012.

Comprehension

Task 6

Answer these questions about the text.

a. Why has this information come into the public domain?
b. What do you think is the difference between overweight and obesity?
c. What is the main reason councils say they take children into care?
d. What point does the National Obesity Forum make about children's weight?

Task 7

A financial year in the UK runs from 6 April to 5 April. According to this article, how many children and teenagers were taken into care wholly or partly because of their obesity, during each of the following time periods?

a. 2007   b. 2009–2010   c. 2010 onwards

Discussion

Task 8

In groups of three to four, discuss these questions.

a. What do you think data protection laws are?
b. What do you think that the phrase "only as a last resort" means?
c. In your opinion, is it right to take children into care because they are obese, even if there are no other causes for concern? Give at least two reasons for your opinion.

Grammar

Conditional II – What would happen if ...?

We use Conditional II (If Clause Type 2) to talk about a different possible world. It is used to describe things which are either not likely to happen, or are improbable.

Form	
If clause	**Result clause**
If + simple past tense	would / might / could + infinitive of main verb
e.g. *If you **took** more exercise, you **could eat** more carbohydrates.*	
e.g. *If you **didn't eat** so many sweets, you **wouldn't need** so many fillings in your teeth.*	

Task 9

With a partner, think of endings for these sentences.

a. If children ate less fast food, ...
b. There wouldn't be so much childhood diabetes if ...
c. If the fast food industry wasn't so powerful, ...
d. The average child in Britain might be more active if ...

Case studies – Two cases of unhealthy eating

Case study A
Maggie Olwen is a nutritional adviser, and she has just started to work with the Charlton family. The family's eleven-year-old daughter Jodie is overweight and has been diagnosed with childhood diabetes. They have two younger children aged six and four who are also heavier than average for their age. The news of the diabetes has been a great shock, and the family really wants to make changes in their lifestyle.

Case study B
Peter Clarke is also a nutritional adviser and he's been asked to meet with the Edwards family, whose two young children Shawn, two, and Chantel, four, are overweight. The whole family loves fast food, and they eat takeaways at least five times a week. They tell Peter that they can't imagine eating differently, and none of them likes fruit or vegetables.

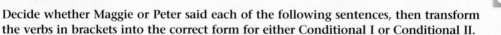

Task 10

Decide whether Maggie or Peter said each of the following sentences, then transform the verbs in brackets into the correct form for either Conditional I or Conditional II.

a. If you (eat) more pulses and beans, your bodies (digest) food better.
b. If you (not buy) so much fast food, you (save) money.
c. If you (cook) with olive oil, your bodies (process) the fat better.
d. If you (find) at least one or two vegetables you all like, it (help).

Jamie's kitchen nightmare: his show is getting the chop

1 He crossed the Atlantic with a can-do attitude, a suitcase full of silly clothes, and the naïve conviction that a few flashes of that cheeky-chappy smile and some judicious use of Mockney would help him make it big in Hollywood. But, like so many other British stars, Jamie Oliver has discovered that American entertainment is a cut-throat business.

5 A year after he launched a "food revolution" that aimed to convince the world's fattest schoolchildren to rein back their daily intake of burgers, pizza, chicken nuggets and chocolate milkshake, the Naked Chef's career on US television appears to be collapsing like an overblown cheese soufflé.

On Tuesday, hours before this week's third episode of Oliver's latest culinary TV series was 10 due to hit the airwaves, ABC announced that it had been pulled from its prime-time slot, because of disappointing ratings. In place of Jamie Oliver's Food Revolution, in which he was attempting to improve the calorie-laden diets of the under-privileged inhabitants of Los Angeles, the network decided to air a one-hour recap of Dancing With the Stars. [...]

Call this dumbing down, but the show's decline is perhaps also Oliver's fault, for deciding 15 to film his second series in southern California. Last year's debut series was shot in Huntington, West Virginia, where the relative novelty of media attention, along with the supportive attitude of local lawmakers, helped create a city-wide buzz that led to some signal achievements. He even persuaded local schools to take pizza off their breakfast menu.

20   Los Angeles is a tougher nut to crack. The size of the metropolis has made it tricky for Oliver to gain media attention. And his requests to film inside school canteens have been consistently denied by the LA Unified School District, a huge and famously dysfunctional body responsible for running the city's schools.

That has left a gaping narrative hole in the show that has at times seemed impossible to plug. On occasion, Oliver has even accused local bureaucrats of deliberately attempt-
25   ing to deprive him of shooting locations. [...]

Oliver is clearly in the right: the proportion of obese children in Los Angeles has increased from 18 to 25 per cent in the last decade, while a typical LA school lunch consists of "hot and spicy chicken chunks", "beef steak fingers in gravy" and a pudding of "peanut butter and jelly pockets". The problem is that so far this series, his cameras
30   have been unable to film a proper exposé. The School District in this series, for its part, has run an effective propaganda campaign, with officials appearing on Fox News to argue that Los Angeles is an unsuitable location for a "food revolution," and that Oliver was only motivated to film there because he's hoping to launch a Hollywood career. [...]

Extract from: Guy Adams: Jamie's kitchen nightmare: his show is getting the chop, in: Independent, May 5, 2011, www.independent.co.uk/news/media/tv-radio/jamies-kitchen-nightmare-his-show-is-getting-the-chop-2279005.html#, accessed July 3, 2012.

Comprehension

Task 11

In pairs, answer the following questions.

a. What was ABC's reason for taking Jamie Oliver's show off the air?
b. What has left a big hole in the show?
c. What mistake does the article say that Jamie Oliver made?

Task 12

Find phrases in the text which have the same meaning as the words in *italics* below.

a. Removing free preschool care leaves a *big gap* in children's services.
b. Some insiders say that the fast food industry can be a *ruthless* business.
c. He needs to *control* his appetite for chocolate and sweets.
d. The television channel is *appealing to a less educated audience* with its reality shows.

Writing

Task 13

a. Jamie Oliver is doing a school dinners' TV programme in Germany and he's looking for kindergartens which already have good practice in healthy eating. You work in a nursery; write to him saying why he should choose your workplace to be in the show.

b. Your kindergarten has been chosen, and Jamie and his team are going to visit to make a film. You need to plan a menu for five lunches for the children at the nursery so that they eat five healthy, balanced meals. Plan and write out this menu.

Module 2: Attention Deficit Hyperactive Disorder

Myths and facts about ADHD

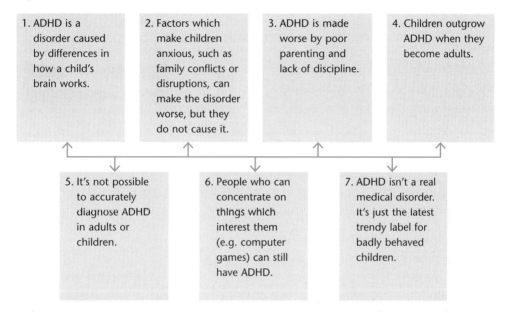

1. ADHD is a disorder caused by differences in how a child's brain works.

2. Factors which make children anxious, such as family conflicts or disruptions, can make the disorder worse, but they do not cause it.

3. ADHD is made worse by poor parenting and lack of discipline.

4. Children outgrow ADHD when they become adults.

5. It's not possible to accurately diagnose ADHD in adults or children.

6. People who can concentrate on things which interest them (e.g. computer games) can still have ADHD.

7. ADHD isn't a real medical disorder. It's just the latest trendy label for badly behaved children.

Task 1

Do the quiz in groups of three to four. Decide if the statements in the seven boxes above are myths or facts.

Can a bad diet and too many additives cause ADHD?
1 There are many people who believe that unhealthy food, and additives in particular, cause ADHD. However, despite many studies which have looked for links between the illness and different food elements, most scientists agree that there is no conclusive evidence to support any kind of causal connection. On the other hand, some reports have
5 shown that food allergies can play a role in making ADHD worse if a child already has a tendency towards it. A child or an adult may be allergic to any type of food; an additive can be the culprit, but so can something natural like milk or wheat flour.

Certain foods are less likely than others to cause allergies. These include rice, vegetables and meat, so if you want to try to plan an allergy free diet, this is what you should stick
10 to. And as for the safest drink? Well, that would be water!

Comprehension

Task 2

Does the text say that there is or there isn't a link between ADHD and food?

Task 3

In pairs, look at the food nouns in the two texts above, and make lists of all the countable words and all the uncountable words.

Examples:

Countable	–	additives
Uncountable	–	wheat flour
Can be both	–	food / foods

Grammar

Countable and uncountable nouns with *some / any, much / many, a lot of*

Use	Examples
Countable nouns	
These nouns can be counted.	*He has 1,500 books.*
They have a plural form.	*They have three children.*
We use a / an with the singular form.	*There is a problem here.*
Uncountable nouns	
These nouns can't be counted.	*I'd like some tea.*
These nouns can only be singular.	*We need some information.*
We don't use a / an.	*He loves music.*
Nouns which can be both	
Some nouns can be both, depending on the meaning:	
Specific meaning (countable)	*Children can react to a range of foods.*
General meaning (uncountable)	*Food can contribute to a child's problems.*
Some	
Some is used in positive sentences.	*He has some general research to do.*
	They think they took some good photos.
Some is also used in requests and offers.	*Could I have some coffee please?*
Any	
Any is used in most questions.	*Do you have any questions?*
	Does he do any exercise?
Any is used in negative sentences.	*I didn't bring any money.*
No means the same as *not any*.	*He has no friends (he hasn't got any friends).*
We also use *any* with the meaning	*You can catch any train, they all go to Bristol.*
"it doesn't matter which."	*Q: What do you want to eat? A: Anything you have is fine.*

Much

Much is used with uncountable nouns especially in negatives and questions.

She doesn't eat much pizza.
How much information do you need?

Many

Many is used with countable nouns, in positive sentences but especially in negatives and questions.

My father has many hobbies.
Does he eat many takeaways?
There weren't many people at the meeting.

A lot of

A lot of is used in positive sentences with both countable and uncountable nouns. We can also use *a lot of* in negative sentences, and questions.

My brother has a lot of health issues.
There's a lot of milk left in the carton.
There hasn't been a lot of input.
Are there a lot of new students?

Task 4

Complete the sentences with *some* or *any*.

a. There are ...(1)... foods which may cause allergies.
b. There isn't ...(2)... strong evidence that additives cause ADHD.
c. Do you have ...(3)... food allergies?
d. There is ...(4)... research which suggests a link.
e. Could I have ...(5)... coffee?

Task 5

In pairs, complete the sentences with *much, many* or *a lot of*. Sometimes more than one answer is possible.

a. It is thought that there are ...(1)... contributing factors to ADHD.
b. She can't be healthy with a diet that contains so ...(2)... fast food.
c. Do you have to make so ...(3)... telephone calls?
d. Hurry up, we haven't got ...(4)... time left.
e. I don't know how ...(5)... fruit she eats.
f. You shouldn't put so ...(6)... salt on your food.

Task 6

Find and correct the mistake in each of these sentences.

a. He gave me a lot of informations.
b. Come and visit me some time you want to.
c. They think there are too much people in the classroom.
d. Could I have any coffee please?
e. Q: What does surplus mean? A: It means there are too much of something.
f. The doctor gave him too much prescriptions.

Activity

Task 7

Copy this word map into your notebooks
Write down all the words connected to the word *prescription*
that you can think of.

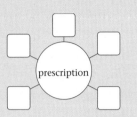

Hints:

- What are the verbs and adjectives connected to the word *prescription*?

Discussion

Task 8

Ritalin – the debate

1 The use of medication such as Ritalin (methyl-
phenidate hydrochlors) to treat ADHD has been a
rising trend in both the USA and in Britain over
the last 20 years. In the same period, Germany
5 too has seen a sharp rise in the numbers of children who are diagnosed with ADHD and then
prescribed the drug.

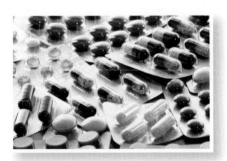

Student A: You are *for* the use of Ritalin. Use the language for expressing opinions in Unit 4, and the following information:

- Used properly research has shown that Ritalin is safe, as safe as aspirin. Many doctors and scientists say that Ritalin is helpful to children and adults with ADHD.
- Some doctors over-prescribe, and some mis-prescribe, but this doesn't mean that the benefits of a helpful drug should be overlooked. We shouldn't throw the baby out with the bathwater!
- Parents of children with ADHD swear that the drug helps their children, and that without it their children would not get through school.
- Ritalin should only be correctly used in combination with talking therapies, the education of the parents and the child, and lifestyle modification.
- Stimulants have been successfully used to treat what we now call ADHD since 1937. This is not a new phenomenon.

Student B: You are *against* the use of Ritalin. Use the language for expressing opinions in Unit 4, and the following information:

- There is a dangerous trend towards medicalising child behaviour.
- Ritalin is a strong drug; it can make changes to a child's body and personality. There is no proof that it is not addictive.
- It can't be true that suddenly there are so many children with ADHD, compared to only 30 years ago. Some cases are simply bad behaviour or bad parenting, or both.
- Some doctors prescribe Ritalin without a proper diagnosis.
- The parents of children with ADHD need to be educated, for example to encourage them to read their children bedside stories rather than letting them play electronic games all the time.

Activity

Task 9

Role-play

In groups of four, role-play a meeting between the parents of a young boy and two kindergarten workers. The parents think that their son is just naughty, but the kindergarten workers believe he might have ADHD. When he is at kindergarten, the little boy can't sit still, and never pays attention to a story or an activity, but always gets up and walks around. He is always picking up one toy after another, and playing with it for a few moments only, then dropping it and moving on to grab another toy.

- Two of you play the parents, imagine you have a very active little boy. You have lots of questions about his behaviour in the kindergarten and about ADHD.
- Two of you play the kindergarten workers. You should ask questions about the boy's behaviour at home and try to explain ADHD using the language in this module.

Module 3: Autism

Q&A: Autism

1 Sarah Boseley explains who is affected and the treatment they receive.

Q. What is autism?
A. Autism is a lifelong condition that
5 impacts on the development of individuals. It is often referred to as autism spectrum disorder, as it affects some individuals far more than others. People with the condition have difficulty
10 understanding and relating to others.

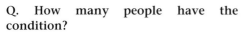

Q. How many people have the condition?
A. Around 500,000 have been diagnosed in the UK.

Q. What are the characteristics of people with autism?
15 A. They do not have an instinctive understanding of how people feel. They may find it hard to understand somebody's facial expression or tone of voice and may not recognise a joke. Some people with autism may not speak at all and those who do may find it hard to participate in conversation. They may appear to say or do things which are insensitive or rude and behave recklessly in, for instance, running across a road
20 because they do not understand danger. They like systems and routines and can be distressed by unusual or unexpected events.

Q. Is Asperger's syndrome a form of autism?

A. Yes, it is on the autism spectrum. Generally people with Asperger's function at a higher level, can speak better and often have above average intelligence. They are
25   more able to cope in society, but they may be aware of the difficulties they have in relating to other people, which makes them anxious.

Q. What causes autism?

A. Nobody knows for sure, but it appears to be triggered by a combination of genes (it runs in families), and environmental factors (there have been cases of identical twins
30   where one is autistic and the other is not).

Q. How soon is it diagnosed?

A. Not soon enough. Parents may be aware that something is wrong from early on, but it is quite common for a child not to be diagnosed until he is more than a year old. Often it takes even longer. Asperger's may not be diagnosed until a child
35   is three or four years old.

Q. Is there a cure?

A. Not at the moment. There are therapies, however, that can be helpful.

Article from: Sarah Boseley: Q&A: Autism, in: The Guardian, January 12, 2009, www.guardian.co.uk/ society/2009/jan/12/autism-health, accessed February 16, 2012.

Comprehension

Task 1

Find words in the text which mean the same as:

a. to manage
b. unhappy, suffering
c. dangerously and without taking care
d. making a connection
e. affects

Two professionals who work with autistic children

Ben Grey

1 Ben is a primary school teacher in the UK, who teaches the reception class (ages four to five). There are autistic twin boys in his class, and Ben gets help from a support assistant, Karen. Here, Ben is talking about work-
5 ing with autistic children:

"The twins are extremely bright, and they are lovely boys. The most important thing when working with them is keeping to a routine so they know what to expect. A visual timetable is essential because if they
10 don't know what is planned for each day they might not be able to cope. In early years' education the

learning is less structured, so this may be hard, but it's still important to find a way to keep the boys in a routine that they know about and understand. We also use the Social Use of Language Programme (SULP). This is a programme which helps children learn
15 about social communication skills, and how to have more awareness of themselves and other people. Without learning about these things, autistic children can really struggle to interact with their peers."

Pat Currie

Pat is a Speech and Language Therapist who
20 works with autistic children from the ages of two to seven.

"The aim is for many autistic children to attend mainstream school, but there are also special schools for the children whose autism
25 is more severe. Keeping to a routine is really important. If there's something which adhers from the normal school day, for example when a photographer visits, an autistic child who has not been well prepared could become
30 very upset and agitated. An important part of autistic children's development is to learn to interact with others. We also use SULP, and we make use of role plays whenever possible. For example, we might get a small group together including one autistic child and some of his or her classmates, and get them to act out a social situation. We also make use of drama, and find that the children
35 respond very well to that. Autistic children also often have other communication issues which benefit from treatment, such as unclear speech."

Comprehension

Task 2

Are the following statements true or false?

a. Autistic children like it when there is a change to their normal day.
b. Most autistic children in the UK go to special schools.
c. There are often other language problems which co-exist with autism.
d. Children with autism find it really easy to make friends with other children.

Task 3

With a partner, find words from the two texts which can replace the words in italics in these sentences.

1. She needs to be trained to *react* well in these situations.
2. It's very important to have some *understanding* of what autism is.
3. He hopes that taking this job will *be good for* his career.
4. The little girl became very *troubled* when her parents left her for the first time.

Task 4

Find all the words in the text which express the following:

a. The possibility of something happening.
b. The probability of something happening.

Grammar

Modal auxiliary verbs to express *possibility* and *probability*

	Form	Example	Meaning
P r e s e n t	must + infinitive	*The children **must be** very tired.*	I really think this.
	might / might not + infinitive	*They **might need** some quiet time.*	Possibly true.
	may / may not + infinitive	*They **may not understand** what we expect of them.*	Possibly true.
	could + infinitive	*They **could be** confused because it's different today.*	Possibly true.
	can't + infinitive	*They **can't be** hungry, they just ate.*	I really don't think this is true.
Please note – the opposite of **must** here is **can't**.			
P a s t	must have + past participle	*He **must have had** a good reason to miss the meeting.*	I really think this.
	might/might not have + past participle	*He **might not have seen** the email.*	Possibly true.
	could have + past participle	*He **could have been called** to an emergency.*	Possibly true.
	may/may not have + past participle	*He **may have sent** a message which we didn't get.*	Possibly true.
	can't have + past participle	*He **can't have** just **forgotten** about it.*	I really don't think this is true.
	couldn't have + past participle	*He **couldn't have known** that we changed the room.*	I really don't think this is true.
Please note – the opposite of **must have** here is **can't have**.			

Task 5

Put the verbs in brackets into the correct form, using a modal auxiliary verb.

a. The little girl (have) ADHD, she seems to have a couple of the symptoms.
b. He (be) very happy that he got the new job.
c. The nutritionist (say) that we haven't been trying to improve our diet.
d. His parents (not like) us giving him food with sugar in it.

Task 6

Write five sentences using the modal auxiliary verbs *must have, may have, might have, could have* or *can't have* to express possibility or probability in the past.

Writing

Task 7

Look back at the two articles in Module 1 – Council "put child, five, into care for being obese" and Jamie Oliver show loses US primetime TV slot. With a partner, choose one of them and summarise it, using the framework below.

When summarising a text, you need to choose only the most important information, and you also need to keep your summary brief.

1. Name of article, plus source and date.		4. Give a little background information.	*Why do you think that the story was written?*
2. What was the main theme or point of the article?	*This should be described in one or two short sentences.*	5. Choose two or three of the most important details.	*For example: key events / key statistics / key quotations.*
3. What type of article was it?	*For example: a news story / a biographical piece / a report on a scientific study / a report on a cultural development.*	6. Think of one question to give to your classmates to discuss this topic	*This should not be too long. Make sure to choose something where there might be two different opinions, not something which everyone agrees on.*

Activity

Task 8

Find a newspaper article relating to any of the three modules in Unit 8. Use the framework to summarise it, then present it to your class.

Unit 9:
Disability and illness

Module 1: What is disability?

Comprehension

Look at this word cloud. In pairs, put the words into three different groups.

hearing impairment   blind   sign language
muscle weakness   visual impairment
guide dog   limb disability   paralysis
lip reading   lack of manual dexterity
hearing aid   Braille   mobility impairment
partially sighted   speech therapist

Writing

Task 2

In groups of four, write a survey to find out about attitudes to disability.

1 Your survey should have five questions. Think about the information you want to get. An example question might be: How would you feel if one of your siblings was planning to marry somebody with a disability: very comfortable, quite comfortable, quite uncomfortable, very uncomfortable? Why?

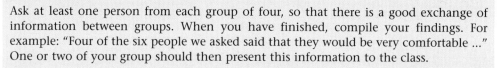

Activity

Task 3

Move around the class and conduct your survey on your classmates.

Ask at least one person from each group of four, so that there is a good exchange of information between groups. When you have finished, compile your findings. For example: "Four of the six people we asked said that they would be very comfortable ..." One or two of your group should then present this information to the class.

The social and medical models of disability

1 The diagram below shows the *medical model* of disability. This is the traditional way of viewing disability. It centres on the lack of functional ability – physical, sensory or mental. It sees a disabled child or adult as passively receiving different services which are aimed at treating or managing their impairment. Emphasis is put on the diagnosis and on the label,
5 so that the disability, and not anything else about the child or adult, becomes the focus of attention.

An alternative way of viewing disability led by a disability rights group, has developed since the 1970s. This different way of looking at disability is known as the *social model*.

The social model says that the problem is not the disability, but society's barriers. These
10 barriers stop people with impairments or disabilities from taking part in society in the same way as other people. In this model, the disabled child or adult is valued, and resources (for example money) are made available to services when those services are needed.

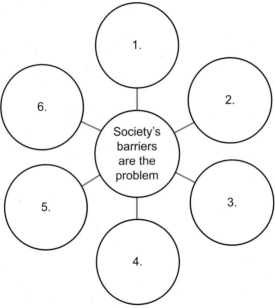

Comprehension

Task 4

Looking at the social model diagram, what do you think might be in circles 1–6?

Discussion / Writing

Task 5

In groups of three to four, write down your answers to the following questions.

a. What do you think are the advantages of using the social model of disability?
b. Can you think of five barriers that are faced by disabled children and their families?

Three case studies from the UK

A. Jonathan is a four-year-old boy with cerebral palsy. He goes to a nursery for children with special needs called Winnie the Pooh nursery. Here the children are seen by therapists (speech therapists, occupational therapists and physiotherapists) at least once a week. Activities and play are tailored to the needs of each child and their development. Opportunities are given to the children to explore and value the differences and similarities between themselves and others, and children are encouraged to express their needs by talking, pointing, eye contact, use of pictures and signing.

B. Maylin is a five-year-old girl who has a severe hearing impairment. She is in the reception class at Kingston Primary School. Children are left to play a lot of the time, and learning activities are designed to be fun, for example, maths sessions may be number rhymes. Maylin has a teaching assistant who works with her through signing, so that she can take part in the activities and play with her classmates.

C. Sinead is a three-year-old girl with Down's syndrome. She attends Little Acorn Nursery in her home town of Hull. Little Acorn is an inclusive nursery. The children spend their time playing, but they are also taught pre-reading and pre-number skills as they play. The children listen to stories and are encouraged to paint and draw. With Sinead, tasks are broken down to basics to help her learn the same skills as her peers.

Comprehension

Task 6

Answer the following questions.

a. Which of the children is educated alongside children without disabilities?
b. Which of the children has its own specific worker to help him/her?
c. Which of the children is taught basic numeracy?

Task 7

With a partner, answer the following question.

What do you understand by the phrase: "Opportunities are given to the children to explore and value the differences and similarities between themselves and others"?

Grammar

The Passive Voice

Use
We use verbs in the active voice to say what the subject of the sentence does.
e.g. *The children **go** to the local kindergarten.*

We use verbs in the Passive Voice to say what happens to the subject of the sentence.
e.g. *The children **are looked after** at the kindergarten.*

In the Passive, the person or thing who / which performs the action is often not known, or not of primary importance. If we want to say who or what performs an action, we use *by*.
e.g. *The children **are looked after** by the staff at the kindergarten.*

Form

The Passive is formed by the verb *be* and the Past Participle (the third part of the verb).
Be changes its tense, the Past Participle stays the same no matter which tense is used.

e.g. *The nursery **is cleaned** every day.*	Present Simple of *be* + Past Participle
e.g. *The nursery **is** currently **being cleaned**.*	Present Progressive of *be* + Past Participle
e.g. *The children **were taught** yesterday.*	Past Simple of *be* + Past Participle
e.g. *The boy **has been seen** by a doctor.*	Present Perfect of *be* + Past Participle

Task 8

Look back at the three case studies of Task 5. Make a list of all the verbs which are in the Passive Voice, and all the verbs which are in the Active Voice.

Working in an inclusive Berlin kindergarten

Ritvan Celik works in an inclusive nursery in Berlin. He talks about the daily routine and the work he does there.

Our day begins at 8.30, when the first children arrive. A little after 9 we give the children breakfast. There are three groups of children and I work with the oldest group, the Little Einsteins. After breakfast the children clean their teeth and then we take them through to the play room for the Morning Circle, where they sing songs and play speaking and count-ing games, for example practising the days of the week. We encourage each child to take part but we don't force any of them, and if they make mistakes we use positive modelling rather than correction. Between 10 and 12 we lead the children through activities which are different every day, for example one day they might do sport and another day music. Alternatively, we help them to work on a special individual or group project. Our work fits in to a city-wide curriculum, and each activity has clear aims and objectives which we explain to the children.

At 12 we have lunch, and then after lunch the group has a quiet time while the younger children take a nap. We also have Book Hour, when the children look at books, or one of us reads a story to them. Later in the afternoon they have free play.

We're constantly observing each child's progress and evaluating that progress against previ-ously agreed objectives. All the children get their own individual Sprachlerntagebuch which is full of things such as interviews and photos. They also get different projects to work on and record in their books, projects which are always guided by their own interests, curiosity and skills. The children who come to the kindergarten are from different ethnic backgrounds, and there are also disabled children. Of course, we treat the disabled children in exactly the same way as the other children. Each child is an individual with skills and strengths and we take these into account (rather than focussing on something which perhaps they can't do) when planning the children's objectives.

Re-write the sentences from the text in the Passive Voice.

a. We give the children breakfast.
b. We encourage each child to take part, but we don't force any of them.
c. We use positive modelling rather than correction.
d. One of us reads a story to the children.
e. We're constantly observing each child's progress, and evaluating that progress against previously agreed objectives.
f. In planning the children's objectives we've taken these strengths into account.

Discussion / Writing

Task 10

Why have inclusive kindergartens? In groups of three or four, discuss the advantages and disadvantages, and then write four sentences giving your group's opinion either for, or against, inclusive kindergartens.

Module 2: Children in hospital

If your child has to go to hospital

1 Hospitals can be strange, frightening places for children. Being ill or in pain can also make them upset. You might feel helpless, but there are things you can do to comfort your child.

Prepare your child as much as you can

5 Play doctors and nurses or operations using teddies and dolls, and read stories about being in hospital. It's good to do this even if your child isn't due to go to hospital. Many children have to go into hospital at some stage, and many are an emergency case. Explain as much as possible to your child. Even young children need to know what's happening to them. It's important to be truthful. What children imagine is often worse
10 than reality. Don't say that something won't hurt when it will.

Some hospitals arrange visits for children and their families before a child is admitted for a planned treatment or operation. It's also important to let your child know when they'll be able to see you and whether you'll be staying with them. Explain to your child
15 what being in hospital will be like. Tell them they'll be sharing a ward with other children of their own age and that it'll be different from their own bedroom at home.

Stay with them

20 It will help your child if you visit them in hospital as much as possible and, with young children especially, sleep there. Do all you

can to arrange this. All children's wards in hospital now offer the possibility for parents
to stay overnight with their children. Talk to hospital staff beforehand. Be clear about
25 the arrangements and what will happen.

Talk to the hospital staff
Talk to one of the nurses or doctors who will be treating your child about anything you
think is important. Inform staff of any special words your child uses (such as for needing
to go to the toilet) and any particular ways you have of comforting them.

30 Take their comforter
Let your child take a favourite teddy or comforter with them into hospital. Be prepared
for your child to be upset by the experience. They may continue to be upset for some
time afterwards. Give them as much reassurance as you can. [...]

*From: If your child has to go to hospital, in: NHS choice, July 29, 2011, http://www.nhs.uk/Planners/
birthtofive/Pages/Ifchildgoestohospital.aspx, accessed March 22, 2012.*

Comprehension

 Task 1

Answer the following questions.

a. Give two reasons, from the text, for how parents can use objects to help to make
   hospital less frightening and upsetting for their children.
b. Give two ways that the text says parents can use language to help make hospital less
   frightening and upsetting for their children.

 Task 2

**Write an English sentence using the phrase *in pain*, and
another using the verb *to hurt*. Compare your sentence
with the person next to you.**

Language

 Task 3

**Many illnesses have the same or very similar names in English and German, for
example mumps, asthma, meningitis or conjunctivitis. Others have different names.**

**The box contains the names of four common childhood illnesses, and below it are
descriptions of the illnesses. In pairs, match the illness to the symptoms described.**

flu – measles – whooping cough – chicken pox

a. A fever may be present, followed by a rash which appears on the body and head and
   spreads to the arms and legs. The rash starts as red spots which become itchy blisters.
b. Children may have a low fever and a mild cough at the start, but this develops into
   fast violent coughing fits. Children cough again and again until their lungs are void
   of air, which gives the cough a characteristic sound. This can last for several weeks.

c. Symptoms include fever, sneezing, an aching body, coughing, a runny nose, a sore throat, a headache and exhaustion. Vomiting and diarrhoea can also occur.

d. This can start with fever, a runny nose and a cough. A red blotchy rash begins on the face between the third and seventh day of illness, and spreads to the rest of the body.

Task 4

With a partner, discuss the phrases *life-limiting illness* and *life-threatening illness*. What do you think the difference in meaning could be?

Listening

Sometimes children aren't going to get better

1 Joanna Giles works as a nursery nurse in a children's hospice in Chester. This is an interview about her work.

Could you tell us about the hospice and the
5 **people who work there?**
The hospice provides support and treatment for local children who have life limiting and life-threatening conditions. This can be in the hospice, but what a lot of people don't realise is that we also do a lot of our work in the children's homes. The team here is made up of doctors, nurses and therapists, as well as family support workers, bereave-
10 ment counsellors, psychologists and social workers plus me and two other nursery nurses. A lot of our support is for the families of the ill children, for example we have sessions for sibling support.

Tell us something about the children you work with.
People have the idea that most of the children we work with have cancer, but the reality
15 is different. Of course we work with children with illnesses such as cancer, there are some conditions which are life-threatening and which can be treated, although the treatment may not work. However, we also work with many children who have illnesses in which early death is inevitable, but where treatment can help to prolong life. An example would be cystic fibrosis. As well as this, we work with children who have pro-
20 gressive conditions with no curative treatment options. These are illnesses such as muscular dystrophy, where treatment is palliative and may go on for many years.

Could you tell us a little bit about your daily routine?
It's important that the children the hospice cares for achieve as much as possible. Many of the children have special needs such as hearing or sight impairment, and others have
25 limited mobility and / or learning disabilities. We have special equipment to meet the children's needs, and of course we provide the toys, books and crafts that you find in all nurseries. We try to vary the activities and we have as many outings as possible, sometimes we go to the park or to the zoo. You'd be wrong to think that a children's hospice is always a sad place. At times it is of course, but this is a great place to work
30 with a strong ethos of friendliness and support.

What qualities does a good hospice worker need?
You need good communication and listening skills. Of course qualifications and training are important, but being the right kind of person is even more so. You need to be a car ing person who has insight into, and empathy, for what the families are going through.
35 Teamwork and flexibility are both really important too.

Comprehension

Task 5

Listen to the interview twice, and then answer these questions.

a. Where do the hospice workers do their work?
b. Name three of the jobs from among those in the team who work at the hospice.
c. What is a common misconception that people have about children in a hospice?
d. What kinds of special needs do the children in the hospice often have?
e. Name three of the qualities which Joanna says that a hospice worker needs.

Language

Task 6

Make sentences to explain these words connected with hospitals. Use one word or phrase from each of the three boxes. The first one has been done as an example.

nurse – ambulance – patient – X-ray – physiotherapist

person	takes sick people to hospital
machine	is sick or ill
person	cares for sick people
vehicle	treats people with mobility problems
person	takes a picture of the body showing the skeleton

e.g. A *nurse* is a *person* who *cares for sick people.*

Grammar

Identifying relative clauses

A Relative Clause is a part of a sentence. An Identifying Relative Clause identifies a noun or a noun phrase. In other words it tells us *which* or *which type of* person or thing is meant.

e.g.   A man works next door. He is an occupational therapist.
      Which man is an occupational therapist?
      *The man **who works next door** is an occupational therapist.*

Pronouns

For *people*, we use the pronouns *who* or *that*:

e.g.   People work with young children. These people often love their jobs.

   People w**ho work with young children** often love their jobs.

For *things*, we use the pronouns *which* or *that*:

e.g.   The nursery uses activities. These activities help children to learn their numbers.

   *The nursery uses activities **that help children to learn their numbers.***

Note: we can't ever use *what*.

e.g.   *The **problems what he is facing. (incorrect).***

   ***The** problems **that / which** he is facing.* (correct)

Identifying the object of who, that or which

Often the noun we want to identify is the object of *who, which* or *that*:

e.g.   *The book **that Alan read** was very popular with the children.*

   Alan = subject   the book = object

In these cases, if we want to we can leave out *who, which* or *that* from the sentence.

e.g.   *The book **Alan read** was very popular with the children.*

Prepositions in Relative Clauses

If the relative clause includes a preposition, this will normally be at the end of the clause.

e.g.   Those are the children. I work with them.

   *Those are the children **(who) I work with**.*

e.g.   You have applied *for* a job. The job is in Birmingham.

   *Is the job **(which) you have applied for** in Birmingham?*

Only in very formal written English (not spoken English), can the preposition go at the beginning of the clause. In this case, *who, which* or *that* can't be left out.

e.g.   *The **job for which I am applying** is the one working with disabled children.*

Task 7

Write out these sentences again, leaving out *who*, *that* or *which* when it is possible.

a. The boy who missed this morning's session has special needs.
b. I'm working with a little girl who wants to be a doctor.
c. It was the worst job interview that I've ever had.
d. The key which opens this door is the one which is missing.
e. All the people who I met at the clinic were very friendly.

Relative clauses which give us extra information

The second type of relative clause gives us extra information about something. We already know which thing it is. We need to use commas to separate this clause from the sentence.

e.g. *My school, **which is one of the best in the county**, is in Wakefield.*
e.g. *You can stay at the local hotel, **which is very comfortable**.*

Pronouns

For *people*, we use the pronoun *who*. We sometimes use *that*.
e.g. *The manager, **who is from Sweden**, is very supportive.*
For *things*, we use the pronoun *which*. We can't use *that*.
e.g. *Marian told me about the training course, **which she enjoyed very much**.*
We cannot leave out *who* or *which* in any of these sentences.

Prepositions

As with identifying relative clauses, these usually go at the end of the clause.
e.g. *She showed me the garden, **which had plenty of room for children to play in**.*

Compare the two types of Relative Clause.	
*The man **who lives upstairs** is a teacher.*	*John, **who lives in London**, is a teacher.*
This tells us which man is being talked about.	Even without the clause, we know who we are talking about – John.
• We don't use commas. • We can use **who / that** or **which / that**. • We can leave out **who / that / which** when it's with the object.	• We use commas to separate the clause. • We can only use **who** or **which**. • We can't leave out **who** or **which**.

Task 8

Read the information below and complete the sentences, using a relative clause. Decide which type of clause you need to use. The first one has been done already.

Example: There is a woman living upstairs. She's French.
       The woman who lives upstairs is French.
a. Olu was looking for some paints yesterday. She has found them now.
       Olu has found ...
b. Jane has a sister. She showed me a photograph of her. She is a lawyer.
       Jane showed me ...
c. Martin applied for several jobs last month. He's been offered one of them.
       Martin has been offered ...
d. There was an electrical problem. It crashed all the computers. It's now been fixed.
       The electrical problem ...
e. Daisy is one of my closest friends. I've known her for ten years.
       Daisy ...

Module 3: Learning disabilities

When the disabled were segregated

1 Today the emphasis in Britain and America is on inclusion and independent living for disabled people. Most (though sadly not all) disabled people who want to do so are able to live in their own
5 homes. But this wasn't always the case. For much of the twentieth century, it was common in the UK and the USA to segregate disabled people from the rest of society.

Large numbers of British and American disabled
10 people were put away in institutions on the grounds that it was for their own good and the good of society. For example, in 1913, the passing of the Mental Incapacity Act in Britain led to around 40,000 men and women being locked away, having been deemed "feeble-minded" or "morally defective." Many disabled people living in hospitals, special schools and care homes are known to have suffered severe emotional and physical
15 abuse. [...]

In the late 1960s, a report by Margaret Oswin on a British hospital which provided long-term residential care for children with "severe chronic handicaps" was highly critical of the service the children received. Her research discovered an impersonal regime where the children's possessions were numbered and staff did not play or talk effectively with
20 the children. Not only did the institution have sub-standard toilets but children in the upstairs wards had no access to the grounds.

A woman who lived in a British "mental deficiency institution" for 16 years from 1952 was interviewed by D. Atkinson, M. Jackson and J. Walmsley for their book *Forgotten Lives*. She remembered, "The worst thing was I couldn't wear my own clothes. You had
25 to wear other people's." The beds were so close together there was no space for each resident to have his/her own locker. They had to help themselves to clothes from one big cupboard in the ward. [...]

Institutions sometimes had humiliating admissions rituals. One care home for people with learning disabilities used to forcibly cut girls' hair when they arrived. A girl recalled
30 with sadness: "I had lovely hair right down my back and they cut it." If residents put up resistance, they were tied in a chair while the cutting took place and then locked in a dark room for up to half an hour before receiving an injection. [...]

Institutionalisation is not a phenomenon of the dim and distant past either. The move towards widespread independent living in the community is a relatively recent develop-
35 ment. Although criticisms of residential care grew in the years after 1945, there was ironically an expansion of segregation of disabled people after World War II. [...]

During the 20th century, disabled people forced to live in institutions in Britain and America were often mistreated and denied the opportunity to make basic choices about how they lived their lives. Staff accounts, official reports, academic research and the
40 testimonies of disabled people themselves all provide plentiful evidence of inhumane practices and violations of fundamental human rights. [...]

Extract from: Victoria Brignell: When the disabled were segregated, December 15, 2010, in: The New Statesman, www.newstatesman.com/society/2010/12/disabled-children-british, accessed April 12, 2012.

Comprehension

Task 1

Answer the following questions using the text.

a. Find three terms which were used in the past for those with learning disabilities.
b. Find three examples of abuse suffered by disabled people in institutions.
c. Find a word which is a homonym (a word which has two different meanings).

Case study – How things are today

1 Fidelia Charles has a four-year-old son, Javel, who is learning disabled. She talks about how she manages.

"Javel was diagnosed with global developmental delay six months ago. I live in Walton in Liverpool
5 and my family are mainly all back home in Africa. I go to the local children's centre with Javel and we get a lot of support there. The centre is co-run by Scope, which is one of the leading UK disability charities, so they have really good facilities for fami-
10 lies with disabled children.

Javel goes to the inclusive nursery there, and every week I go to their session called "Me Time" which
is a support group for parents and carers of disabled children. Through the centre, I've also been able to organise a short break, whereby Javel was cared for while I got a chance
15 to get away for a few days. It made such a difference to me and Javel to get the opportunity to recharge my batteries."

Activity

Task 2

In groups of three to four, discuss the following questions.

- Do you think that the words we use to name
  learning disabilities make a difference?
- Do you think it makes sense to use such a broad term as learning disabled, which covers everything from dyslexia to profound and multiple learning disabilities?
- What do you think the word *labelling* means and what do you think that *labelling* theory is?

Writing

Task 3

Write three sentences to describe the ways in which the lives of learning disabled children were different 50 years ago.

e.g. Children didn't usually live in their family homes, but in institutions.

Grammar

Reporting with Passive Verbs

When we want to report something we can use one of two special structures with a verb in the passive. These are often used in news reports.

e.g. ***It is reported that*** *many nurseries in the UK are losing funding due to government cuts.*
Or: *Many nurseries in the UK **are reported to be** losing funding due to government cuts.*

Other verbs often used with this structure are: *said, thought, believed, considered, known, expected, alleged, understood.*

e.g. *It is **expected** that the nursery will close soon.*
Or: *The nursery is **expected** to close soon.*

Task 4

Rewrite these sentences using the alternative passive reporting structure.

a. It is thought that many childcare workers are now unemployed.
b. A crowd of people is reported to be outside the court building already.
c. A young man is alleged to have stolen the car from outside the shop.
d. It is considered to be one of the best schools in the city.
e. The social worker is known to have a very high caseload of children.

Activity

Task 5

Role-play the following situation with a partner.

Student A: You work in an inclusive kindergarten, where disabled and non-disabled children are educated together. You want to convince Student B that this is a good thing.

Student B: You are the mother or father of a little boy with Down's syndrome. You want to find out about the nursery, you're not sure if an inclusive nursery is best for him.

Comprehension

Task 6

Mencap is a leading UK charity which campaigns for and with people with learning disabilities. The following extract is adapted from Mencap's website, from the page which describes important dates in their history.

The dates have been removed and the important events have been jumbled up. In pairs, decide which date from the box at the top fits in which gap near the beginning of each sentence.

1946 – 1955 – 1958 – 1969 – 1995 – 2006 – 2009

- In ...(1)... the Disability Discrimination Act was passed. It aimed to end the discrimination faced by many disabled people and to guarantee their civil rights. [...]
- In ...(2)... the National Society launched a ground-breaking project called the Brooklands Experiment. This compared the progress of children with a learning disability who lived in hospital with a group of children who were moved to a small family environment and cared for using educational activities modelled on those in "ordinary" nurseries. After two years, the children in the home-like environment showed marked improvements in social, emotional and verbal skills. The success of the experiment was published around the world. [...]
- In ...(3)... the UK finally ratified the United Nations Convention on the Rights of Persons with Disabilities. It reaffirmed that disabled people have the same human rights as non-disabled people. [...]
- In ...(4)... Judy Fryd, a mother of a child with a learning disability, formed "The National Association of Parents of Backward Children" – which later became "Mencap." She wrote to Nursery World magazine inviting other parents to contact her. Many wrote back to Judy expressing their anger and sorrow at the lack of services for their children. [...]
- In ...(5)... the society shortened its name to "Mencap." [...]
- In ...(6)... Mencap celebrated 60 years as the leading UK charity for people with a learning disability. [...]
- In ...(7)... the association changed its name to "The National Society for Mentally Handicapped Children" and opened its first project, the Orchard Dene short-stay residential home. [...]

Extract from: Timeline, in: Mencap, www.mencap.org.uk/about-us/our-history/timeline, accessed April 12, 2012.

Unit 10:
Ethnic diversity

Module 1: The changing face of society

Integration and multi-culturalism in Germany

1 Before the advent of air travel and mass communication, it was the norm to live in ethnically homogeneous communities. The inhabitants of a village or a city all shared the same traditions and customs, and they spoke the same language. Everyone lived their lives according to the same rules. The presence of outsiders was rare, and the native
5 inhabitants thought nothing of tolerating those who were different, as they were foreigners.

Today we live in societies which embrace people of different social, cultural and ethnic backgrounds. Most metropolitan areas in Europe have large populations of ethnic minorities from Asia, Africa and the Middle East, as well as many people from other
10 European nations.

The question of integration is still being hotly debated in Germany. Are Germany's diverse ethnic communities properly integrated in German society? Are these communities assimulating into the dominant culture, or are these people living in "parallel societies"? Can a society such as Germany's be regarded as multi-cultural – one in which
15 people feel united rather than divided by their differences? In this unit we will explore ethnic diversity and what it means to belong to a minority group.

Discussion

Task 1

Reflect and write a short comment on the following questions. Discuss your answers with a partner or in a small group.

a. Brainstorm the terms "ethnic diversity" and "integration".
b. Why, in your opinion, has the face of society changed over time?
c. How do you think the face of society will continue to change?
d. What are the advantages/disadvantages of these changes?

Listening

Task 2

Where do you think these people in the pictures come from? Give reasons for your answers. Now, listen to the four people pictured and describe their lives in their home or host countries. Match the descriptions you hear to the pictures. The transcription of the audio can be found on page 208.

Task 3

Answer the following questions on the text above.

a. Why might Can not be considered German despite his German citizenship? Why might Can not be accepted as Turkish when he is in Turkey?
b. Selma is relieved that no one seems to object to her wearing a headscarf. Why do you think she anticipated this as being a problem in the United States?
c. Why might Germans think Amelia is German? What does this tell us about how people perceive and define foreignness?
d. What aspects of living in Germany made Katherine feel alienated?

Discussion

Task 4

Reflect on the following questions with a partner. Then discuss your ideas with the rest of the class.

a. Katherine complains that she felt like an outsider while she was living in Germany. What steps could she have taken to feel more comfortable in her host culture?
b. Some ethnic minorities are reluctant to integrate themselves into German society. Do you think these communities are reluctant to assimilate by choice, or is it because there's a resistance on the part of Germans to accept them?

Grammar

Adverbs of frequency

Adverbs of frequency tell us how often an action is performed or an event occurs.

Some of the most common frequency adverbs are: *always, never, usually, often, sometimes, occasionally, rarely* and *seldom*. Phrases like *every month* or *once a day* are also frequency adverbs.

*Selma **always** wears her headscarf in public, but I have **often** seen her without it when I have visited her at home, as she **usually** takes it off there.*

Note the position of the adverbs in the example. We prefer to place frequency adverbs between **the subject** and the **main verb**:

Selma *always* **wears** *her headscarf in public.*

Or between the **auxiliary verb** and **main verb**:

I **have** *often* **seen** *her without it.*

Some frequency adverbs can also be placed at the beginning of a sentence, before the subject:

Sometimes / Occasionally *I visit Selma at home.*

This is a matter of preference, depending what the speaker wants to emphasise in the sentence. Note though, that ***always*** and ***never*** are never used at the beginning of sentences.

Task 5

Using the adverbs of frequency listed above, describe the frequency with which you do the following activities, giving a reason why.

I often watch foreign films because I am interested in how people from different cultures view the world.

How frequently do you:

a. get the chance to speak a foreign language?
b. visit other countries?
c. go to a Chinese or Indian restaurant?
d. attend a multicultural festival?
e. donate money to a charitable cause?
f. make friends with someone from a different country?

The changing face of the UK

1 Britain is a multi-cultural country. On the streets of every town in Britain you will encounter all kinds of people from a wide variety of different cultures. The great majority of these people are
5 British but they all look and dress differently because Britain is a multi-racial society. Britain has this in common with that other great melting pot culture, the United States. One of the interesting features of British society is that while Britons
10 share a common national identity, their manners, attitudes and style of speech are often influenced by aspects of their ethnic background. A Sikh will speak with a London accent and support his local football team, but will continue to wear a turban and listen to the traditional music of his community.

Cultural crossover is a common phenomenon in Britain and as can be seen by the devel-
15 opment of such musical genres as Bangra, which is a blend of Punjabi folk music and Western pop. The group *Cornershop* had a hit with their song "Brimful of Asha" which fused Western rhythms and Indian melodies with electronic dance beats. The song is about an Indian singer and mixes Punjabi and English lyrics. Its commercial success and appeal to music lovers of all ethnic groups can be seen as a metaphor for the way in
20 which British society has succeeded in embracing diversity and creating a unified, inclusive and constantly evolving identity from this multiethnic mix. Whether your background is Anglo-Saxon or Punjabi, it is just as British nowadays to enjoy a Mutton Vindaloo as it is to tuck into a plate of fish and chips. Indian customs and cuisine have become very much a part of the British way of life.

25 Britain has always been a multi-ethnic society. The Romans, Normans, Vikings and Saxons invaded the island and settled it earlier in its history. The Irish began immigrating in large numbers to Britain from the mid-nineteenth century on. During the 1950s and 1960s people from former British colonies and other places came to Britain seeking a better life.

30 However, despite all of this, it would be wrong to assume that Britain is – or ever was – a paradise of racial harmony. Casual racism was very prevalent up to the 1970s when even a people as similar to the British as the Irish were openly discriminated against in areas such as employment and housing. Even today, race riots occasionally break out. On the whole though, Britain has managed quite well to assimilate its diverse peoples into a
35 common sense of cultural identity. The road to a tolerant multi-cultural society has however proven to be a long, slow and sometimes painful one.

Activity

Task 6

With a partner, use Internet sources to research the current demographic compositions of Britain and Germany. Compare the demographic statistics and note some of the countries' differences. How do you account for these differences?

Writing

Task 7

In recent decades, Germany has become a multi-cultural society and home to many diverse ethnic communities. Do you think these communities have been integrated into mainstream German society, or do they exist separately alongside it? Write an essay of about 250 words, outlining your ideas and opinions. Use examples to help support and illustrate your arguments.

The changing face of Germany

1 **An interview with Dilek Yalniz, a 29-year-old woman who was born and raised in Berlin.**

Tell me a little bit about you and your background.

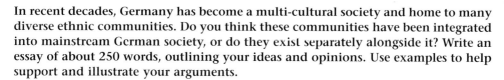

5 **Dilek:** I was born in Berlin and my parents come from Adana, Turkey. My mother came to Berlin when she was 14 because her parents were immigrant workers in Berlin. They sent for her when they decided to stay in Berlin.

10 **What was your childhood like, particularly the time you spent in preschool?**

Dilek: I started preschool when I was three years old. I remember liking all of my teachers. The children were all from mixed backgrounds, Turkish, Arab etc. but all of the teachers were German and only spoke German. At home, 15 we only spoke Turkish. It was a good combination. In preschool we celebrated German holidays – Christmas, Easter, and I wanted to do the same at home. I remember correcting my mother's German when she didn't pronounce something correctly. We kids had more contact with Germans and the German language, and so it was natural for us to correct her.

20 **Did you have any bad experiences in preschool?**

Dilek: I remember only one negative experience during my preschool years. My preschool had to close for some reason and we had to go to another one for two months. It was lunch time and we were going to eat a vegetable casserole. I asked one of the adults whether there was pork in it and she said "no", and so I ate the lunch. Afterwards 25 I asked again if there had been pork in it. She said there had been and asked me whether it had been that bad. I thought it was cruel of her to trick me like this.

Do you think there is such a thing as a typical Berlin family?

Dilek: I don't think so. Maybe mine is a typical Turkish family in Berlin. It's typical for a Turkish 30 child in Germany to grow up between two cultures. It isn't easy. I was only influenced by my families values and customs up to a certain age. Then I was introduced to German culture through my experience of attending kindergarten and later 35 school. I have tried to take the most positive things

from both cultures and feel I manage with this mixture very well. I don't think of my family as a typical Berlin family, but as typical of a family that lives in two different cultures, with its children developing in both.

How do other people react to you?

40 **Dilek:** People generally regard me as German. I feel most comfortable in Berlin as I was born and raised here. My family is here. For me, Turkey is a place to visit for a holiday. I do have a special connection to Turkey, though. I can identify with Turkey but I don't want to live there. I feel secure and safe here in Berlin, whereas in Turkey, I feel emotions on a level which I don't experience in Germany.

Comprehension

 Task 8

Answer the following questions.

a. Where does Dilek come from?
b. What might have motivated the woman Dilek mentions to trick her into eating pork?
c. What does Dilek feel is typical of her family?
d. Why does Dilek regard her exposure to two cultures as a positive experience?
e. Explain the differences in the way Dilek relates to Germany and Turkey respectively.

Discussion

 Task 9

a. Together with a partner make a list of what you consider to be the similarities and differences between German and Turkish cultures.
b. Dilek talks about taking the best from each culture and developing a complex sense of identity through blending the values, customs and outlooks of both. Think of some clear examples in which the experience of being raised in two cultures can be both enriching and problematic. Share your ideas in an open discussion with the rest of the group.

Module 2: Growing up bilingual

What is bilingualism?

1 In countries such as Germany and Britain, where it is common for just one language to be used in the home, parents and educational professionals often feel it is better for children to learn just one language when they are growing up. But experts disagree over the issue of whether it is confusing or enriching for young children to be exposed to
5 more than one language. Some linguists feel that learning more than one language delays language development, but many believe that children have no difficulty acquiring any number of languages from a very young age.

In societies such as Singapore, bilingualism is the norm and multi-lingualism is not uncommon. Speaking more than one language is a necessary competence as Singaporean society is made up of people from a wide variety of ethnic communities, all of whom speak different native languages. There, multilingualism is a required social skill that enables people to communicate with one another across different cultures, thus helping to preserve social harmony. Parents in such a culture expect their children to pick up the languages they need, and aren't concerned about issues of delayed development.

It is sometimes the case that a child's first language is the second or third language of his parents. Children always adopt the dominant language of the society they live in as their native tongue, regardless of the languages their parents speak to them at home. Amir lives in Berlin with a French father and an Iranian mother. French is the language used at home when the family sits down to eat or goes on a Sunday outing, but mother and son speak exclusively Farsi to one another when alone together. Amir, however, speaks German as his native language. Although he speaks the languages of both his parents very proficiently, German is the language through which he perceives and construes the world. This is because German is clearly the dominant language in his environment and therefore, the one Amir uses most.

Even if a child grows up in a home in which two languages are spoken, this does not mean that the child will learn to speak both languages with equal fluency. Jennifer lives in Cologne with her German mother and American father. Her mum speaks only German to her, while her dad makes a point of talking to her in English. Jennifer, however, usually responds to her father's questions in German and tends to use English only when she wants something from him, like pocket money or an ice cream. When she speaks English, she makes all the characteristic errors of German native speakers. She uses "false friends", German sentence constructions, German tense usage and direct translations of German expressions. Instead of saying, for example, "what time is it", she will say "how late is it", "gloves" are "handshoes", and verbs are sometimes placed at the end rather than at the beginning of sentences. This is because Jennifer is working from within the structures of her first language to acquire her knowledge of the second.

Comprehension

Task 1

Find words and expressions in the text that match the definitions below.

a. people who study how languages work and are used
b. the ability to speak two languages to a high degree of fluency

c. the capacity to speak a number of languages to a high degree of fluency

d. your mother tongue, the language in which you feel most at home

e. typical mistakes

f. the language spoken in Iran

g. an adjective which describes your ability to do something extremely well, such as playing the piano or speaking a language

h. a small sum of cash that children receive from their parents every week or month

i. a word that seems similar to another word in a different language, but which has a different meaning, e.g. the German word "brav" and the English word "brave"

Task 2

Answer the following questions on the text in your own words.

a. What issue do linguists disagree over concerning the language learning of children?

b. Why is the ability to speak more than one language the norm in Singapore?

c. What is one of the benefits of multilingualism to a multiethnic society?

d. Why does Jennifer speak English like a German learner, even though her father is a native speaker of English and talks to her in his own language every day?

Discussion

Task 3

With a partner discuss whether children should learn more than one language from a young age. Do you think foreign parents should speak the dominant language of the community rather than their own native language to their children? Discuss your views and ideas with a partner, then share your conclusions with the rest of the group.

Grammar

The Past Perfect Simple

The Past Perfect is formed using *had* + the Past Participle of the verb:

I / you / he / she / it / you / we / they *had spoken.*

The Past Perfect is used to refer to completed actions which occurred before another event in the past:

Simple Past:	When I arrived at the room, the meeting *began.*
	(I arrived at the room, and then the meeting began. I was on time.)
Past Perfect:	When I arrived at the room, the meeting *had* already *started.*
	(The meeting began before I arrived at the room. I was late.)

Task 4

Complete the following sentences using *because* + Past Perfect and *so* + Simple Past.

When I left the school, there was no one there ... (lock up) / (everybody / leave).
- *... so I locked up.* (subsequent event, Simple Past)
- *... because everyone had left.* (previous event, Past Perfect)

a. The playroom was in a mess (I / clean up / it) / (the children / it / not tidy up).
b. James couldn't speak French (he / decide to learn / it) / (he / not have / it / at school).
c. Jack was in a great mood (he / got the job) / (he / celebrate / with his friends).
d. I performed a play with the children (I / write one) / (they all / dress up).
e. Henry could speak Spanish (live / in Spain) / (teach it / at the preschool).

Case study

1 Paul is five years old. His father is English and his mother German. They moved to Berkshire, England, three months ago and Paul has been attending the local preschool since they arrived. He's a clever child who's doing his best to integrate and to get along with the other children. Paul can communicate in English but seems to prefer speaking
5 in German. Paul's carer thinks that these problems have to do with his language skills and has referred him for testing.

Background information was gathered from Paul's carer and parents. His carer says that Paul does not always follow instructions, is often reluctant to participate in activities, and usually takes more time to complete tasks than the other children. He enjoys inter-
10 acting with the other children, but often switches from English to German when playing.

Following language testing, Paul's language abilities were assessed as being equal to those of native English speaking children of his age in the area of concept words. Concept words are terms that relate to language areas such as texture, social awareness, time
15 and sequence (the order in which events occur). Paul's level of competence in these categories can be explained by the fact that this is the kind of language taught at school, but not usually reinforced at home by parents.

Comprehension

Task 5

Match the words and expressions below with their equivalents in the text.

a. to be sent for medical treatment or testing by a doctor or psychologist
b. to be unwilling to do something
c. to take part
d. to play, talk, communicate with other people

e. to exchange, swap or move from one thing to another
f. terms that relate to abstract rather than concrete ideas
g. the way something, like a piece of fabric, feels
h. to make stronger, or to teach something repeatedly until it is fully understood

Discussion

Task 6

Imagine you and your partner are preschool teachers. Discuss the case of Paul and think of things you could do to help him communicate more effectively.

Should you talk to his parents and find out more about his family background and home life? What else could be done? Write down your ideas.

Writing

Task 7

Write a short progress report on the ideas you developed in Task 6. In your report explain the language, communication and social issues facing Paul, and include some recommendations about what you think should be done to address these issues.

Module 3: Racism and stereotyping

1 **Ethnic stereotypes – why do they matter?**
Sabine Beyer runs training courses on equality and diversity awareness for
5 social workers and early years' practitioners in Mannheim. Here, she talks about the damage that can be done by stereotyping people due to their ethnicity.

10 **What is an ethnic stereotype?**
Sabine: It's a generalised representation of an ethnic group, based on what are *perceived* to be typical characteristics of members of the group. These generalisations are often not based on facts, but on myths or *skewed* perceptions. An example might be the
15 stereotype that white people don't have rhythm and can't dance very well.

Are there other types of stereotypes as well as those to do with ethnicity?

Sabine: Stereotypes exist in all cultures and in all aspects of life. For example we see a man or a woman wearing a smart suit and make *assumptions* about him or her. It can be argued that stereotypes are useful – even necessary – tools to help us sort the constant
20 flow of new data in our day-to-day lives. However, once race or ethnicity is involved, stereotypes have the potential to do great harm.

Are they ever harmless?

Sabine: There is an argument that when stereotypes are applied by one group to another group with more or less equal status in the world (for example between the British and
25 the French) they are harmless. However, even in these situations stereotypes are based on ignorance and they mean that we ignore differences between individuals and assume things which are often not true. Because stereotypes – in common with any forms of *prejudice* – are fixed beliefs, someone who believes in them is less open to recognising the truth when it presents itself.

30 **When do stereotypes become racist?**

Sabine: Stereotypes become most dangerous when they are applied by a majority group in a society towards a minority group within that same society. This is especially true if the positions of power are held by people from the majority group. Then, stereotypes become *interwoven* with, and often *indistinguishable* from, racism. An example might be
35 a white British person believing that a young black man is probably involved with crime or drugs. Another example could be a white German person thinking that a young German man of Turkish origin probably can't speak good German.

If people have only limited social contact with another group, they are more likely to have negative perceptions of them. This can grow into an "us and them"-mentality
40 where the minority group is blamed for society's problems, even if in reality these problems stem from somewhere else.

Comprehension

Task 1

Find a word in italics in the text which can replace the words in italics in the following sentences.

a. The differences between this book and the other one are *imperceptible*.
b. It's normal to make *guesses* about things when we don't have all the information.
c. Her original ideas were now *intertwined* with those of her mentor.
d. People sometimes *see* what they expect to *see*, rather than what is actually there.
e. The man was said to have a strong *bias* towards Muslims, which is also known as Islamophobia.
f. His views have been completely *distorted* on the matter, ever since he was the victim of a robbery.

Discussion

Task 2

In groups of three to four, discuss the following questions.

a. What stereotypes exist about the Germans, French, British and Italians?

b. What can we do to combat racism, stereotyping and discrimination? Think of three concrete actions that could be taken up at your workplace or college.

Friends launch anti-racism first in city nurseries

1 Children as young as three are to become the first line of defence in the battle against racism. [...]

Glasgow has become the first local authority in Scotland to introduce a dedicated anti-racism curriculum in its nurseries. Staff will be taught how to tackle incidents, explain
5 differences in skin colour and help children develop the skills to handle attacks.

Research shows racist attitudes can be picked up by children as young as two. A similar programme in 170 city primary schools in 2005 led to a slight drop in the number of racist incidents. Other local Scottish authorities have adopted the primary and the new early years programme has already attracted interest from several other councils.

10 Kubriya Binjamin's daughter Ambreen, 3, goes to Kinning Park Nursery, where around 60 % of pupils are Asian. Born in Glasgow, the 29-year-old mum-of-three said, "I think there is still a lot of work to be done but it's much better now. There are so many different communities in Glasgow which has helped."

As well as large Asian communities, Glasgow is home to more than 5,000 asylum seekers
15 from countries such as Iraq and 7,000 people from the EU accession countries including Poland. Council executive spokesman for education Gordon Matheson said, "This report is about addressing race issues at a young age specific way so that children grow up celebrating diversity."

*Friends launch anti-racism first in city nurseries, March 30, 2012, in: Evening Times, www.eveningtimes.co.uk/
friends-launch-anti-racism-first-in-city-nurseries-1.955634, accessed May 1, 2012.*

Comprehension

Task 3

In pairs, think of alternative ways to express these phrases from the text in English.

tackle incidents – handle attacks – attract interest – address issues – pick up attitudes

Grammar

Reported speech

We use *reported* or *indirect speech* when we want to express what other people say, think or believe.

Form	Examples
In order to write reported speech we change the verbs from the present to the Simple Past .	The 29-year-old mum-of-three said, "I **think** there **is** still a lot of work to be done but it **is** much better now." *The 29-year-old mum-of-three said that she **thought** there **was** still a lot of work to be done but that it **was** much better now.*
can => could will => would	Paul said, "I **don't think** that I **can** do it." *Paul said that he **didn't think** that he **could** do it.* Jaz said, "My colleague **will** see you soon." *Jaz said that her colleague **would** see them soon.*
In compound tenses, the auxiliary or helping verb is the one which changes.	Mia said, "Peter **has given up** his job." *Mia said that Peter **had given up** his job.*
If the verb is already in the Simple Past, we can either leave it the same, or change it to the Past Perfect.	Jim said, "I **woke up** early yesterday." *Jim said that he **woke up** early yesterday.* *Or: Jim said that he **had woken up** early yesterday.*
You can also leave out "that".	*Mia said Peter had given up his job.* *Jim said he woke up early yesterday.*

Task 4

Rewrite the sentences below using reported speech.

a. Amy said, "My boss wants to organise a party for Eid, but she doesn't have the staff."
b. Lidia said, "Our team has made great progress towards combating racism."
c. Ade said, "You'll need to work within the anti-discrimination policy."
d. Devon said, "I've been living in Britain since the 1950s, when my family came from Jamaica."
e. Joanna said, "Paco and Julio normally speak Spanish together, but today they're speaking English for the benefit of the visitors."

Language

Presenting your argument

Preparation

- Make sure that you have a clear structure to your argument. Think of it as though you're writing an essay. Include an introduction, a middle part and a conclusion.

- Get as many facts as possible to back up your argument. What you're looking for is evidence such as statistics from a reputable source. Ideally cross-reference your facts from different sources.
- You can use some opinions too, but remember you need to be convincing to persuade others to agree with you, so be ready to back up your opinions with facts.

During a debate

- Listen. You won't convince anyone if you don't listen to the other person, or team. React to what they say and comment on it, to show that you are listening and taking their points on board.
- Stay calm. Don't get too emotional. Present your arguments in a clear controlled voice, and keep your body language under control, for example, don't wave your arms around.

Activity

Task 5

In groups of four, prepare for a debate.

In recent years there has been an influx into Berlin of people from the USA, the UK, Spain, France and Italy.

Group A: You feel that this benefits the city and makes it a more vibrant place, and you believe that it will also bring more much-needed jobs to the German capital.

Group B: You feel that the foreigners have encouraged gentrification and forced rents and other prices up, so that local people can no longer afford to live in the areas where their families live.

Unit 11:

Social learning and behaviour

Module 1: The importance of play

Listening

Before you listen to the following text, look at these words and find their meanings.

a. reward	1. to be occupied or involved in an activity
b. gratification	2. the act of imitating or imagining something real
c. to resist	3. something received in return for good behaviour
d. temptation	4. to deal with (a problem) effectively
e. to distract	5. natural or inherent, e.g. an ability
f. correlation	6. describing something that has not been changed or altered in any way
g. self-regulation	7. a desire to do something, particularly something unwise
h. to cope with	8. to divert someone's attention
i. to engage in	9. the interdependence or relationship between two variables or outcomes
j. innate	10. pleasure or satisfaction derived through fulfilling a desire or task
k. make-believe	11. to withstand an action
l. unadulterated	12. the ability to control one's own behaviour

The marshmallow experiment

1 In the late 1960s a man named Walter Mischel, a father of three young girls, discovered that his four-year-old had suddenly developed the ability to wait before receiving a promised treat – a sweet reward. Before the age of four, she didn't know how to cope with desires that weren't immediately fulfilled. Mischel discovered that this
5 was generally true for most four-year-olds, but some children were better at controlling themselves than others.

In 1968 Mischel started a longitudinal experiment at Stanford University that became known as the marshmallow
10 experiment. A group of kindergarten children aged four to six were invited to participate in the study. They were left alone one at a time in a small bare room, only containing a desk and a chair. On
15 the table was a treat – a marshmallow or an Oreo cookie, and a bell. The children were made an offer: they could either eat the treat right away, or if they were

willing to wait until the adult returned to the room, they would be rewarded with a
20 second treat. If the child rang the bell, the adult would return, but the child would not get a second treat.

Most children were able to resist the temptation for several minutes; only about thirty per cent of the children successfully delayed gratification until the adult returned – a quarter of an hour later. Video footage of these children during the experiment shows
25 that the ones who were successful used creative strategies to resist eating the treat. Some would turn themselves away from the treat, while others would talk or sing to themselves. Mischel called this skill the "strategic allocation of attention". Instead of focusing on the "hot stimulus", patient children can distract themselves to avoid thinking about the object they desire.

30 Over the next forty years after the initial experiment was conducted, Mischel maintained regular contact to the participants, requesting that they, their parents and teachers complete questionnaires that would provide valuable information about their social and emotional development. When Mischel and his research team began analysing the results, they realised that there was a correlation between the outcome of the experi-
35 ment and later patterns of social behaviour. The participants who surrendered and ate the treat straight away were more likely to have behavioural problems; they weren't as successful at school, and often had difficulties maintaining relationships. Later studies confirmed that they even had higher body mass indexes as adults, and were more likely to have problems with drugs. Mischel and his colleagues concluded that self-regulation
40 is, in fact, a better predictor of academic performance and success than IQs. The marshmallow experiment, Mischel argues, was not about measuring will power or self-control; it was about the cognitive skills needed to think strategically and to develop ways of coping with stressful situations.

How do children develop self-regulation? Is it an innate ability, or is it a skill children
45 can learn to develop? According to Laura Berk of Illinois State University, children can develop self-regulation skills through make-believe play. When children play make-believe they are engaged in private speech; they talk to themselfs, mapping out what they are doing as they do it. They lay out rules for themselves in private speech, and this helps them learn how to regulate their behaviour. This is how adults manage their
50 emotions and regulate their self-control, too.

Berk stresses the importance of giving children enough *Spielraum* - the time and space to engage in imaginative play. The child's play should not be disrupted or regulated by

well-meaning adults. Supervised or organised activities are, in fact, counter-productive, as they do not allow children to negotiate the terms of their play by themselves, unadult-
55 erated imaginative play is indeed the most valuable tool for a child's social and emotional development.

Comprehension

Task 2

Are the following statements true or false? Correct the sentences so that they are true.

a. Most three-year-olds can delay gratification.
b. The marshmallow experiment assessed the cognitive skills children need to develop strategies for coping with stressful situations and regulating their own behaviour.
c. There was no apparent correlation between the outcome of the experiment and the participants' success in school and later life.
d. Self-regulation is an intuitive skill that cannot be learned.
e. Make-believe play stimulates private speech, which is an important tool for developing self-regulation.

Task 3

Answer the following questions based on your understanding of the story.

a. What was the most significant discovery of the marshmallow experiment?
b. What is the correlation between the outcome of the experiment and the children's social and emotional development?
c. Why is imaginative play so important?

Task 4

a. What are the benefits of play? Discuss with a partner whether the descriptions below are accurate.
b. Can you name any other benefits of play? Share your ideas with the group.

- Play can enhance problem-solving skills.
- Play can help advance language development and communication skills.
- Play can occupy children while their parents work.
- Play can improve children's grades at school.
- Play can divert a child's attention away from learning.
- Play can teach children cooperation and consideration.
- Play can improve children's motor skills.
- Play can help children cope with traumatic experiences.
- Play can help relieve stress.

Task 5

Look at the developmental milestones and match them to the three children according to their age abilities.

Lilly, 1

Samantha, 3

Megan, 5

a. plays simple games requiring memory
b. likes to hide and seek objects
c. forms first friendships
d. plays independently on the playground
e. prefers playing with a parent
f. likes to play make-believe
g. understands the object of games and rules
h. prefers playing with same-sex peers

Writing

Task 6

What kind of play, or which kind of game did you most enjoy as a child and why? Write a paragraph of no less than 150 words.

Language

1 **Phrasal Verbs**
Phrasal Verbs are two-part verbs: a verb that is followed by an adverbial particle or a preposition that has a slightly different meaning than the verb by itself. For example, the verb *grow* means to increase in size or amount. When *grow* is followed by an preposi-
5 tion, the verb phrase means something else.

*Parents help their children **grow up** to become responsible adults.*
*Babies **grow out of** their clothing quickly.*

The Phrasal Verb can also have an idiomatic meaning that is very different from the meaning of the verb by itself.

10 *They were best friends as children, but **grew apart** as they got older.*

Some Phrasal Verbs are not followed by objects; they are intransitive: *What time do you **get up** in the morning?* Intransitive Phrasal Verbs are always inseparable.

Other Phrasal Verbs are transitive: *The children **put away** their toys.*
Some of these Phrasal Verbs are separable, i.e. the prepositions particles can go either
15 before or after the noun objects: *The nanny helped the children **put** their toys **away**.*
Or: *The nanny helped the children **put away** their toys.*

Other transitive verbs are inseparable: *We asked a babysitter to **look after** the children.*
Not: *We asked a babysitter to look the children after.*

When the object is long noun phrase, we prefer to put the Phrasal Verb after the
20 particle:

*We have **put** our trip to the zoo **off** until next week.* (This sounds awkward.)
*We have **put off** our trip to the zoo until next week.* (This sounds better.)

When the Phrasal Verb is followed by a pronoun object rather than a noun, the adverb
participle goes after the pronoun object:

25 *We **put the toys away**. Or: We **put them away**.*
Also: *We **put away the toys**. But not: We put away them.*

Task 7

Complete each of the sentences using an appropriate Phrasal Verb in the box.

get along – name after – pick up – put off – put on – run out – set up – take after – throw
up – turn off

a. Our son's name is Benjamin. He was …
b. He is nothing like is mother. He …
c. Ben has made a lot of new friends since he's been at the nursery. He …
d. In fact, Ben likes nursery school so much he begins to cry when his mother …
e. "Can he dress himself yet?" "He can take off his jacket and shoes, but he refuses to …"
f. Ben was ill today. After breakfast he …
g. We wanted to do an art project for Easter today, but we…
h. We teach the children to conserve energy. They should remember to …
i. Because of the poor weather, our trip to the zoo has been …
j. The children like to play house. So, in one corner of the room, we …

Generation of "play deprivation"

1 Play is a serious business – and a lack of play opportunities for children is becoming a
form of deprivation, say play organisations. All too often the subject of play has been
trivialised, says Penny Wilson of the Play Association Tower Hamlets – consigned to local
newspaper pictures of bouncy castles and "gappy-toothed children with their faces
5 painted like clowns".

"This has nothing to do with what play is about," says Ms Wilson.

Play is an instinctive and essential part of childhood, she says, which is becoming more
and more under pressure, with evidence that a lack of spontaneous play leaves a long-
term social legacy.

10 "Play allows children to work out their emotions. When you're playing you're finding
out about who you are," she says.

"Play isn't about fun. Even with very small children, you can see there is a symbolism
to their play, there's a meaning to it."

Scheduling parents

15 But she warns that the world of play is being encroached upon from many different directions.

There are ambitious middle-class parents who over-schedule their children's lives – so there is no time left for children to play their own imaginative games. Outdoor play in the streets and parks has become much more limited – with anxious parents afraid about 20 safety.

"Children's worlds are shrinking," she says. [...]

And the design of modern cities has left fewer spaces for play. She shows some bleak pictures of modern housing developments with only the most token of play equipment. These play spaces, which can become threatening hang-outs, can even become places 25 that children avoid.

"Play deprivation" is a problem that is also being addressed in the United States – and Ms Wilson has been hired to advise on projects in New York, Chicago and Washington which are "trying to reintroduce the concept of play".

Stress

30 "I'm really frightened about the generation of children who are growing up without having played," she says. [...]

But how can play be under threat when every shopping centre has a barn-sized toy shop – and children's bedrooms are creaking with toys and gadgets?

"There's a direct correlation, because with many of the toys we buy, the toys do the 35 playing, not the child. Play shouldn't be based on ownership," she says.

This consumerist approach has taken away the initiative from children, she says. [...]

But there is also now a growing awareness of the importance of independent play. As an academic discipline, playwork can be studied to PhD level – and organisations are working to create more playable spaces.

40 The Play Association Tower Hamlets has worked on estates to try to create areas where children can play safely, not just in designated playgrounds. [...]

The Glamis Adventure Playground in Shadwell, which has won the London adventure playground of the year, is a multi-coloured play area, surrounded by grey flats and traffic rumbling through east London. Whatever the worries of the streets outside, in this pro-45 tected space children up to the age of 15 can run around and make up their own games, using the climbing frames, walkways and quirky equipment, including a landlocked boat. For inner-city children whose parents are afraid to let them play outside, this is a chance for healthy outdoor play. [...]

"If play is a serious aspect of children's health and well-being, then we need to take the 50 spaces available for them seriously" says Ms Wilson.

Extract from: Sean Coughlan: Generation of "play deprivation", in: BBC News, September 25, 2007, news. bbc.co.uk/2/hi/uk_news/education/7007378.stm, accessed July 9, 2012.

Comprehension

Task 8

Answer the following questions about the text in your own words.

a. What is play deprivation?
b. Why does Penny Wilson consider play "a serious business"?
c. Why are children not playing as much today as they used to?
d. What does Penny Wilson do as a playworker?

Activity

Task 9

Look for an Internet video showing an adventure playground in the United Kingdom. Try to describe the concept in your own words and explain how it is different than a traditional playground. Discuss your answers as a group.

Module 2: Taking responsibility for self and others

Writing

Task 1

Do you have a pet, or did you have a pet as a child? Have you ever wanted a pet? Write a short paragraph about your pet and the pleasures and problems of keeping a pet. Then find a partner and talk about your experiences.

Case study – pets in the classroom

1 This week was pet project week in Mrs Marlow's reception class. The children who had pets at home were asked to bring them in on Monday to show and talk
5 about. Abigail brought in her goldfish, and Ethan presented his puppy. Noah showed the class his cat, and Emma let everyone pet her guinea pig. Mrs Marlow surprised the children with their own
10 class pet turtle. They named it Cecil and put it in a terrarium in the science corner.

On Tuesday, Mrs Marlow arranged for the local veterinarian to come and talk to the children about the importance of animal health. He taught the children everything they needed to know about turtles and how to care for Cecil properly. The children took turns

15 feeding the turtle cut up vegetables and pieces of fruit. Mrs Marlow also set up a weekly schedule, so that each of the children would have a turn taking care of Cecil. On Wednesday, Mrs Marlow showed the children pictures of different species of turtles and their environments. Then they talked about Cecil's natural habitat. Mrs Marlow asked the children to draw pictures of Cecil, which she hung up around the room. At the end
20 of the day Mrs Marlow read Aesop's fable "The Tortoise and the Hare".

Thursday was arts and crafts day. The children decorated the backs of paper plates with different colourful materials to create tortoise shells, then pasted on a head, a tail and some arms and legs to the back. Some of the children modelled turtles out of clay.

On Friday, Mrs Marlow took her class on an excursion to the aquarium. A caretaker from
25 the aquarium showed the children some of the different species of turtles they had and explained how they were all different and similar. The caretaker also let the children help him measure and weigh all of the turtles. The children were quiet, observant and asked many questions.

Comprehension

Task 2

Answer the following questions about the case study.

a. Why do you think Mrs Marlow decided to adopt a pet for her reception class?
b. What could be the advantages of having a pet in the classroom? Make a list.

Task 3

Visit the website www.petsintheclassroom.org and collect information about The Pet Care Trust. Write a summary about their programme. Then, watch the video you see on the website and make a list of the educational benefits of having a pet in the classroom. What kinds of skills do children learn?

Activity

Task 4

You are a reception teacher and you would like to adopt a pet for your class. You want your students to decide which animal is best suited as a classroom pet. Devise a scheme to help your students explore the possibilities and reach a common decision. What are the learning outcomes of such a task? Create a power point presentation to share your ideas with the rest of the group.

Writing

Task 5

Write a letter to an organisation that sponsors classroom pets. Apply for grant money for a classroom pet. Your letter should include which pet you would like to adopt and why you feel this animal is best suited for your classroom. Also state which supplies you will need to purchase for your pet. Your letter should be no longer than one page.

Module 3: Does gender matter?

Writing / Discussion

| Task 1 |

Make a list of skills you think women are better at performing than men. Do the same for men. Discuss your ideas as a group, and try to explain your reasons for believing in these differences.

Is the gender difference a delusion? Or, should we be teaching boys and girls differently?

1 The widespread belief that the differences between men's and women's abilities are innate is now being contested by a growing number of scientists. "Neurosexism", as they call it, has had major implications on the education and social upbringing of boys and girls, these researchers suggest. If parents believe their sons have poorer chances of
5 acquiring verbal skills, and their daughters will probably never excel at mathematics, they will never attempt to help their children challenge and overcome their intellectual deficits.

According to Cordelia Fine, author of *Delusions of Gender*, there are no significant neurological
10 differences between the sexes that can explain certain strengths and weaknesses in ability. Contrary to popular belief, our gender or genetic predisposition has no decisive impact on our intellect.

15 Lise Eliot of Chicago Medical School confirms the recent findings; she says the hard-wired differences between the male and female brain is a myth. Eliot claims the behavioural and intellectual differences are not inherited, but rather learned. As we grow older our behaviour becomes increasingly gender-oriented
20 because we assume the social roles in our gendered culture. Girls' and boys' behaviour is the result of what we expect it to be. Boys develop better spatial skills not because of an inherent superiority, but because they are encouraged to perform well in sports that require throwing and catching. Similarly, girls are perceived as more emotional and communicative than boys, and so parents and teachers focus their attention on language
25 skills. While Eliot does not deny that there are differences between boys and girls, these differences, she says, are far smaller than the stereotypes we propagate.

Parents and educators find these recent findings hard to believe. They observe considerable differences in boys' and girls' behaviour and learning aptitudes every day. Reception teacher, Steve Mynard, feels that teachers need to treat boys and girls differently in order
30 to give them equal opportunities at school. Practitioners, Mynard asserts, need to understand the developmental differences and plan a curriculum that will take these gender

differences into consideration. The Early Years Foundation Stage (EYFS) framework recognises gender differences and endorses providing girls and boys with gender-specific opportunities. Taking their activity preferences and different learning styles into account
35 is, paradoxically, viewed as the non-discriminatory approach to teaching.

Comprehension

Task 2

Find the words in the text that can replace the words in italics in the following sentences. Use a thesaurus to help you.

a. The question whether the gender differences in children's behaviour are a result of nature or nurture is an issue that has been *disputed* among educators for years.
b. Because of neurosexism, researchers claim, boys and girls do not *try* to develop certain skills to their greatest potential.
c. The differences in performance of certain skills are no longer attributed to *naturally inherent abilities* in men and women.
d. The outcome of the experiment had no *significant* correlation with the participants' social development later in life.
e. Most of the traits that make us unique individuals have actually been *passed on* to us by our parents and grandparents.
f. Society expects boys to *do* well in athletics, and girls in languages.
g. Most educators contend that girls and boys do have different gender-specific *abilities*.
h. The league for Early Years professionals *recommends* encouraging gender-oriented activities for boys and girls.

Task 3

Answer the following questions about the text in your own words.

a. What was the popular belief about the differences in men's and women's intellectual abilities up until most recently?
b. What have scientists recently discovered to discredit this former belief?
c. How do researchers explain why there are such differences in the way men and women behave?
d. Why are the recent findings so hard for educators to believe?

What are little boys made of?
"Snips and snails, and puppy dogs tails
That's what little boys are made of!"
What are little girls made of?
"Sugar and spice and all things nice
That's what little girls are made of!"

– Traditional English nursery rhyme –

Grammar

Gerund or infinitive

Non-native speakers of English usually find it difficult knowing whether to use the infinitive or gerund verb form after the main verb. Infinitives and gerunds are verb forms that can be used to replace a noun as the object in a sentence. Some main verbs are followed by infinitive verbs, while others are followed by gerunds (the -ing form).

I like **working** with children.   (gerund)
I like **to work** with children.   (infinitive)

Sometimes both forms are possible without a difference in the meaning of the sentence.

The verb *like* can be followed by both forms; there's no difference in the meaning. Other verbs, however, can be followed by either a gerund or infinitive, but not without a slight difference in meaning. Compare the following sentences:

Maria didn't remember **to pack** her toothbrush.
Maria didn't remember **packing** her toothbrush.

Do you understand the difference in meaning?
The first sentence means: Maria forgot to pack her toothbrush.
The second sentence means: *Maria forgot whether she had packed her toothbrush or not.*

Unfortunately there is no patent way of knowing when to use the gerund or the infinitive. It is easiest to learn them gradually through practise.
Here are some of the common verbs that are followed by a gerund:

admit – appreciate – complete – consider – delay – deny – discuss – enjoy – involve – look after – look forward to – mention – postpone – recall – recommend – risk – suggest – take care of

These are some of verbs that are followed by infinitives:

agree – appear – arrange – care – decide – expect – learn – neglect – need – offer – plan – prepare – pretend – promise – refuse – seem – wait – want

With some special verbs the -ing form is used when the main verb is followed by the preposition *to*. Examples of these verbs are: *look forward to, object to, be used to.*
We **aren't used to walking** this far.

It should be noted that some auxiliary verbs contain the preposition *to* (e.g. have to, used to) but this should not be confused with the infinitive *to*. In this example the infinitive form of *play* is used without the *to*, i.e. **used to + play** (not: used + to play).
We **used to play** in the woods behind the barn.

Only infinitives are used after indirect objects (a noun or pronoun) following main verbs.
We **expect the children to put** away the toys when they're done with them.

We usually use a gerund, not an infinitive, when the verb comes after a preposition.
Look both ways **before crossing** the street.
We're thinking **about redecorating** the rooms.

Task 4

Complete the sentences by putting the verb in the brackets in the gerund or infinitive form.

a. We look forward to (meet) the new children in September.
b. The children must learn (do) things by themselves.
c. Alex was proud of himself for (take) off his shoes.
d. We cannot risk (lose) one of the children in the crowd.
e. Nina and Felicia are pretending (be) princesses.
f. Just as we got outside, it started (rain).
g. Each boy denied (hit) the other.
h. A playworker's job is to encourage children (play) freely and (use) their imaginations.
i. We can't prevent them from (do) what they want to do.

Sweden's "gender-neutral" preschool

1 Some have called it "gender madness", but the Egalia preschool in Stockholm says its goal is to free children from social expectations based on their sex.

On the surface, the school in Sodermalm – a well-to-do district of the Swedish capital – seems like any other. But listen carefully and you'll notice a big difference.

5 The teachers avoid using the pronouns "him" and "her" when talking to the children. Instead they refer to them as "friends", by their first names, or as "hen" – a genderless pronoun borrowed from Finnish.

It is not just the language that is different here, though. The books have been carefully selected to avoid traditional presentations of gender and parenting roles. So, out with 10 the likes of Sleeping Beauty and Cinderella, and in with, for example, a book about two giraffes who find an abandoned baby crocodile and adopt it.

Most of the usual toys and games that you would find in any nursery are there – dolls, tractors, sand pits, and so on – but they are placed deliberately side-by-side to encourage a child to play with whatever he or she chooses. At Egalia boys are free to dress up and 15 to play with dolls, if that is what they want to do.

For the director of the preschool, Lotta Rajalin, it is all about giving children a wider choice, and not limiting them to social expectations based on gender.

"We want to give the whole spectrum of life, not just half – that's why we are doing this. We want the children to get to know all the things in life, not to just see half of it," she 20 told BBC World Service. [...]

Last year a Swedish couple provoked a fuss in the media by announcing that they had decided to keep the gender of their young child, Pop, a secret from all but their closest family members. There was a similar case recently in Canada with a baby called Storm.

But is it not confusing for a young child to blur gender boundaries like this?

25 It is a criticism that Egalia director Lotta Rajalin has heard many times before, but she contests it vigorously.

"All the girls know they are girls, and all the boys know that they are boys. We are not working with biological gender – we are working with the social thing."

The verdict of child psychologists and experts in gender is divided – with most support-
30 ive of the aims, but questioning the means.

"The sentiments are excellent, but I'm not sure they are going about it in exactly the right way," says British-based clinical psychologist Linda Blair.

"I think it's a bit stilted. Between the ages of three and about seven, the child is searching for its identity, and part of their identity is their gender, you can't deny that," she told
35 BBC World Service.

But Sweden takes gender issues seriously, and for a number of years now, the government has been taking its battle to the playground. Gender advisers are now common in schools, and it is part of the national curriculum to work against discrimination of all kinds. Sweden is often praised as being one of the most equal countries in the world when it
40 comes to gender, but there are critics at home who think things have gone too far. [...]

Extract from: Cordelia Hebblethwaite: Sweden's "gender-neutral" preschool, in: BBC News Europe, July 7, 2011, www.bbc.co.uk/news/world-europe-14038419, accessed July 9, 2012.

Comprehension

Task 5

Complete the sentences based on your understanding of the text.

a. The Egalia preschool in Stockholm encourages ...
b. The teachers at Egalia use language that ...
c. The children's books at Egalia ...
d. The teaching staff at Egalia want boys and
   girls ...
e. Egalia director Lotta Rajalin insists that ...
f. Not all child psychologists and experts ...
g. The gender issue in Sweden ...

Activity

Task 6

In a debate two teams will consider the question: Is a gender-neutral upbringing and education favourable or detrimental for a child's social development? The affirmative team will argue that gender-neutral education is favourable, while the negative team will argue it is detrimental. Each team presents two constructive speeches and two rebuttal speeches. At the end of the debate, take a class vote to see whether more students endorse gender-neutral upbringing and education or oppose it.

Unit 12:

Emergencies in daily life

Module 1: Health and safety issues in the preschool

Preschool danger zones

1 As in the home or the workplace, the preschool environment presents potential dangers to the health and safety of children. Preschool children are at an age where their sense of danger has not yet fully developed. They don't always exercise the degree of caution they should when faced with possible hazards in their environment. There are many
5 areas in their immediate surroundings where the rambunctious preschool child needs to be protected from accident and injury, such as the bathroom, the classroom, the traffic on the way to and from school, and the playground. In this unit, we will explore typical dangers for the preschooler as well as examining ways in which these dangers can be reduced or eliminated altogether.

10 **Areas of danger**

The preschool classroom presents threats to the safety of children. Obvious dangers include damaged chairs which cannot bear the weight of the child, desks with broken edges and sharp corners, and badly-designed, or broken, toys and playthings. Poorly-designed furniture as well as improperly secured mats and rugs can also cause accidents. Windows that
15 cannot be closed properly or that can be fully opened by a child also pose safety risks.

The health of children may also be endangered by poorly ventilated rooms, or by malfunctioning heaters and thermostats that fail to maintain the temperature at the right level. The presence of lead in the water supply of older buildings can also impair the health of children.

20 Rooms should be properly equipped with functioning fire alarms and smoke detectors, and fire exits kept clear at all times. Entrances and exits to the building should be properly watched and monitored to ensure that younger children cannot leave the building, and that unauthorised persons cannot enter.

25 Especially in city preschools, traffic presents an immediate threat to safety whenever the children are taken outside on an outing. The volume and speed of traffic can be underestimated, not only by children but by their adult carers as well. A preschool may be located in an area where the pedestrian crossings are few in number, and impatient or
30 impulsive children could be tempted to cross the street in a dangerous place, rather than take the time to walk to the pedestrian crossing at the end of the street.

Drowning is one of the most common causes of death in children of preschool age. Young children can drown in
35 less than 15 cm of water, and particular care must be taken to ensure that buckets of water for mopping the floor, or basins of water for washing up are never left unattended, or are promptly emptied after use. It is also important to ensure that the hard, tiled floors of bathrooms are never
40 left wet, as slippery floors can cause falls that may result in serious injury.

As in the home, the kindergarten kitchen poses all sorts of hazards to the unwary child. Sharp knives left lying on countertops, kettles containing boiling water and ovens with red hot hobs and heating elements all present serious threats to the safety of the child.
45 Electrical sockets also pose a danger to curious children, who may electrocute themselves by inserting metal objects, such as knives or skewers, into the outlet.

The playground is another area which presents an obvious risk of injury to children. Defective, damaged, poorly-designed or inadequately secured equipment can cause bad accidents. Swings need to be properly anchored into the ground, slides provided with
50 guardrails, and bars on climbing frames spaced close enough together to ensure that small children don't fall through or get stuck between them. Protective surfacing such as rubber mats or mulch should also be generously placed around play equipment to help save falling children from serious injury.

Comprehension

Task 1

Find words and terms in the text above which match the definitions below.

a. device designed to regulate the temperature in a room
b. to damage or harm
c. to closely watch, observe, keep track of or supervise
d. people who do not have the required permission to enter restricted areas
e. a field trip or visit to somewhere outside the preschool, such as the zoo or a museum
f. the amount, mass or number of something.
g. death caused by asphyxiation due to the inhalation of water.

h. to be fixed or secured into the ground
i. barriers designed to lower or eliminate the risk of falling
j. organic material intended to protect against injuries

Task 2

Collocations are commonly used verb-noun combinations. In the above text there are a number of collocations used, which express the idea of being exposed to risk.

Verb	Noun
to expose to	risk, danger
to present	a risk, a threat, a danger, a hazard
to pose	a risk, a threat, a danger, a hazard

Examples:
Unemptied buckets can *pose a risk* of drowning to small children.
Busy streets can *expose* children *to the risk* of being run over.
Unprotected playground equipment can *present a danger* of falling.

Make a list of the types of dangerous situations presented by the following areas in and around the preschool: the bathroom, the kitchen, the classroom, the playground and the streets outside the preschool.

Then, using the collocations above, describe the kinds of risk which these situations potentially present.

Preschool safety checklist

1 It's important that preschool teachers and teachers' assistants are aware of all the potential dangers that the preschool environment presents. Making out a checklist is an effective
5 means of identifying hazards with regard to developing a health and safety plan that will help prevent accidents from happening.

Toys used in the classroom should meet the health and safety requirements set out by the
10 relevant government body or local authority. Toys should be made from safe, high quality materials and be manufactured to a high standard. Teachers should ensure that the toys are free from harmful chemicals and do not contain parts that break off or can be detached easily. Playthings such as dinner and tea sets should be disinfected after use to prevent the transmission of disease, as children
15 may put the plastic cutlery into their mouths. It is also important to remember to store toys safely. Heavy boxes should not be placed on shelves that can be reached by children who may pull these heavy objects down upon themselves. Children should also be instructed and encouraged to use toys safely and appropriately. Building blocks, for example, should not be used to stand upon, nor thrown at other children. In games
20 involving water, children should be discouraged from pouring water onto the floor, as wet floors present the risk of slipping.

Caregivers also need to be conscious of the dangers posed by the electricity supply. Exposed sockets should be secured using readily and cheaply available protective
25 covers. Electrical cords should not be left exposed as they present both a tripping hazard as well as exposing children to the danger of electrocution. Cords should be mounted on walls, out of reach of the tallest child in the group and secured against skirting boards or placed
30 beneath the floor boards of the room.

Cleaning supplies present a serious risk of poisoning and should always be securely locked away when not in use.

Smoke and fire alarms should be regularly checked and properly maintained. Fire extinguishers need to be frequently tested and certified for use by fire inspectors. A fire drill should be
35 drawn up, taught to the children and regularly practised. This can be done in a fun way as a learning activity to encourage the children to learn what procedures to follow in case of fire. Children should also be taught the emergency numbers of fire and ambulance services in case, for example, their caregiver should have an accident and lose consciousness.

The most important precaution of all though is to ensure that the children are ade-
40 quately supervised in an environment that has been made as safe for them as possible. Children should never be left alone, even for short periods of time, without supervision. Supervision does not have to be obtrusive or invasive. Children can be given the free-dom they need to play independently with one another while still being discreetly supervised by a caregiver.

Language

Task 3

Find words in the text which match the fol-lowing definitions.

a. to make sure
b. to clean or chemically treat an object to rid it of germs
c. the communication or contraction of illness
d. knives, forks, spoons and other eating utensils
e. suitably, to do something in the right way
f. to receive an electric shock

Writing

Task 4

With a partner draw up a list of all the possible dangers children are potentially exposed to in the preschool environment. Then complete the checklist below on a separate sheet of paper with recommendations on how to counter these dangers. Some examples have been included.

Area	Risk	Countermeasure
Street	Fast moving traffic	Ask local authority to install speed bumps to slow cars down
	Distant pedestrian crossing	
Kitchen	Tables with sharp edges	Apply soft padding to the edges
Classroom		
Electricity	Exposed electrical cords	Place cords beneath floor boards
Playground	Hard ground	
Bathroom		
Fire Safety	Fire exits not clearly marked	

Grammar

Conditional III

The Conditional III is used to talk about imaginary events in the past, i.e. events that did not take place but which might have affected the present situation if they had occurred.

Read the following sentences about a past action and the result of that action.

Jennifer did not prepare well for the interview for the position of preschool director. She did not get the job.

This is what actually occurred. But we can also imagine a different past situation, which might have produced a different outcome:

*If Jennifer **had prepared** well for the interview, she **would have got** the job.*

In the Conditional III, the **Past Perfect** is used in the "if" clause and the **past tense** of "would" in the remainder of the sentence:

If Clause	Would Clause
Past Perfect tense: **had (not) + Past Participle** (third form of verb)	Past tense of would: **would (not) have + Past Participle** (third form of verb)
If **we had dried** the kitchen floor properly, ...	... Anna **would not have slipped** and **fallen**.

Task 5

Look at the following past situations and their results and express them as Conditional III statements, i.e. say what would have happened if the situation had been different.

Example:
Jackie climbed onto the table. She fell off.
If Jackie **had not climbed** *onto the table, she* **would not have fallen off.**

a. Peter left the sharp bread knife on the table in the kitchen. Paul accidently cut himself with it.
b. Kevin stuck a fork into the electrical socket. He received an electric shock.
c. John forgot to lock the door to the kindergarten before he left. The cash box in the office was stolen.
d. Joshua didn't look both ways before he crossed the road. He was run over by a car and taken to hospital.
e. We installed a smoke detector in the kitchen. We heard the signal when the fire started last week.

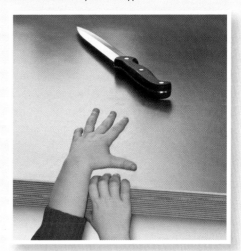

Mixed Conditionals

If we talk about a past action and its result in the present, we use Mixed Conditionals:
Past action: John took a two month drama course.
Present result: Now he can do drama classes with the children.
Mixed Conditional: If John **hadn't taken** *the drama course, he* **couldn't do** *drama classes with the children.*

In Mixed Conditionals, the **Past Perfect** is used in the "If" clause and the **present tense** of "would" in the remainder of the sentence.

If Clause	Would Clause
Past Perfect tense: **had (not) + Past Participle** (third form of verb)	Present tense of "would": **would (not) + infinitive** (first form of verb)
If Andrew **had not installed** *the protective matting in the playroom, ...*	*... the children* **would have** *more accidents.*

Task 6

Express the following sentences as Mixed Conditional statements.

a. Jack received his passenger van licence last week. Now he can take the children out on drives.
b. Jim spent two years studying Farsi. Now he can talk to the Iranian children we have here in their native language.
c. We applied to the education board for more funding. This means we now have enough money to purchase new classroom equipment.

 Task 7

Conditional review: Read the following sentences. Decide whether they are Conditional I, II, or III or Mixed Conditionals, and complete them using the appropriate forms.

a. We (take) he children to the museum today, if it (be) open on Mondays. I'll check on the internet and find out.
b. I (attend) the workshop at the weekend, if I (not have to) look after my sick relative.
c. If I (drive) to work yesterday instead of taking public transport, I (arrive) on time.
d. If I (not have) the experience of looking after so many younger brothers and sisters when I was growing up, I (not be) so good with children now.
e. I (apply) for a higher position in a year or two, when I (gain) more experience in this job.
f. Dagmar (repair) the chair in the classroom last week, if she (know) it was broken, and Max (not fall) through it.
g. I (set) up my own kindergarten, if I (have) the money, but the bank won't offer me a loan.

Module 2: Teaching children about safety

Helping children to learn about safety

1 One of the most effective ways of preventing accidents in the preschool is of course to make the children more aware of the potential dangers around them, as well as to teach them to behave and play safely with one another. Play activities can be used to encourage children to be more safety conscious. Children learn most easily and effectively through
5 games, play and role-playing activities. Approaching the issue of safety in this way also presents the advantage of being able to teach children about danger and the risk of accident, without unduly frightening them. It is important to teach children about safety in a context that allows them to feel that they have control over their environment and can act to protect themselves and others from accident and injury.

10 Drafting a set of safety rules for the kindergarten provides the basis for the development of a comprehensive programme designed to prevent accidents. A good way of making children aware of the dangers present in the preschool environment is to take them into each room and ask them to imagine how they could hurt or injure themselves there. A

list of their responses can be taken. For example, in the
15 kitchen, Jennifer might mention how she once cut her
hand on a knife that was left on the kitchen table at
home. Max might reply that the same thing happened
to him, and Paul might add that he once hit his head
on the corner of the table in the kitchen and bled from
20 the cut. The caregiver can note down each of these
remarks.

The children can then be brought back to the classroom
and asked how these accidents could have been
prevented. They may well respond with a variety of sug-
25 gestions, such as, "We should always put the knives back
in the drawer when we're not using them", or "We don't
need sharp knives, we shouldn't have them in the
kitchen", or "Mum puts a plastic guard on the blade of
our sharp knives so we don't cut ourselves". The car-
30 egiver can then take each of these suggestions in turn
and discuss them with the group. She may ask the children questions such as "Must we
always return knives straight to the drawer when we're not using them? I prepared
breakfast this morning and cut up some tomatoes. Then I left the knife I was using on
the chopping board because I needed it to cut the cheese while I made some tea. Should
35 I always put it away immediately, as soon as I stop using it?", or "But if we have no sharp
knives in the kitchen, how can we cut up and chop food. Paul, you tried cutting a piece
of bread yesterday with a butter knife. Did that work for you?"

Questions such as these may lead the children to the conclusion that there can be no
such thing as a totally safe environment, where all potential dangers are put out of
40 harm's way. The children may then start to think in terms of what they need to learn
and how they need to behave in order to avoid injuring themselves and causing accidents in the kitchen. The teacher's comments and questions can elicit responses from
the children like, "We should make sure that the knife is left on a safe place on the table
and warn other children that it is there until we are finished using it and ready to put
45 it away"; or "We should always pick up the knife by the handle and never by the blade";
or "We should never point a knife at anyone", or "Sometimes it's more dangerous to use
a knife that's not sharp. When I tried to use the butter knife to cut the bread, the knife
slipped and I hurt my finger". Getting children to reflect on their own experience to
find solutions to the problems they encounter in their environment encourages them
50 to think independently and to develop a sense of responsibility for their own actions
and behaviour. This process leads in turn to increasing the children's sense of control
over their own environment and enables them to learn that they have the power to
prevent accidents and make their surroundings safe for both themselves and others.
Making children aware of their ability, as well as their responsibility, for taking care of
55 themselves and others is a meaningful and effective way of minimising the risk of accident. Asking questions that evoke responses to the issue of safety can also be instructive
for caregivers who may not have considered some of the novel solutions that the imagi-
nativeness and inventiveness of children can yield! Caregivers can also learn from this
kind of interaction with their charges that a safety plan does not have to consist only
60 of a list of dos and don'ts.

Once the children are conscious of the risks posed in the kitchen, they can then be actively involved in preparing a safety programme that addresses the issues and problems they themselves have identified. Thus they end up preparing their own programme for their own use. This sense of having done it all by themselves can encourage them to
65 abide by the rules that they have formulated for themselves and their peers.

The preparation of the programme can be carried out as a play activity. The children can, for example, be given drawing materials, cardboard and paper to make signs for the kitchen that alert and remind people of the potential dangers. Signs can be attached to cupboard doors and drawers, reminding users to make sure they've shut them properly.
70 A "Danger – Wet Floor!" placard can be made from laminated cardboard and a child appointed to hang it on the kitchen door whenever the floor has been mopped. In this way children can also be introduced to behavioural routines that increase and maintain their daily awareness of the risks their environment presents.

Comprehension

Task 1

Find the words and expressions that match the definitions below.

a. to be aware of risks and how to minimise or eliminate them
b. wide-ranging, inclusive, thorough
c. a wooden or plastic tablet used for cutting vegetables, meat or bread
d. to draw out answers from a person by asking them directed questions
e. to think about, e.g. an experience or event in order to learn from it
f. to suddenly meet with a person or a problem
g. a word which means one's immediate environment
h. an experience you can learn from can be described in this way
i. the ability to find novel solutions to problems or to create ingenious ideas

Task 2

With a partner discuss the following questions.

a. Is it always a good idea to involve young children in the drafting of a safety programme?
b. To what extent should children be permitted to determine the procedures and precautions the plan should contain?
c. In what sorts of situations would it be justifiable to simply issue children with instructions and impose prohibitions, without discussing the safety issues with them beforehand?

Dialogue between a caregiver and two children.

1 **Maxine:** Hi kids. How did you get here today?
  Pia: Mum drove me here on her way to work.
  Paul: I came with my dad on the bike. We almost had an accident on the way.
  Maxine: Oh really, Paul! Please tell us what happened.

5 Paul: Well, we were cycling on the bike track. Then we stopped at the crossing and crossed when the light turned green. But even though our light was green, a car came and almost ran us over. Dad was really angry and shouted at the **10** driver. Then we got on our bikes again and cycled the rest of the way.

Maxine: Oh, that was terrible. You must have had quite a shock! Has that ever happened to you, Pia?

15 Pia: Yes, I was nearly hit by a car not so long ago. But I crossed when the light was red.

Maxine: Why did you do that?

Pia: The kid next to me crossed and I thought that it would be OK. But she was nearly hit by the car, too. The driver honked his horn really hard. It was really **20** scary and I cried!

Maxine: If you're at a pedestrian crossing, you should always look to see if the light is green?

Pia: Yes, you should always check to see. That's how you know it's safe. You have to check and not just run across the road without looking. Then you won't **25** get knocked down.

Maxine: But Paul, you and your dad looked and the same thing happened to you? Why was that, do you think?

Paul: I don't know. The car shouldn't have driven because his light was red. It was our turn to across.

30 Pia: I crossed too though, although the light was red – like the driver who almost hit you, Paul. Even though I shouldn't have, I did it anyway. The red light can't control you!

Paul: No, even if the man is green, it doesn't mean there's nothing coming. You can't just look at the lights and cross when they go green. The green light **35** means you're allowed to go, but not that it's safe to go. You have to look yourself and check anyway. You have to make sure it's safe to cross.

Pia: Yes, I'll make sure to look both ways in future, up and down the street, before I cross. Otherwise I might get killed!

Maxine: Do you think all the other kids here know how to cross the street safely?

40 Paul: No, Max told me he sometimes runs across the road without looking especially where there's no crossing. He said he had seen other kids do it and nothing happened to them. I told him he was stupid!

Maxine: Maybe he's not stupid. Perhaps he just doesn't know the right way to do it. After all, you and Pia have just told me you've made mistakes, too. Even your **45** dad forgot to look both ways when you were cycling here this morning, Paul!

Paul: Yes, we should tell the other kids what we talked about today. We could make a sign and hang it on the back of the front door to remind the kids of what they should do at the crossing before they go out. I saw something like that at my brother's school. He helped make a big sign in art class and it was a lot **50** of fun! Even big kids sometimes forget what they should do to cross the road safely.

Maxine: That sounds like a great idea, Paul! What do you think, Pia? Even adults need to be reminded of how to cross the street. I think a sign would be a big help to us all. Shall we start making it now? What do we need? Some cardboard **55** and paints …

Activity

Task 3

Split up into groups of three. One of you will play the role of caregiver and two of you the roles of five-year-old children, as in the above dialogue. Choose an area of health and safety that the children should be made aware of and taught about, e.g. fire safety; safety in the bathroom; safety in the playground.

a. First of all, think about how the caregiver should introduce, lead and guide the discussion. Consider the questions she should ask and how these questions should be phrased and addressed. The questions should be open enough to give the children the scope and freedom they need to think independently, while being stimulating enough to prompt them into generating their own ideas and solutions.

b. Then reflect upon how five-year-old children think. Consider the things children might think about, and how they might express their thoughts, ideas and opinions.

c. Next improvise an exchange between you, and the children which will lead to the preparation of a safety plan or strategy for the area of risk you have chosen. For example, first allow the children to identify the potential dangers of the chosen area, and then give them the opportunity to suggest ways of dealing with these dangers.

If you wish you can note down the dialogue you have improvised to help you remember it later. The dialogue should conclude with a suggestion for an activity designed to produce a plan to reduce danger in the risk area under discussion.

In the above text, for example, the caregiver and teacher agreed to make a sign. Other activities could, for instance, be determining out the steps of a fire-drill and performing it as a dramatic scenario or making up a song about avoiding danger in the kitchen or bathroom. Perform your role-play in front of the group.

d. Discuss each others' role-plays. Offer feedback based on the following criteria.
   • Did the discussion elicit useful, imaginative responses from the children?
   • Did the teacher guide the discussion well, or was it too unstructured, or, too overly programmed?
   • Did the children really develop an increased awareness of the dangers and risks of their environment?
   • Was the activity suggested at the end of the discussion useful or appropriate to the task of developing a safety strategy for the safety issue under discussion?

e. In your original groups, prepare, perform or carry out the activity that you agreed upon in your role-play and present it to the rest of the class.

Module 3: Dealing with emergencies

Accidents will happen!

1 Inevitably accidents do occur no matter how much we try to avoid them. In a preschool containing up to 30 or 40 children, accidents, cuts, falls and bruises are simply a part of daily life. No safety programme, no matter how comprehensive, detailed or thoroughly

applied can prevent all instances of accident or injury. Serious accidents are, thankfully,
5 rare in a well-run preschool, but they do still occur, and caregivers have to be prepared
to deal with them when they do. In this module we will be looking at what can be done
when a child starts choking and how to place a child in the recovery position, as well
as what is involved in writing out an incident report. In all cases of accident and injury
an incident report will have to be completed, detailing the circumstances under which
10 the accident happened. This is necessary in order to have a clear record of exactly what
occurred, especially if medical personnel or emergency services need to be involved. It
is also reassuring for parents to know that the preschool management and staff take the
issue of safety seriously, and are prepared to deal responsibly with crises when they occur
in accordance with established procedures.

Dealing with choking

1 One of the most distressing occurrences preschool staff have to deal with is when a child
suddenly begins to choke. The sight of a child unable to catch its breath can be sufficient
to induce panic or paralysis in a carer and it is important for this reason that staff are
fully trained and ready to deal with this eventuality should they be confronted with it.

5 For a child (approx. one year to puberty)

1. If the child is unable to cough up the obstruction, give back blows.
2. Bend the child forward.
3. Give up to five sharp blows between the shoulder
10   blades with the heel of the hand.
4. Check the mouth for dislodged objects. If the child is still choking, perform the steps below.

1. If the child is still choking, give abdominal thrusts.
2. Place a fist above the belly button.
15 3. Grasp your fist with your other hand. Pull inwards and upwards four or five times.
4. Check the mouth for dislodged objects.
5. If they are still choking, give three full cycles of back blows and abdominal thrusts, checking the mouth
20   after each cycle.
6. Call an ambulance if they are still choking and repeat cycles of back blows and abdominal thrusts until medical help arrives. If the child loses consciousness, give CPR (cardiopulmonary resuscitation).

Choking Factsheet, in: British Red Cross, no publication date, http://childrenfirstaid.redcross.org.uk/assets/Uploads/Choking-factsheet.pdf, accessed April 10, 2012.

The recovery position

1 When a child loses consciousness because of heatstroke or in the aftermath of an epileptic fit, they should be placed in the recovery position. This is a position which allows

the child to breathe freely, helps prevents injury should they experience a fit, and greatly reduces the risk of suffocation should they vomit.

5 1. Place arm nearest to you at a right angle, with palm facing upwards.

2. Move other arm as shown, keeping the back of the hand against the child's cheek. Get hold of knee furthest from you and pull up until foot is flat on
10   the floor.

3. Pull the knee towards you, keeping the child's hand pressed against their cheek. Position the leg at a right angle.

4. Make sure that the airway remains open by tilting
15   the head back, then check breathing by feeling and listening for breath.

Recovery Position Factsheet, in: British Red Cross, no publication date, http://childrenfirstaid.redcross.org.uk/ assets/Uploads/Recovery-position-factsheet.pdf, accessed April 10, 2012.

Comprehension

Task 1

Find words or expressions in the texts "Accidents will happen!" and "Dealing with choking". that match the definitions below.

a. a document which details the circumstances of an accident
b. a word which means "happening"
c. a blockage that needs to be removed

d. to strike someone, e.g. to free their airway of a blockage
e. either of two large, flat, triangular bones located in the top left and right corners of the back
f. the raised part of the palm of the hand nearest the wrist
g. objects that have been loosened or freed
h. sharp movements of the hand into the upper stomach area, as used in the procedure to prevent choking
i. a tightly clenched hand

Activity

Task 2

Split into pairs. Using the information above, as well as other sources such as videos and images from the internet, prepare a short presentation demonstrating *on a doll or pillow* how to perform either the anti-choking procedure, or how to place someone in the recovery position to an audience of carers who need to learn these techniques as part of their training to work in a kindergarten.

Please note that performing this procedure on a person could result in serious injury.

Your presentation should consist of:

* A general introduction outlining the importance of learning these techniques and the situations in which you may be required to use them.
* The main part in which you demonstrate in clear steps how the technique is carried out.
* A conclusion in which you summarise the most important points to note.

If you are familiar with Microsoft PowerPoint or Apple Keynote, prepare a slideshow to help illustrate and support the points you wish to make.

Task 3

If a child has suffered a serious accident in your kindergarten, you will need to call its parents to inform them of what has happened. It is important in such situations to remain calm and communicate as clearly, reassuringly and sympathetically as possible. It is essential to be open and honest about what has happened and to answer questions as directly and as comprehensively as possible.

With a partner perform a telephone role-play based on the scenario below. One of you will play the parent and the other the carer making the call.

Robert, a five-year-old, slipped on the kitchen floor and cut his forehead. You and another member of staff managed to stop the bleeding and put a bandage on the wound, which was not too deep. When Robert became unconscious you immediately called an ambulance and he was taken to hospital. The ambulance arrived within five minutes of your call and Robert had already started to regain consciousness before it arrived. The paramedic examined the wound and told you it would need some stitches, but reassured you that the cut was not serious. He also said that Robert would probably suffer some mild concussion and would need to rest at home for a few days. Your colleague accompanied Robert in Dublin Street in an ambulance. [0]

Incident Report Forms

When an accident involving a serious injury occurs, an incident report detailing the circumstances of the accident and the nature of the injuries incurred must be filled out.

Sample Incident Report

Incident Report – Elysium Kindergarten	
Name of Child: Michael Wright	**Date of Birth:** February 2, 2007
Details of Incident	
Time / Date: 10.15/March 30, 2012 **Type (accident, illness etc.):** Accident resulting in injury **Location** (playground, classroom etc.): Playground	
Details of Incident: Michael was playing in the playground with the other children during the break. He was climbing up the ladder to the top of the slide when he lost his footing and fell to the ground, a distance of about two metres. He fell badly onto his arm and cried out in pain. Kindergarten staff immediately called for an ambulance. The other children were taken back to the Kindergarten. Two members of staff remained with Michael, covered him with a blanket and comforted him while waiting for the ambulance, which arrived shortly afterwards. **Injuries incurred / Nature of illness:** Michael suffered a broken forearm, and some scratches and bruising to the face as a result of the fall. **Medical treatment / services:** Staff called emergency services at 10.15, as soon as the accident occurred, and an ambulance arrived within 10 minutes, shortly before 10.25. Michael was examined and treated by paramedics where he was lying, before being taken to the accident and emergency at the children's hospital in Dublin Street.	
Parent / Relative / Other Contacted: **Name:** Sylvia Wright (Mother)	**Time / Date:** 10.30/ March 30, 2012
Witnesses: **Name(s):** Karen Fiedler, Jackie Baggot (Kindergarten staff members). **Note:** Karen travelled in the ambulance with Michael to the hospital and remained there with him until his mother arrived.	
Signature: *J. Baggot*	**Time / Date:** March 30, 2012
Recommendations for future prevention: Place rubber foot grips on the rungs of the slide ladder and extend protective matting around the area of the slide.	

 Task 4

Together with your partner from Task 3, write an incident report, modelled on the sample report above, which describes the details of the accident suffered by Robert in Task 3 above. When completed read out your report to the rest of the class.

Unit 13:

Conflict management

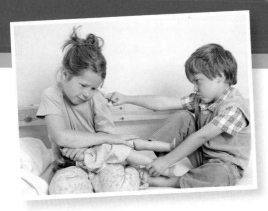

Module 1: Resolving conflict

Are children the best people to resolve their own conflicts?

1 Norma Hunter works in the Behaviour Support Unit of a primary school in Manchester. Here, she talks about what causes conflict among young children, and how the children themselves can often find a solution to the problem.

Why do children fall out?
5 Conflict is a part of life for people of all ages and of course young children are not immune. Finding ways to resolve conflict is a very important part of a child's development. In the UK, part of the national curriculum is known as SEAL (Social and Emotional Aspects of Learning) and its second theme is called Getting On and Falling Out. Conflict in preschool education tends to arise over such issues as sharing toys, taking
10 turns, personal space, who the children play with and who they don't, and sometimes due from not fully understanding what is happening. Young children are very focused on what they want, not on what the children around them want.

What does a teacher or an educator need to do?
Don't ignore it or avoid it. Step in fast enough to prevent children from getting hurt,
15 but don't rush into imposing a solution of your own. Keep calm, if you get angry it will definitely make things worse. Avoid responding with a threat or an ultimatum. If that's the only model of conflict resolution the children learn, it won't be helpful to their development. Use differentiated responses which are appropriate for the individual children involved.

20 Children want adults to be clear and concrete. Vague concepts of "kindness" and "niceness" don't mean much to a three-year-old. Caring about others and empathy have to be developed and coached, you cannot just tell the child "let's all be friends."

What is the best way to resolve the disputes?

In most cases, the children can come up with the solutions themselves if the adult
25 facilitates this in the right way. For a start, wait until they've calmed down. Acknowledge
and accept their emotions, don't tell them "you shouldn't be angry or upset." To them,
the emotion is very real and important, so give them a little time to be angry or upset.
After they've calmed down ask them "What's the problem? What happened exactly?"
Listen, and repeat it back so that it's very clear for everybody. For example "You wanted
30 the book which Charlene had. You took it from her. Charlene wanted to keep the book."
Then ask what ideas the children have as to how the problem can be solved. You'd be
surprised how often and how well children can come up with good ideas for the resolution of the conflict.

Comprehension

Task 1

Decide if these statements about the text are true or false.

a. Young children are focused on the needs of other children around them.
b. Teachers and educators should react fast and try to find a solution as quickly as possible.
c. It can be useful to respond by making a threat.
d. Teachers and educators should use different responses depending on their knowledge of each child.
e. It's a good idea to tell the children to stop crying because there is really no reason for them to be upset.

Task 2

Replace the word or phrase in italics in these sentences with a synonym from the text.

a. The children usually *alternate with each other* in using the slide.
b. I think that the manager *dictates* the ethos and objectives of the kindergarten without consulting parents and staff.
c. We generally make sure that we *make a distinction* between the needs of all our children.
d. Maya is our administrative assistant. She really *assists* the progress of our group.
e. You have to make sure that you *recognise* everybody's contribution.

Activity

Task 3

Role-play the following situation in pairs.

Student A
You are the mother, or father, of a boy who has been involved in a fight at his nursery. Your son bit and hit another child in a conflict over a toy. You believe strongly in letting children find their own solutions to conflict, and in letting the children express what they are feeling rather than telling them what to do or not do. You don't like to tell your son that one or other type of behaviour is "wrong."

Student B
You are the grandparent of (and main carer for) a child who has been involved in conflict at her nursery. She has been hit and bitten by another child. You are not convinced by the theory of letting children resolve their own disputes. You think that children need boundaries and clear rules about what is acceptable behaviour and what is not, and they look to adults for this information. You think that sometimes it is important to tell a child that a certain type of behaviour is unacceptable.

Discussion

Task 4

In groups of four, brainstorm to come up with a list of all the skills which children could develop from finding solutions to conflict themselves.

Grammar

Review of tenses

Task 5

Decide which of the pairs of sentences is correct.

a. I am living in Dresden since I was ten.
b. I have lived in Dresden since I was ten.
c. She was speaking to her brother on the phone when the doorbell rang.
d. She spoke to her brother on the phone when the doorbell was ringing.
e. The doctor told us that he had already sent the tests away to the laboratory.
f. The doctor told us that he already sent the tests away to the laboratory.

g. We normally work until 5 p.m. but this week we finish at 4.30.
h. We normally work until 5 p.m. but this week we are finishing at 4.30.
i. May is in hospital for a planned operation, I'm going to visit her tomorrow.
j. May is in hospital for a planned operation, I will visit her tomorrow.

Task 6

In pairs, rewrite the following sentences, using the words in brackets and other words which you can think of. Don't change the form of the word in brackets.

a. Understanding every word isn't the most important thing.
   It ...(matter)... if you don't understand every word.
b. Oh no, it's still raining.
   Oh no, ...(yet)...
c. I knocked on your classroom door yesterday – why didn't you answer?
   What ...(doing)... yesterday?
d. John arrived there. The game of football was over.
   The game ...(already)... when John arrived.
e. I can hear Peter and Lawrence talking, but what language is that?
   What is that language ...(which)...?

Task 7

Identify all the tenses used in the sentences in Task 6, and say why you used each one.

Module 2: Conflicts between children and parents and caregivers

Is positive reinforcement of children manipulation? Should you use praise and rewards to get children to cooperate?

1 Working with young children, toddlers especially, can be very frustrating. Trying to *coax* a toddler into doing things you'd like him to do requires a lot of patience. Both parents and caregivers readily admit being hesitant about how to respond to a child who cannot – or does not want to – cooperate. Although we all may disagree with applying certain 5 methods of punishment, such as spanking or forcible isolation ("time out"), we may dif-
fer on the usefulness of doling out rewards and *praise* for positive behaviour. Because young children haven't yet learned to distinguish between good and bad behaviour, admonishment for not 10 cooperating doesn't seem to be as appropriate, or effective, as positive reinforcement is, for cooperative behaviour. But can too much positive reinforcement be a form of manipulation? Could it even have a *detrimental* effect on a child's social 15 development?

Verbal rewards are used to reinforce desirable behaviour patterns; they are intended to get children to comply with our requests or instructions. Although it can be effective in conditioning a child to behave appropriately, it is doubtful whether a child will learn to recognise why this type of behaviour is necessary and appreciated in particular
20 situations.

The more a child is rewarded for doing something well, the less interested the child becomes in the activity itself; instead, the child will only focus on receiving the reward. A study conducted by Joan Grusec (1992) at the University of Toronto discovered that children who were frequently praised for being *generous* to others became progressively
25 less generous; they were, in fact, less interested in sharing or helping than those children who were not praised for the same behaviour. The acts of generosity were no longer seen as something valuable in their own right, but rather omit as a means of getting a reaction from an adult.

Similar studies reveal that children who are praised for doing a creative task well are less
30 likely to be as competent at the next creative task. Researchers suggest that praise puts children under pressure to produce praiseworthy work. The more a child anticipates praise, the less likely he or she is to take the risks that are necessary to be creative.

Children need unconditional love and support. By over-indulging a child with praise for positive behaviour, we are teaching the child to believe that our affection for the child
35 *is* conditional. But what is the most effective alternative to using positive reinforcement in order to *discourage* misbehaviour? If a child is doing something it shouldn't be, rather than threatening or bribing, you should ask the child how his problematic behaviour can be corrected. Allowing the child to participate in the decision-making process conveys the message that you take his ideas and feelings seriously. And children who are
40 treated with more respect will in turn show more respect for others.

Rather than simply saying, "Good job!" for doing a good deed, recognise the child's accomplishment with an evaluation-free statement like, "You did it!" If the child has done something generous, drawing his attention to the positive effect of his action will reinforce its purpose. Instead of showing him that he has made you proud, he sees
45 reason to be proud of himself. Encouraging children to do tasks successfully and to behave well is not about spoon-feeding them positive reinforcement, but more importantly about recognising the worthiness of their tasks and deeds.

Comprehension

Task 1

Find one word in the following sentences that is used incorrectly. Correct the sentences by replacing the word with one of the appropriate words in italics from the text.

a. Many parents use bribery as a reliable method of conveying a child into doing something favourable.

b. A child is more likely to be genuinely selfish if he is made aware of the virtue of his generosity.

c. Some experts say that too much positive reinforcement has a desirable effect on a child's social development.

d. One way to encourage misbehaviour is to show a child more respect for his ideas and feelings.
e. Children who are constantly bribed for doing good deeds do not learn to recognise the worthiness of their deeds.

Task 2

Answer the following questions in your own words based on your understanding of the text.

a. Why are verbal rewards not effective in teaching children appropriate behaviour?
b. What message does frequent praise convey to children?
c. What are more effective alternatives to positive reinforcement?

Discussion

Task 3

Read the scenario descriptions below and discuss with a partner the mistakes the teachers make in resolving the conflicts. How could the conflicts be resolved more effectively?

a. After the children had all worked hard to put away the toys at the end of the day, Emil (2 ½) overturned a bin of building blocks and proceeded to play with them. The nursery school teacher scolded Emil and made him clear up the blocks all by himself. All of the other children were sent outside to the playground.
b. Max (4) chose to ignore his nursery teacher's requests to stop playing and to go inside. His teacher said that if he did not stop playing immediately, he would not receive a snack when they went inside.
c. Sarah (3) needed help taking off her jacket and shoes. Her childminder told her that she should be able to do that at her age, adding "only babies need help getting undressed."
d. Two five-year-old girls in Ms Slade's reception class are having a row about who should take care of the baby doll. The girls play tug-of-war with the doll, shouting at each other "It's mine!" until Ms Slade comes over. She tells the girls that if they can't agree, neither of them will get the baby doll to play with. She takes the doll away and hands it to a younger bystander.

Language

Talking to parents

1 A childcare professional must have good communication skills, especially when working with parents. It can be challenging for a practitioner to raise concerns and sensitive issues with a parent. This requires good listening skills, empathy and tact on the part of a childcare professional. Mutual respect and trust are the keys to establishing a good
5 working relationship with parents and this can be achieved through clear communication.

As a childcare provider, you must assume that all parents want to hear good news about their child. They want to be proud and hopeful of their child, and want to have the feeling that
10 they are good parents. So, it's important that you carefully select your words and try not to blame someone or be judgemental. If a parent challenges your opinion, resist the temptation to become defensive. Instead, acknowledge their viewpoint and concerns. Tell them that you value their
15 opinion.

Here are some techniques for positive communication with parents:

"It's a funny thing about mothers and fathers. Even when their own child is the most disgusting little blister you could ever imagine, they still think that he or she is wonderful."
Roald Dahl, *Matilda*,
1st ed. Edition.
Jonathan Cape, London 1988

Parents like to hear positive qualities about their child, so before you express criticism, find a positive attribute about
20 the child you can praise.

> "Adam is particularly good at ..., but he does have difficulty with ..."

Instead of saying, "your child will never be able to ...," you should say, "your child may have trouble with ..."

25 When a parent comes to collect their child at the end the day, you should not wait for a family member to initiate conversation. Instead, you should freely comment on the child's experiences that day. If you are asked how a child's day was, avoid just saying "fine." Instead, give a parent a clear picture of the day's events using adjectives to help describe the child's experiences.

30 When you have something difficult to say, it's a good idea to introduce your intent with a phrase like,

> "I think you should know ..."
> "I thought you'd like to know ..."
> "I think it's important for you to know that ..."
35 > "I'd like to talk to you about ... When would be a good time to talk?"

Show a parent you are sincerely concerned:

> "I am a little worried about Adam. He stopped what he was doing and started crying several times throughout the day."

Don't make assumptions about the causes of a child's behaviour. Instead, allow parents
40 to maintain control over the conversation by asking them for a possible explanation for their child's behaviour.

> "I've noticed that ... Do you have any idea what the cause of this could be?"

And finally, avoid blameful questions like, "Why can't you bring Adam to nursery on time?" Instead be polite when you make requests:

45 > "It would be very helpful if you could bring Adam to nursery a little earlier."
> "I'd like to ask you to ..."
> "Could I ask you to ..."
> "We'd greatly appreciate it if ..."

Task 4

Read the following comments and try to rephrase them using more diplomatic language.

a. If you cared about Emily, you wouldn't allow her to do that.
b. Unlike the other children his age, Jamal isn't capable of using a pair of scissors.
c. Michael's behaviour is very disappointing.
d. I doubt Charlotte will be ready to enter school by autumn.
e. It's obvious that Dean isn't getting enough attention at home.

Activity

Task 5

Choose one of the statements in Task 4 and create a dialogue which demonstrates positive communication between a childcare professional and a parent. Role-play your dialogue together with a partner in front of the class.

Module 3: Is disciplining necessary?

Listening

Listen to three young adults speaking about their upbringing. How much can you understand when listening? Take notes as you listen. Then, try to answer the questions below. Try to do this exercise without reading the transcript.

How my parents raised me

Elizabeth, 35

1 My parents were strict, especially my father. I wouldn't necessarily say that they were authoritarian, but they certainly were authoritative. My father set limits and enforced rules with a very resolute voice and used physical discipline if necessary. Although I might not have realised it at the time, my parents – both educators – were responsive
5 and nurturing, and my sister and I lacked for nothing. My parents recognised the value of a good education and instilled in us the importance of diligence and achievement.

Everything that could possibly distract us from our studies and jeopardise our prospects was not tolerated. There were rules we found hard to understand; in fact, it seemed there was no rationale to them at all. We were not allowed to get our ears pierced, wear make-
10 up, apply nail polish or date boys until we turned 16. For two girls in puberty, these rules seemed both harsh and archaic to us in the 1970s and 80s. The older I got though, the better I got at finding ways to get around these nonsensical rules my parents had laid down for us. Although I respected my parents' authority, I had also developed a strong self-esteem and confidence. I had to test my limits for myself. Now, I would say that I
15 am a successful person because my parents taught me respect and self-respect, discipline and self-discipline.

Sibel, 30
I grew up in a traditional Muslim family with four siblings. My parents immigrated to Germany from Turkey in 1978 and my brothers and I were born shortly thereafter. I am
20 the middle child; I have three brothers and one younger sister. My sister and I were raised to obey my father and our brothers. Although my mother was responsible for my rearing and education, she had no authority in our home. When I turned 10, my mother said that I would have to wear a headscarf to protect my female integrity. This was the custom in our family, and it never occurred to me to question the validity of this Islamic
25 "sacrament". My father was very domineering – authoritarian. He did not allow me to leave the house, to play with my friends, or to go to the cinema without the chaperon-age of my brothers. I grew up in fear. My father would often beat me, my sister and my mother, and he permitted my brothers to beat us, too. It was all about power and con-trol, not about discipline. My father wanted me to become a devout Muslim woman
30 who would obey and serve her husband. I feared the consequences of not becoming this woman, but I could not respect my father for being such a cruel and brutal person either. So, I have always had to live my life in secret, hiding my talents and passions from my family. Even today in the company of my friends, I feel uncomfortable unveiling my true colours. I only wish my family could be proud of me for who I really am. I feel alone
35 without a family I can trust.

James, 25
My parents were hippies. They believed in raising me and my brother as equal counterparts to themselves. We were a democratic family, and my parents never imposed
40 rules upon us that we disagreed with or couldn't under-stand. My brother and I never really lived by rules. We did what we wanted when we wanted to – and we still do! My parents firmly believed that life itself would teach us all the lessons we needed. They never preached
45 or scolded, but they would explain the consequences of our actions when we made poor decisions. For a child, having anti-authoritarian or permissive parents is great: no bedtime, no television limits, no curfew. However, the downside of this kind of upbringing was that I got
50 bad grades in school; my parents said that it was my responsibility to do my homework, which I routinely
neglected to do. Instead I would hang out with my mates and get into mischief. Now as an adult, I find it difficult to set limits for myself, and I find it hard to decide what is necessary and important for me to do. I jump around from one job to the next. If I'm

55 honest with myself, I lack discipline and diligence, and I lack self-control. My parents undoubtedly love me, and I believe they were convinced they were being the best parents they could be.

Comprehension

Task 1

Are the following statements true or false?

a. Elizabeth says her father would occasionally smack her as a young child for being disobedient.
b. Sibel is the eldest of five children.
c. James's parents are teachers.
d. Elizabeth's parents taught her to be a hard worker.
e. Sibel was allowed to go to the cinema by herself.
f. James was allowed to stay up as long as he wanted.
g. Elizabeth accepted her parents' rules, but didn't always follow them.
h. Sibel grew up in a religious family.
i. James says he is successful today because he had to learn to be responsible for himself at a young age.

Task 2

Discuss the following question with a partner. Then, share your ideas with the group.

a. Which three types of upbringing methods were mentioned by the speakers?
b. How do you think these peoples' upbringings has affected their personal development?
c. Which person do you think is most well-adjusted? Least well-adjusted? Explain.
d. Which upbringing method would you endorse?

Grammar

We use the Simple Present tense to talk about permanent situations, or things that happen on a regular basis. However, when we want to talk about things that occurred routinely in the past, we use the modal verbs *would* or *used to* + infinitive. See the examples from the text:

*My father **would** often **beat** me …*

Task 3

Can you find any other examples in the text?

Task 4

Rewrite the following sentences using *would + infinitive* or *used to + infinitive* to show that these events happened routinely in the past.

a. My parents always let me make my own decisions.
b. I was scared of the dark.
c. I went to bed whenever I wanted to.
d. She sucked her thumb until she was ten.
e. My parents always went out on Saturday evenings while I stayed home with the babysitter.

The parenting gap: why French mothers prefer to use the firm smack of authority

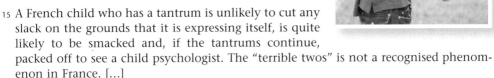

1 [...] In her book *French Children Don't Throw Food*, out this month, American mother-of-three Pamela Drucker-man, who lives in Paris, asks how the French manage to raise children who, unlike many of their US or British
5 counterparts, sleep through the night at two months, are not picky eaters, do not throw tantrums in the supermarket and go to bed without making a fuss, while their mothers "continue looking so cool and sexy". [...]

In France a child is rarely considered an equal, but a
10 small human being ready to be formatted, partly by its parents, but mostly by the state education system. It has to be *encadré*, kept within a clearly and often rigidly defined framework that places disciplines such as manners and mathematics above creativity and expression.

15 A French child who has a tantrum is unlikely to cut any slack on the grounds that it is expressing itself, is quite likely to be smacked and, if the tantrums continue, packed off to see a child psychologist. The "terrible twos" is not a recognised phenomenon in France. [...]

20 Druckerman places emphasis on how French children are taught to be better behaved in public and social situations. Passengers on the Eurostar can often identify a child's nationality without hearing them speak. You can more or less bet the one running up and down the carriage screaming his head off will not be French.

Bénédicte Lohe-Le Blanc, 38, a teacher originally from Brittany, and her husband Vincent,
25 39, live with their three children, Sten, 11, Yaelle, nine, and Kenan, six, in west London. She believes British parents are lax with their children.

"I was at an English friend's house and her six-year-old son was thumping the piano as we were trying to speak. His mother said 'yes that's lovely, but not so loud'. He just carried on. I said to myself, if this were France, the child would have been hauled off to
30 another part of the room and made to stop. British parental culture is very relaxed, while we terrorise our children."

She is convinced this is a backlash from the laissez-faire attitudes that prevailed in France after the May 1968 student riots that brought a form of the swinging 60s to French society.

"In the wake of May 68 we were more relaxed and we rejected authority. But my genera-
35 tion saw the damage that lack of limits did to children and how it ultimately caused
them problems, so we went back to being authoritarian."

She added: "We consider our children to be small people, but they are not equal to an
adult. They need authority, they need rules and they need to be kept in line. A child is
a child and has his place. In France we see authority as a form of affection and believe
40 that a child blossoms because of, not in spite of, that authority. The bottom line is my
child can have his own opinion, but it's me who decides." [...]

*Extract from: Kim Willsher: The parenting gap: why French mothers prefer to use the firm smack of
authority, in: The Observer, January 1, 2012, p. 25.*

Comprehension

Task 5

**Find the appropriate vocabulary from the text
to conclude the sentences.**

a. A child who eats almost everything is not a ...
b. A child who cries and screams uncontrollably
   is having a ...
c. A parent who hits the child on its bottom is
   giving it a ...
d. Parents who are not strict are said to be ...
e. French parents believe that children need rules to be kept ...

Task 6

**Answer the following questions in your own words based on your understanding
of the text.**

a. Describe the differences in young children's behaviour in England and France.
b. Explain why the British and French approaches to child-rearing are so different.
c. How does the German child-rearing approach compare to those of the British and
   French?

Grammar

Compound prepositions

When we want to show that something has happened as a result of something else, we use
the compound prepositions *due to, owing to, on account of* or *because of* before noun phrases,
but not preceding independent clauses, i.e.:

I cannot go to work today **owing to** *my son's illness.* (correct)
I cannot go to work today **due to** *my son is sick.* (Not correct, because "... *my son is sick*" is
an independent clause.)

Due to can be used after the verb *be*, but *owing to* cannot.

*His absence today was **due to** illness.* (correct)
*His absence today was **owing to** illness.* (incorrect)

*We were unable to go on our excursion **on account of** the poor weather.* (correct)
***Because of** the poor weather, we were unable to go on our excursion.* (correct)

Task 7

Rewrite these two sentences as one sentence using one of the Compound Prepositions. Make any other necessary changes.

a. Many children are hospitalised each year. They are abused by family members.
b. Our kindergarten will be closed this summer. They will be expanding and modernizing the building.
c. Most three-year-olds cannot write their names. They lack hand-eye coordination.
d. We cannot disclose personal information. We have a confidentiality policy.
e. We could not hire Ms Peters. She did not have the required qualifications.
f. Rebecca cannot have any food with nuts in it. She has a nut allergy.

Activity

Task 8

Have a cross-cultural classroom debate on discipline. Split up into two teams. One team will support the French approach to child-rearing, while the other team will support the British parenting style. Before you open the debate discussion, each team should collect and prepare their arguments. Once both teams have presented their arguments, decide as a group which team was most persuasive.

Writing

Task 9

How did your parents raise you? Were they too strict, or not strict enough? Would you do anything differently as a parent? Write a short composition of no more than 200 words.

Listening-Transcriptions

Unit 1, Module 3

Finding a job

Sandra Hare

1 My name is Sandra Hare and I'm 55. I had studied Early Childhood Education and I worked as a preschool teacher for 24 years and I loved every minute of it. Because working in preschool is very strenuous work that requires a lot of energy, I'm looking around for a new employment opportunity better suited to my age. You see, my husband died
5 about a year ago and I'm caring for my elderly mother at home now. I just don't have the same amount of energy as I used to, but I'm not ready to retire yet; I don't want to sit at home. But I don't want to work full-time anymore either. And besides, I need an income. Whatever it is, working with children is an absolute must!

Geoffrey Madden

10 I'm Geoffrey Madden, 28 years old, with a degree in social work with a focus on education. I finished my college education three years ago and have been working until now in temporary positions. I'm looking for a permanent full-time position, preferably working with adolescents. My experience has been in local education authority settings and recreational facilities for troubled youths. I've thought about working in approved
15 homes or with at risk youths. I grew up in a multi-cultural environment in London myself and can appreciate the difficulties teens of minority backgrounds have in society. Naturally my native language is English, but I understand a bit of Bengali, too.

Julia Martens

My name is Julia Martens and I'm 19 years old. I'm currently attending the local vocational
20 college, studying Early Childhood Education. As I haven't finished my studies yet, I'm not exactly sure what kind of job I want. I love working with people, especially children – young children. When I was a child, I wanted to become a nurse. I spent a lot of time in hospital and the nurses who cared for me were my role models. I do have experience working as a summer camp counsellor, so I'm able to plan and facilitate group activities.
25 I'm qualified in First Aid and CPR.

Claire Peters

Claire Peters is my name. I'm 42 years young and a full-time mum of two children, eight and ten. I've been unemployed for ten years, since the birth of my oldest daughter. Now, that my kids are older and more independent, I feel it's time for me to go back to work.
30 I'd like flexible part-time employment during the day in the field in which I got my training: Early Childhood Education. My first working experience after college was working with children with learning disabilities. I did that for about for about six years before I decided to have kids of my own. It would be nice to work with infants, although it's been a while since I comforted little babies!

Unit 7, Module 1

Teenage confessions

35 **Emma, 17**

I don't like looking at myself in the mirror. All I see is a fat, ugly girl looking back at me. I turn sideways and see the bulge below my waist. I see a huge bum and protruding hips and thighs. I hate my body.

It all started when I was about 13. I was fond of a lad at school at the time, and I thought
40 if I looked really good, better than any of the other girls, he would finally notice me. I started dieting.

Genetically, I was never predestined to be thin. Because my mum is overweight and my father used to be overweight, my parents were very conscientious about what we eat. Whenever I wanted to eat something high in calorie, like ice-cream or pizza, my mum would
45 always make me feel guilty for it, as if I were committing a sin. I began to believe it myself.

At the beginning, dieting required a lot of self-discipline. It was frustrating at first, but when I finally lost my first stone, I was really proud of myself. Now, I measure my success according to my weight. Seeing the scale go down makes me feel really good about myself. I'm so scared of gaining weight. I don't want to be a failure and I'm completely
50 fixed on not letting myself succumb to my weakness. There's always a little devil looking over my shoulder – a voice in my head that scolds me for eating something I shouldn't.

Whenever my schoolmates invite me to come over for a movie night or a party, I don't go because I don't want to be tempted by the food and drink. I try to think of all kinds of excuses to decline food. And when I am forced to eat, I feel like I am betraying myself
55 and then I hate myself all over again.

Stephen, 18

As soon as I come home from school, I turn on my computer. On weekdays, I play for about five or six hours at a time. But at weekends I may spend up to 15 hours online. Once I get started, I just can't stop. I sit there in front of the screen and I'm in a totally
60 different world, where times stands still. In the virtual world I can create new roles for myself and take on superhuman powers. Sometimes I get so involved in my role I forget to eat, drink and sleep; I lose track of time. When I play I forget all of my problems; it's like escaping reality for a few hours.

My parents are concerned that I'm shutting myself off from my friends. But I'm not!
65 Online games are actually quite social. When you play online, you play with different people from all over the world. It's even easier to make friends online than in real life. You work together as a team; it gives you a sense of belonging as you work towards a common goal. Sometimes I organise game parties; I invite my friends over and we play together.

70 My parents think I'm an addict. I wouldn't say I'm addicted; there are plenty of people who watch telly for five or six hours a day. The game makes you want to keep playing; it's hard to let go because it's potentially never-ending. With each new quest or each new level, you always try to top yourself and your opponents. You always have to set yourself a new goal, and every time you reach that goal, you feel rewarded. That's what
75 I live for. It's awesome.

Jane, 16

When Amy Winehouse died, it really shook me up. I really don't want to end up like her. I'm 16 and I weigh 16 stones and yet I can drink ... well – more than you might expect.

80 I go out with my friends to the pubs at the weekends. It's the only thing to do around here really. We're a big circle of friends, and we each pony up for a round of pints. So, by the end of the evening, we've all had at least six pints and are really wasted. Whoever drinks the most is like the paragon, so it becomes kind of competitive. We all have a good time together while we're there, but I usually don't remember anything by the morning. Sometimes I regret it, when I hear about the things I've said and done the next day. I've 85 tried to imagine what my life would be like if I stopped drinking, but to tell you the truth, I wouldn't want to miss hanging out with my mates. They're like family to me.

My parents got divorced when I was 13. My father drank, and he would get pretty aggressive. My mum set him an ultimatum, but he just couldn't stay sober. I stayed with my mum, but we've had a rough time, the two of us. I want to make her proud of me, 90 so I put myself under a lot of academic pressure. But it can be so overwhelming at times. I look forward to the weekends to relieve stress and numb the pain.

Unit 10, Module 1, Task 1

Can

1 I am 23, and I live in Berlin. I recently decided to become a German citizen and to give up my Turkish citizenship. This will make living in Germany easier even though most Germans don't consider me German. When I visit my extended family in Ankara, most people there think I am German. So, I'm not really Turkish, but not really German either.

5 Selma

I just moved to the United States because my husband got a good job in Boston in a big company. Most people here don't even seem to notice my headscarf. I am quite relieved about that!

Amelia

10 Most people assume I am German until they talk to me. Then they realise that I must be Scandinavian. I actually come from Denmark, but I have spent most of my life in Australia – so I consider myself Australian. I was able to get a very good position in Germany because of the various languages I can speak. I've made a lot of new friends in Germany, and I enjoy living here. I plan on staying for at least the next five years.

15 Katherine

I have been living in Ottawa, the capital of Canada, for the past two years. I enjoy living here because most people take it for granted that I am Canadian. Everybody here has mixed roots, and most people think positively of the fact that mine are Lebanese. I grew up in Cambridge because both of my parents work at the university there. I also lived 20 in Düsseldorf for a few months, but because of the language and cultural differences there, I felt like an outsider.

Vocabulary
English – German

Unit 1: Working with children – working for institutions of childcare

after-school care club	[ˌɑːftə ˈskuːl kɜə klʌb]	Hort
approved school (UK)	[əˈpruːvd ˌskuːl]	Erziehungsheim
childminder	[ˈtʃaɪld ˌmaɪndə]	Tagesmutter
child-rearing	[ˈtʃaɪld ˌrɪərɪŋ]	Erziehung
coin	[kɔɪn]	(ein Wort) erfinden/prägen
compulsory	[kəmˈpʌlsəri]	verpflichtend
conducive	[kənˈdjuːsɪv]	dienlich, zu etw. beitragend
contemporaneously	[kənˌtempəˈreɪnɪəsli]	gleichzeitig
CPR (cardiopulmonary resuscitation)	[siː piː ɑː (ˌkɑːdiəʊˈpʌlmənəri rɪˌsʌsɪˈteɪʃən)]	die Herz-Lungen-Reanimation
crèche	[kreʃ]	Kinderkrippe
discriminatory	[dɪˈskrɪmɪnətri]	benachteiligend
early childhood practitioner	[ˈɜːli ˈtʃaɪldhʊd prækˈtɪʃənə]	Erzieher/-in
educator	[ˈedʒuːkeɪtə]	Pädagoge
equipment	[ɪˈkwɪpmənt]	Anlage, Ausrüstung
found sth.	[ˈfaʊnd ˌsʌmθɪŋ]	etw. gründen
infant	[ˈɪnfənt]	Säugling
Makaton®	[ˈmækətɒn]	eine Gebärdensprache
meagre	[ˈmiːgə]	ärmlich, mager
merely	[ˈmɪəli]	lediglich
monitor	[ˈmɒnɪtə]	beaufsichtigen, überwachen
preferential treatment	[ˌprefəˈrenʃəl ˈtriːtmənt]	bevorzugte Behandlung
prejudice	[ˈpredʒədɪs]	Vorurteil, Befangenheit
provision	[prəˈvɪʒən]	Bereitstellung, Beschaffung
reception	[rɪˈsepʃən]	Vorschule
recreation facility	[ˌriːkriˈeɪʃən fəˈsɪləti]	Freizeiteinrichtung
reform school (US)	[rɪˈfɔːm ˌskuːl]	Erziehungsheim
refuge	[ˈrefjuːdʒ]	Schutzort, Zuflucht
retire	[rɪˈtaɪə]	in Ruhestand gehen
unsettling	[ˌʌnˈsetlɪŋ]	beunruhigend
volunteer	[ˌvɒlənˈtɪə]	ehrenamtlich tätig sein

Unit 2: Protecting children

abuse	[əˈbjuːs]	Missbrauch
at risk	[æt ˈrɪsk]	gefährdet
authorized	[ˈɔːθəraɪzd]	ermächtigt
budgeting	[ˈbʌdʒɪtɪŋ]	Haushaltsplanung
congenital	[kənˈdʒenɪtəl]	angeboren
consent	[kənˈsent]	Bewilligung
dietician	[ˌdaɪəˈtɪʃən]	Ernährungswissenschaftler
disadvantaged	[ˌdɪsədˈvɑːntɪdʒd]	benachteiligt
disclose	[dɪsˈkləʊz]	offenbaren

disruptive	[dɪsˈrʌptɪv]	unterbrechend
distressed	[dɪsˈtrest]	bekümmert
excerpt	[ˈeksɜːpt]	Ausschnitt
foster	[ˈfɒstə]	in Pflege haben, fördern
foster child/parents	[ˈfɒstə ˌtʃaɪld / ˈpeərənts]	Pflegekind/-eltern
impact	[ˈɪmpækt]	Auswirkung
impair	[ɪmˈpeə]	beeinträchtigen
inappropriate	[ˌɪnəˈprəʊpriət]	unangemessen
investigation	[ɪnˌvestɪˈgeɪʃən]	Untersuchung
justified	[ˈdʒʌstɪfaɪd]	berechtigt
lawfully	[ˈlɔːfʊli]	rechtmäßig
minutes	[ˈmɪnɪts]	Protokoll
moderate	[ˈmɒdərət]	gemäßigt
monitor	[ˈmɒnɪtə]	überwachen
neglect	[nɪˈglekt]	Nachlässigkeit
overcrowded	[ˌəʊvəˈkraʊdɪd]	überbelegt
praise	[preɪz]	loben
prediction	[prɪˈdɪkʃən]	Voraussage
reassure	[riːəˈʃʊə]	beruhigen
record	[rɪˈkɔːd]	erfassen
refer	[rɪˈfɜː]	verweisen
session	[ˈseʃən]	Sitzung
sharing	[ˈʃeərɪŋ]	Austausch
significant	[sɪgˈnɪfɪkənt]	bedeutend
slight	[slaɪt]	gering
speech therapy	[ˈspiːtʃ ˌθerəpi]	Logopädie
supportive	[səˈpɔːtɪv]	unterstützend
vulnerable	[ˈvʌlnərəbl]	verwundbar
welfare	[ˈwelfeə]	Wohl

Unit 3: Social background

Xadmissions policy	[ədˈmɪʃənz ˈpɒlisi]	Zulassungsverfahren
Xafford sth.	[əˈfɔːd ˌsʌmθɪŋ]	sich etw. leisten
asylum seeker	[əˈsaɪləm ˈsiːkə]	Asylsuchende/-r
attend school	[əˌtend ˈskuːl]	Schule besuchen
chief executive	[ˈtʃiːf ɪgˈzekjətɪv]	Geschäftsleiter/-in
cite	[saɪt]	zitieren
day care facility	[ˈdeɪ ˌkeə fəˈsɪləti]	Kindertagesbetreuung, Kindertagesstätte
depict sth.	[dɪˈpɪkt ˌsʌmθɪŋ]	bildlich darstellen
hardship	[ˈhɑːdʃɪp]	Beschwernis
inner city	[ˌɪnə ˈsɪti]	Innenstadt
job vacancies	[ˈdʒɒb ˌveɪkənsiz]	freie Arbeitsstellen
language proficiency	[ˈlæŋwɪdʒ prəˈfɪʃənsi]	Sprachkompetenz
nursery	[ˈnɜːsəri]	Kindertagesstätte, Kindergarten, Kinderladen
political persecution	[pəˈlɪtɪkəl ˌpɜːsɪˈkjuːʃən]	politische Verfolgung
poverty line	[ˈpɒvəti ˌlaɪn]	Armutsgrenze
poverty trap	[ˈpɒvəti ˌtræp]	Armutsfalle
A prohibitively expensive	[prəʊˈhɪbətɪvli ɪkˈspensɪv]	unbezahlbar, unverschämt teuer

refurbish	[ˌriːˈfɜːbɪʃ]	renovieren
rudimentary	[ˌruːdɪˈmentəri]	elementar
shortage of	[ˈʃɔːtɪdʒ ɒf]	Mangel an
single-raising mother	[ˈsɪŋgl ˌreɪzɪŋ ˈmʌðə]	alleinerziehende Mutter
social housing	[ˌsəʊʃəl ˈhaʊzɪŋ]	Sozialwohnung
temporary accommodation	[ˈtempərəri əˌkɒməˈdeɪʃən]	provisorische Unterkunft
unemployment benefit	[ˌʌnɪmplɔɪmənt ˈbenəfɪt]	Arbeitslosengeld
urgent	[ˈɜːdʒənt]	dringend
vocational college	[vəʊˈkeɪʃənəl ˈkɒlɪdʒ]	Volkshochschule
voluntary worker	[ˈvɒləntəri ˈwɜːkə]	freiwillige/-r Mitarbeiter/-in
vulnerable	[ˈvʌlnərəbl]	schutzbedürftig, verletzlich
workforce	[ˈwɜːkfɔːs]	Arbeiterschaft

Unit 4: Living in a family

accountant	[əˈkaʊntənt]	Buchhalter/-in
average	[ˈævərɪdʒ]	Durchschnitt
avoid	[əˈvɔɪd]	vermeiden
be bullied	[bi ˈbʊlid]	eingeschüchtert werden
be made up of sth.	[bi meɪd ˈʌp əf sʌmθɪŋ]	aus etw. bestehen
be raised	[bi ˈreɪzd]	aufgezogen werden
be teased	[bi ˈtiːzd]	gehänselt werden
biological parents	[ˌbaɪəˈlɒdʒɪkəl ˈpeərənts]	leibliche Eltern
blend	[blend]	(ver-)mischen
breadwinner	[ˈbredwɪnə]	Ernährer
childless family	[ˈtʃaɪldləs ˈfæməli]	kinderlose Familie
consider	[kənˈsɪdə]	bedenken, erwägen
consist of	[kənˈsɪst ɒf]	bestehen aus, aus etw. gebildet sein
divorce	[dɪˈvɔːs]	Scheidung/scheiden lassen
elope with sb.	[ɪˈləʊp wɪð sʌmbədi]	mit jmd. durchbrennen
explore	[ɪkˈsplɔː]	erforschen, untersuchen
extend	[ɪkˈstend]	erweitern, verlängern
honeymoon	[ˈhʌnimuːn]	Flitterwochen
immediate family	[ɪˈmiːdiət ˈfæməli]	engste Angehörige
impairment	[ɪmˈpeəmənt]	Beeinträchtigung, Schwächung
interaction	[ˌɪntərˈækʃən]	Interaktion, Wechselwirkung
judgement	[ˈdʒʌdʒmənt]	Beurteilung, Urteil
lone mother	[ləʊn ˈmʌðə]	alleinerziehende Mutter
maintain sth.	[meɪnˈteɪn ˌsʌmθɪŋ]	etw. beibehalten, aufrechterhalten, instand halten
pass away	[pɑːs əˈweɪ]	sterben, entschlafen
patch	[pætʃ]	Flicken
patchwork	[ˈpætʃwɜːk]	Flickenteppich, Flickwerk
ponder sth.	[ˈpɒndə sʌmθɪŋ]	etw. durchdenken
previously	[ˈpriːviəsli]	vorher
procedure	[prəˈsiːdʒə]	Ablauf
prosperous	[ˈprɒspərəs]	wohlhabend, florierend
same-sex parents	[ˌseɪmseks ˈpeərənts]	gleichgeschlechtliche Eltern
significant	[sɪgˈnɪfɪkənt]	bedeutend, beachtlich
single parents	[ˌsɪŋgl ˈpeərənts]	alleinerziehende Eltern

sperm donor	['spɜːm ˌdəʊnə]	Samenspender
spread out	[ˌspred 'aʊt]	sich ausbreiten
stepchildren	['step̩tʃɪldrən]	Stiefkinder
step-parents	['step ˌpeərənts]	Stiefeltern
surrogate mother	[ˌsʌrəgɪt 'mʌðə]	Leihmutter

Unit 5: Stages of development

ability	[ə'bɪləti]	Fähigkeit, Kompetenz
achieve	[ə'tʃiːv]	erreichen
allow	[ə'laʊ]	erlauben
burden with sth.	['bɜːdən wɪð sʌmθɪŋ]	mit etw. belasten
confidence	['kɒnfɪdəns]	(Selbst-)Vertrauen
context	['kɒntekst]	Zusammenhang
develop	[dɪ'veləp]	entwickeln, kultivieren
differ from sth.	['dɪfə frɒm sʌmθɪŋ]	von etw. abweichen, sich unterscheiden
direct surroundings	[ˌdɪrekt sə'raʊndɪŋz]; [ˌdaɪ-]	unmittelbare Umgebung, Umwelt
enable	[ɪn'eɪbl]	ermöglichen
extend into sth.	[ɪk'stend ˌɪntu sʌmθɪŋ]	in etw. hineinreichen
facilitate	[fə'sɪlɪteɪt]	erleichtern
fidelity	[fɪ'deləti]	Treue
(guilt) feelings	[(gɪlt) 'fiːlɪŋz]	(Schuld-)Gefühle
holistic	[həʊ'lɪstɪk]	ganzheitlich
immediate environment	[ɪ'miːdiət ɪn'vaɪərənmənt]	unmittelbare Umgebung, Umwelt
independence	[ɪndɪ'pendəns]	Unabhängigkeit
inevitable	[ɪn'evɪtəbl]	unvermeidbar
inhibition	[ɪnhɪ'bɪʃən]	Hemmung
interfere	[ɪntə'fɪə]	einmischen
intervene	[ɪntə'viːn]	eingreifen, intervenieren
maturity	[mə'tjʊərəti]	Reife
observe/observation	[əb'zɜːv / ˌɒbzə'veɪʃən]	beobachten/Beobachtung
perform a task	[pə'fɔːm ə tɑːsk]	eine Aufgabe ausführen
permission	[pə'mɪʃən]	Erlaubnis
permit	[pə'mɪt]	erlauben
persevere	[ˌpɜːsɪ'vɪə]	durchhalten, sich beharrlich bemühen
promote	[prə'məʊt]	fördern
purpose	['pɜːpəs]	der Zweck
self-esteem	['self ɪ'stiːm]	die Selbstachtung
self-inhibiting	['self ɪn'hɪbɪtɪŋ]	selbsthemmend

Unit 6: Working with children under three

acquisition	[ˌækwɪ'zɪʃən]	Erwerb
anxiety	[æŋ'zaɪəti]	Sorge
appreciate	[ə'priːʃieɪt]	anerkennen, verstehen
apron	['eɪprən]	Schürze
assertion	[ə'sɜːʃən]	Erklärung, Behauptung
attribute to sth.	[ə'trɪbjuːt tu 'sʌmθɪŋ]	auf etw. zurückführen
benchmark	['bentʃmɑːk]	Maßstab

competency/competence	['kɒmpɪtənsi / 'kɒmpɪtəns]	Fähigkeit, Kompetenz
comply with sth.	[kəm'plaɪ wɪð sʌmθɪŋ]	etw. befolgen
continuity	[ˌkɒntɪ'njuːəti]	durchhalten, Kontinuität
convenient	[kən'viːniənt]	praktisch, gelegen
convey	[kən'veɪ]	vermitteln, zum Ausdruck bringen
cot	[kɒt]	Kinderbettchen, Feldbett
crawl	[krɔːl]	krabbeln
crib	[krɪb]	Kinderbett
disobedience	[ˌdɪsəʊ'biːdɪəns]	Ungehorsam
dispense	[dɪ'spens]	austeilen
disturbed	[dɪ'stɜːbd]	verhaltensgestört
emergence	[ɪ'mɜːdʒəns]	Entstehung, auch: Auftauchen
enhance	[ɪn'hɑːns]	verbessern
equipment	[ɪ'kwɪpmənt]	Ausstattung
evident	['evɪdənt]	ersichtlich
expectation	[ˌekspek'teɪʃən]	Erwartung
exposure	[ɪk'spəʊʒə]	Kontakt
facility	[fə'sɪləti]	Einrichtung
flannel	['flænəl]	Waschlappen
germs	[dʒɜːmz]	Keime, Bazillen
grapple with sth.	['græpl wɪð sʌmθɪŋ]	sich mit etw. auseinandersetzen
grasp	[grɑːsp]	verstehen, begreifen
immune system	[ɪ'mjuːn ˌsɪstəm]	Immunsystem
implicitly	[ɪm'plɪsɪtli]	indirekt
(be) in charge of	[(bi) ɪn tʃɑːdʒ ɒf]	für etw. verantwortlich (sein)
inappropriate	[ˌɪnə'prəʊpriət]	ungeeignet
keen	[kiːn]	stark
marginal	['mɑːdʒɪnəl]	gering
medium	['miːdiəm]	Medium
multiplicity	[ˌmʌltɪ'plɪsəti]	Vielzahl
nappy	['næpi]	Windel
negotiation skills	[nɪˌgəʊʃi'eɪʃən ˌskɪlz]	Verhandlungsgeschick
observe	[əb'zɜːv]	beachten
pacify	['pæsɪfaɪ]	beruhigen
perception	[pə'sepʃən]	Wahrnehmung
potty	['pɒti]	Töpfchen
provision	[prə'vɪʒən]	Bereitstellung, Beschaffung
relieve	[rɪ'liːv]	lindern, abbauen
reluctant	[rɪ'lʌktənt]	zögernd, unwillig
retain	[rɪ'teɪn]	beibehalten
salary	['sæləri]	Einkommen
soiled	['sɔɪld]	verschmutzt
sound	[saʊnd]	heil, stabil
subsidized	['sʌbsɪdaɪzd]	subventioniert
susceptible	[sə'septəbl]	anfällig
transition	[træn'zɪʃən]	Übergang
validate	['vælɪdeɪt]	etw. bestätigen
waste	[weɪst]	Abfall

Unit 7: Growing up

adolescent	[ˌædəˈlesənt]	Jugendliche
A-levels	[ˈeɪlevəlz]	Abitur
amygdala	[əˈmɪgdələ]	Amygdala (Teil des menschlichen Gehirns)
be fixed on sth.	[bi ˈfɪkst ɒn sʌmθɪŋ]	eingenommen sein von etw.
bulge	[bʌldʒ]	Wölbung, Rundung
bullying	[ˈbʊliɪŋ]	Mobbing
bum	[bʌm]	Hintern, Po
conduct	[ˈkɒndʌkt]	Verhalten
deluge	[ˈdeljuːdʒ]	überschwemmen
deprive sb. of sth.	[dɪˈpraɪv sʌmbədi ɒf sʌmθɪŋ]	jmd. etwas entziehen/vorenthalten
device	[dɪˈvaɪs]	Gerät
devote oneself to sb.	[dɪˈvəʊt wʌnˈself tu sʌmbədi]	jmd. hingebungsvoll lieben, sich jmd. Widmen, sich für jmd. aufopfern
disadvantaged	[ˌdɪsədˈvɑːntɪdʒd]	benachteiligt
distorted	[dɪˈstɔːtɪd]	verzerrt
dote on sb.	[ˈdəʊt ɒn sʌmbədi]	jmd. verhätscheln
eagerness	[ˈiːgənəs]	Eifer, Ungeduld
encumbrance	[ɪnˈkʌmbrəns]	Belastung
erratic	[ɪˈrætɪk]	sprunghaft, launisch
erupt	[ɪˈrʌpt]	ausbrechen
exhibit	[ɪgˈzɪbɪt]	aufzeigen
facial expression	[ˈfeɪʃəl ɪkˈspreʃən]	Gesichtsausdruck
futile	[ˈfjuːtaɪl]	aussichtslos
hover	[ˈhɒvə]	über etwas schweben
humiliation	[hjuːˌmɪliˈeɪʃən]	Erniedrigung
inappropriate	[ˌɪnəˈprəʊpriət]	unangebracht
inevitable	[ɪˈnevɪtəbl]	unabwendbar
mature	[məˈtjʊə]	reifen, sich entwickeln
meddle	[ˈmedl]	sich einmischen
mollycoddle sb.	[ˈmɒliˌkɒdl sʌmbədi]	jmd. verhätscheln
mood swings	[muːd swɪŋz]	Stimmungsschwankungen
numb	[nʌm]	betäuben
obstacles	[ˈɒbstəklz]	Hürden, Hindernisse
offset sth.	[ˌɒfˈset sʌmθɪŋ]	etwas ausgleichen
offspring	[ˈɒfsprɪŋ]	Nachwuchs
pamper sb.	[ˈpæmpə sʌmbədi]	jmd. verwöhnen
paragon	[ˈpærəgən]	Vorbild
placid	[ˈplæsɪd]	gelassen, seelenruhig
predestined	[ˌpriːˈdestɪnd]	prädestiniert
premises	[ˈpremɪsɪz]	Räumlichkeiten
prenatal	[ˌpriːˈneɪtəl]	vorgeburtlich, pränatal
preoccupation	[priːˌɒkjəˈpeɪʃən]	Beschäftigung, Vertieftsein
protruding	[prəˈtruːdɪŋ]	hinausragend
self-reliant	[ˌselfrɪˈlaɪənt]	selbstständig
slag (colloq.)	[slæg]	Schlampe (ugs.)
sober	[ˈsəʊbə]	nüchtern

social cues	['səʊʃəl kjuːz]	Signale durch Gesten und Körpersprache
spiteful	['spaɪtfʊl]	gemein, gehässig
stone (plural: stone)	[stəʊn]	6,35 kg (brit. Gewichtseinheit)
stoop to sth.	['stuːp tu sʌmθɪŋ]	sich zu etw. herablassen
succumb to sb./sth.	[sə'kʌm tu sʌmbədi / sʌmθɪŋ]	jmd./etw. erliegen
surveillance	[sə'veɪləns]	Überwachung
swerve	[swɜːv]	plötzlich abweichen
thrills	[θrɪlz]	Kicks, Angstlust
ubiquitous	[juː'bɪkwɪtəs]	allgegenwärtig
undermine	[ˌʌndə'maɪn]	untergraben
unduly	[ʌn'djuːli]	unangemessenerweise
vicariously	[vɪ'keəriəsli]	indirekt
vulnerable	['vʌlnərəbl]	verwundbar, gefährdet
whore (colloq.)	[hɔː]	Hure (ugs.)
YWCA	[waɪ 'dʌbljuː siː eɪ]	Young Women's Club of America

Unit 8: Food and health

accuse	[ə'kjuːz]	anklagen
airwaves	['eəweɪvz]	Ätherwellen
anxious	['æŋkʃəs]	besorgt
appeal to	[ə'piːl tu]	gefallen
benefits	['benəfɪts]	Vorteile
body mass index	['bɒdi mæs 'ɪndeks]	Körpergewichtsindex
collapse	[kə'læps]	einstürzen
concise	[kən'saɪs]	knapp und präzise
consistently	[kən'sɪstəntli]	beständig
crack	[kræk]	Riss
decline	[dɪ'klaɪn]	senken
deprive	[dɪ'praɪv]	aberkennen, entziehen
determining	[dɪ'tɜːmɪnɪŋ]	bestimmend
digest	[daɪ'dʒest]	verdauen
disorder	[dɪ'sɔːdə]	Erkrankung
disruption	[dɪs'rʌpʃən]	Unterbrechung
equivalent	[ɪ'kwɪvələnt]	gleichwertig
impact	[ɪm'pækt]	Auswirkungen haben
initiate	[ɪ'nɪʃieɪt]	einleiten
nutrition	[njuː'trɪʃən]	Essen, Nahrung
nutritional advisor	[njuː'trɪʃənəl əd'vaɪzə]	Ernährungsberater
obesity	[əʊ'biːsəti]	Fettleibigkeit
plug	[plʌg]	verstopfen
pulse	[pʌls]	Hülsenfrucht
ratings	['reɪtɪŋz]	Einschaltquoten
reliance	[rɪ'laɪəns]	Vertrauen
stone (plural: stone)	[stəʊn]	6,35 kg (brit. Gewichtseinheit)
tough	[tʌf]	hart
tricky	['trɪki]	verzwickt
unsuitable	[ʌn'sjuːtəbl]	ungeeignet

Unit 9: Disability and illness

alleged	[əˈledʒd]	angeblich
attitude	[ˈætɪtjuːd]	Gesinnung
barking	[ˈbɑːkɪŋ]	bellend
bereavement	[bɪˈriːvmənt]	Todesfall
blotchy	[ˈblɒtʃi]	fleckig
Braille	[breɪl]	Blindenschrift
conduct	[kənˈdʌkt]	durchführen
dexterity	[deksˈterəti]	Geschicklichkeit
diarrhoea	[ˌdaɪəˈrɪə]	Durchfall
facilities	[fəˈsɪlətiz]	Anlageteile
feeble	[ˈfiːbl]	schwach
framework	[ˈfreɪmwɜːk]	Bezugssystem
geared to	[gɪəd tu]	abgestimmt auf
ground-breaking	[ˈgraʊndˌbreɪkɪŋ]	bahnbrechend
grounds	[graʊndz]	Gelände/Gründe
humiliating	[hjuːˈmɪlieɪtɪŋ]	demütigend
incapacity	[ˌɪnkəˈpæsəti]	Unfähigkeit
inevitable	[ɪˈnevɪtəbl]	unvermeidlich
jumbled	[ˈdʒʌmbld]	durcheinander
limb	[lɪm]	Glied
mainstream	[ˈmeɪnstriːm]	einbinden
measles	[ˈmiːzlz]	Masern
numeracy	[ˈnjuːmərəsi]	Rechenkenntnis
objectives	[əbˈdʒektɪvz]	Ziele
occupational therapist	[ˌɒkjəˈpeɪʃənəl ˈθerəpɪst]	Ergotherapeut/-in
occupational therapy	[ˌɒkjəˈpeɪʃənəl ˈθerəpi]	Ergotherapie
prolong	[prəʊˈlɒŋ]	verlängern
raspy	[ˈrɑːspi]	kratzend
reaffirm	[ˌriːəˈfɜːm]	beteuern
rubella/German measles	[ruːˈbelə / ˈdʒɜːmən ˈmiːzlz]	Röteln
segregated	[ˈsegrɪgeɪtɪd]	getrennt
special needs	[ˈspeʃəl niːdz]	besondere Förderung
tailored	[ˈteɪləd]	angepasst
testimony	[ˈtestɪməni]	Zeugnis
threatening	[ˈθretnɪŋ]	bedrohlich
transformation	[ˌtrænsfəˈmeɪʃən]	Verwandlung
transition	[trænˈzɪʃən]	Übergang
Treasury	[ˈtreʒəri]	Finanzministerium
ward	[wɔːd]	Station
whooping cough	[ˈhuːpɪŋkɒf]	Keuchhusten

Unit 10: Ethnic diversity

acquire sth.	[əˈkwaɪə sʌmθɪŋ]	etw. erwerben
adopt	[əˈdɒpt]	annehmen
advent	[ədˈvent]	Beginn
alienated	[ˈeɪliəneɪtɪd]	befremdet, entfremdet

appeal	[əˈpiːl]	Anreiz
assumption	[əˈsʌmpʃən]	Annahme, Vermutung
citizenship	[ˈsɪtɪzənʃɪp]	Bürgerschaft, Staatsangehörigkeit
dedicated	[ˈdedɪkeɪtɪd]	zweckbestimmt
delayed	[dɪˈleɪd]	verspätet
distorted	[dɪˈstɔːtɪd]	verzerrt
effective	[ɪˈfektɪv]	wirksam
embrace	[ɪmˈbreɪs]	einbeziehen
encounter	[ɪnˈkaʊntə]	antreffen
enrich	[ɪnˈrɪtʃ]	bereichern
homogeneous	[ˌhɒməˈdʒiːnɪəs]	gleichartig
imperceptible	[ˌɪmpəˈseptəbl]	unmerklich
in the midst of	[ɪn ðə mɪdst ɒf]	inmitten von, unter
indigenous	[ɪnˈdɪdʒənəs]	einheimisch
indistinguishable	[ˌɪndɪˈstɪŋgwɪʃəbl]	ununterscheidbar
influx	[ˈɪnflʌks]	Zustrom
inhabitants	[ɪnˈhæbɪtənts]	Einwohnerschaft
instructions	[ɪnˈstrʌkʃənz]	Anweisungen
intertwine	[ˌɪntəˈtwaɪn]	ineinandergreifen
interweave	[ˌɪntəˈwiːv]	verweben
issue	[ˈɪʃuː]	Frage, Thema, Angelegenheit
perceive	[pəˈsiːv]	wahrnehmen
reluctant	[rɪˈlʌktənt]	unwillig
representation	[ˌreprɪzenˈteɪʃən]	Darstellung, Vertretung
reputable	[ˈrepjətəbl]	achtbar
tackle	[ˈtækl]	anpacken
vibrant	[ˈvaɪbrənt]	lebhaft

Unit 11: Social learning and behaviour

ambitious	[æmˈbɪʃəs]	ehrgeizig
aptitude	[ˈæptɪtjuːd]	Fähigkeit
bleak	[bliːk]	duster, trostlos
blur	[blɜː]	verwischen
clay	[kleɪ]	Knete
contest	[kənˈtest]	bestreiten
cope with sth.	[kəʊp wɪð sʌmθɪŋ]	mit etw. fertigwerden
deliberately	[dɪˈlɪbərətli]	absichtlich
deprivation	[ˌdeprɪˈveɪʃən]	Entzug, Mangel
designated	[ˈdezɪgneɪtɪd]	vorgesehen
detrimental	[ˌdetrɪˈmentəl]	schädlich, nachteilig
distract sb.	[dɪˈstrækt sʌmbədi]	jmd. ablenken
endorse	[ɪnˈdɔːs]	befürworten
engage in sth.	[ɪnˈgeɪdʒ ɪn sʌmθɪŋ]	sich mit etw. beschäftigen
fuss	[fʌs]	Aufhebens
gadgets	[ˈgædʒɪts]	technische Spielerei
gratification	[ˌgrætɪfɪˈkeɪʃən]	Belohnung
implication	[ˌɪmplɪˈkeɪʃən]	Auswirkung, Konsequenz
innate	[ɪˈneɪt]	angeboren

make-believe	['meɪk bɪ,liːv]	Fantasie
predisposition	[,priːdɪspə'zɪʃən]	Veranlagung
rebuttal	[rɪ'hʌtəl]	Widerlegung
resist	[rɪ'zɪst]	widerstehen
reward	[rɪ'wɔːd]	Belohnung
self-regulation	[,self regjə'leɪʃən]	Selbstregulierung
spatial skills	['speɪʃəl skɪlz]	räumliche Wahrnehmung
temptation	[temp'teɪʃən]	Verlockung
unadulterated	[,ʌnə'dʌltəreɪtɪd]	ungetrübt, unverfälscht

Unit 12: Emergencies in daily life

accident	['æksɪdənt]	Unfall
ambulance	['æmbjələns]	Krankenwagen
anchored	['æŋkəd]	befestigt
bear the weight	[beə ðə weɪt]	Gewicht tragen
blade	[bleɪd]	Klinge
bruise	[bruːz]	blauer Fleck
cardiopulmonary resuscitation	[,kɑːdiəʊ'pʌlmənəri rɪ,sʌsɪ'teɪʃən]	Herz-Lungen-Reanimation
cause	[kɔːz]	Ursache
checklist	['tʃeklɪst]	Überprüfungsliste
choke on sth.	[tʃəʊk ɒn sʌmθɪŋ]	sich an etw. verschlucken
climbing frame	['klaɪmɪŋ ,freɪm]	Klettergerüst
comprehensive	[,kɒmprɪ'hensɪv]	umfassend
emergency room	[ɪ'mɜːdʒənsi ,rʊm]	Notaufnahme
exercise caution	['eksəsaɪz 'kɔːʃən]	Vorsicht walten lassen
fire drill	['faɪə ,drɪl]	Feuerübung
guardrail	['gɑːdreɪl]	Absturzsicherung
harmful	['hɑːmfʊl]	gesundheitsschädlich
heath and safety	[helθ ənd 'seɪfti]	Sicherheit und Gesundheitsschutz
heatstroke	['hiːtstrəʊk]	Hitzschlag
imaginativeness	[ɪ'mædʒɪnətɪvnəs]	Ideenreichtum, Phantasiereichtum
impair one's health	[ɪm'peə wʌnz helθ]	seiner Gesundheit schaden
incident report	['ɪnsɪdənt rɪ'pɔːt]	Vorgangsbericht
injury	['ɪndʒəri]	Verletzung
lose one's footing	[luːz wʌnz 'fʊtɪŋ]	Halt verlieren
paramedic	[,pærə'medɪk]	Rettungssanitäter
pedestrian crossing	[pɪ'destriən 'krɒsɪŋ]	Fußgängerübergang
playthings	['pleɪθɪŋz]	Spielzeuge
poisoning	['pɔɪzənɪŋ]	Vergiftung
poorly ventilated room	['pʊəli 'ventɪleɪtɪd rʊm]	schlecht gelüfteter Raum
position	[pə'zɪʃən]	Stellung
prompt	[prɒmt]	anregen
public transport	['pʌblɪk 'trænspɔːt]	öffentlicher Personennahverkehr
reassuring	[,riːə'ʃʊərɪŋ]	beruhigend
requirements	[rɪ'kwaɪəmənts]	Anforderungen
scope	[skəʊp]	Spielraum
skirting board	['skɜːtɪŋbɔːd]	Scheuerleiste, Sockelleiste

smoke detector	['sməʊk dɪˌtektə]	Rauchmelder
suffocation	[ˌsʌfə'keɪʃən]	Erstickung
supervise	['sjuːpəvaɪz]	beaufsichtigen, kontrollieren, überwachen

Unit 13: Conflict management

admonishment	[əd'mɒnɪʃmənt]	Ermahnung
anticipate	[æn'tɪsɪpeɪt]	erwarten
archaic	[aːˈkeɪɪk]	altertümlich
blameful	['bleɪmfʊl]	tadelnswert
bribe	[braɪb]	bestechen
coax sb. to do sth.	[kəʊks sʌmbədi tu duː sʌmθɪŋ]	jmd. etw. entlocken; jmd. dazu bringen, etw. zu tun
cut sb. some slack	[kʌt sʌmbədi sʌm slæk]	Nachsicht mit jmd. haben
diligence	['dɪlɪdʒəns]	Fleiß
discourage	[dɪ'skʌrɪdʒ]	entmutigen
domineering	[ˌdɒmɪ'nɪərɪŋ]	herrisch
forcible isolation	['fɔːsəbl ˌaɪsə'leɪʃən]	Time-out-Technik
fuss	[fʌs]	Lärm/Aufhebens machen
generosity	[ˌdʒenə'rɒsəti]	Großzügigkeit
lax	[læks]	locker, lasch
mischief	['mɪstʃɪf]; [-tʃiːf]	Übermut, Unheil
permissive	[pə'mɪsɪv]	freizügig, erlaubend
praise	[preɪz]	Lob
prospects	['prɒspekts]	Erfolgsaussichten
resolute	['rezəluːt]	entschieden, resolut
scold	[skəʊld]	ausschimpfen, schelten
smack	[smæk]	Klaps geben
spank	[spæŋk]	Klaps geben
tact	[tækt]	Takt
verbal reward	['vɜːbəl rɪ'wɔːd]	Lob
well-adjusted	[ˌwelə'dʒʌstɪd]	ausgeglichen

Bildquellenverzeichnis

Fotos

Deutsches Rotes Kreuz, Generalsekretariat, Berlin: 190.1-4

Fotolia Deutschland GmbH, Berlin: S. 7.1 (wildworx), 8 (babimu), 9.1 (Steve Wright), 9.2 (Helmut Brands), 9.3 (Paul Maguire), 9.4 (Kasia Gryniewicz), 10 (micromonkey), 12 (KaYann), 13.1 (nyul), 13.2 (Pavel Losevsky), 18 (Neo Edmund), 31 (Alena Ozerova), 33 (Monkey Business), 36.1 (Kati Molin), 36.2 (gunnar3000), 37 (artivista | werbeatelier), 39.1 (Yuri Arcurs), 39.2 (Hugh O'Neill), 40 (tarajane), 42 (anandkrish16), 44 (Gennadiy Poznyakov), 45 (Monart Design), 47 (pojoslaw), 48 (soupstock), 50 (Andriy Petrenko), 52 (Adam Gregor), 54.1-2 (contrastwerkstatt), 55 (emily2k), 57 (Andreas Wolf), 58 (Elenathewise), 61 (mangostock), 62 (Yuri Arcurs), 63 (Liddy Hansdottir), 64.1 (Monart Design), 64.2 (dubova), 66 (Ignat Lednev), 67 (AGphotographer), 68 (Kzenon), 70 (Monkey Business), 71 (Jessica Diks), 72 (Helder Almeida), 74 (Andrea Berger), 75 (Miredi), 77 (matka_Wariatka), 80 (Grum_l), 82.1 (yanlev), 82.2 (Yuri Arcurs), 84.1 (frankoppermann), 84.2 (Ella), 85 (ChristArt), 87 (lunamarina), 88 (sparkmom), 90 (Markus Bormann), 92 (kentoh), 93 (Galina Barskaya), 98 (Szasz-Fabian Erika), 99 (Tomas Sereda), 101 (Susan Stevenson), 103 (Pelz), 104 (jeecis), 106 (Anita P Peppers), 107.1 (jjpixs), 107.2 (MAK), 110 (David Davis), 111 (Lorelyn Medina), 112 (mogwai), 113 (Elenathewise), 114 (iceteastock), 115 (Monkey Business), 117 (Jasmin Merdan), 118 (st-fotograf), 119 (Marek), 121.1 (Prod. Numérik), 121.2 (Andy Dean), 121.3 (V.R.Murralinath), 121.4 (Mat Hayward), 121.5 (Murat Subatli), 121.6 (Thomas Perkins), 122 (Olga Nayashkova), 123 (Jaimie Duplass), 126 (Johan Larson), 128 (Ieva Geneviciene), 130 (Andrey Kiselev), 131.1 (mangostock), 131.2 (Cheryl Casey), 136 (Jaren Wicklund), 138 (robert mobley), 141 (barneyboogles), 142 (kameel), 143 (pressmaster), 145 (st-fotograf), 147 (philidor), 148.1 (Karen Struthers), 148.2 (moonrun), 149 (lawcain), 150 (philidor), 151 (Franz Pfluegl), 152.1 (Gina Sanders), 152.2 (Yuri Arcurs), 152.3 (Christian Jung), 152.4 (CURAphotography), 154 (rootsartz), 155.1 (Andres Rodriguez), 155.2 (Atlantis), 157.1 (szeyuen), 157.2 (Varina Patel), 159 (Monkey Business), 160 (bojorgensen), 162 (Robert Kneschke), 164 (Monkey Business), 165 (openlens), 166 (Berna Şafoğlu), 168.1 (BlueOrange Studio), 168.2 (Brebca), 168.3 (Kathrin39), 171.1 (elisabetta figus), 171.2 (Paulus Nugroho R), 173.2 (jeancliclac), 174 (Julie Hagan), 176 (Pavel Losevsky), 177 (auremar), 178 (Kzenon), 179.1 (Dron), 179.2 (openlens), 180 (matka_Wariatka), 181.1 (frankoppermann), 181.2 (Marco2811), 183 (BeTa-Artworks), 185 (pegbes), 187 (manu), 188 (fotodesign-jegg.de), 193 (somenski), 194 (somenski), 195 (Marek), 196 (OlgaLIS), 199 (VRD), 201 (Kwest), 203 (Felix Mizioznikov), 204 (Johan Larson), 205 (dedMazay)

Frances Kregler, Berlin: S. 20, 21, 94, 96

ullstein bild, Berlin: S. 78 (The Granger Collection)

Zeichnungen/Karikaturen

Angelika Brauner/Bildungsverlag EINS: S. 7.2, 189.1-2

Oliver Wetterauer/Bildungsverlag EINS: S. 14, 43, 132, 133, 173.1, 200

Umschlagfoto: Fotolia Deutschland GmbH, Berlin (godfer)